Pandemic Policies and Resistance

Pandemic Policies and Resistance

Southern Feminist Critiques in Times of Covid-19

Edited by Masaya Llavaneras Blanco and
Damien P. Gock on behalf of DAWN

BLOOMSBURY ACADEMIC
LONDON • NEW YORK • OXFORD • NEW DELHI • SYDNEY

BLOOMSBURY ACADEMIC
Bloomsbury Publishing Plc
50 Bedford Square, London, WC1B 3DP, UK
1385 Broadway, New York, NY 10018, USA
29 Earlsfort Terrace, Dublin 2, Ireland

BLOOMSBURY, BLOOMSBURY ACADEMIC and the Diana logo are trademarks of
Bloomsbury Publishing Plc

First published in Great Britain 2025

For legal purposes the Acknowledgements on p. xxi constitute an extension
of this copyright page.

Cover design by Grace Ridge
Cover images: FotografiaBasica, oxygen, Gerard McAuliffe via Getty Images

Bloomsbury Publishing Plc does not have any control over, or responsibility
for, any third-party websites referred to or in this book. All internet addresses
given in this book were correct at the time of going to press. The author and
publisher regret any inconvenience caused if addresses have changed or sites
have ceased to exist, but can accept no responsibility for any such changes.

A catalogue record for this book is available from the British Library.

A catalog record for this book is available from the Library of Congress.

ISBN: HB: 978-1-3505-1360-0
       PB: 978-1-3505-1361-7
       ePDF: 978-1-3505-1363-1
       eBook: 978-1-3505-1362-4

Typeset by RefineCatch Limited, Bungay, Suffolk
Printed and bound in Great Britain

To find out more about our authors and books visit www.bloomsbury.com
and sign up for our newsletters.

To every person who lost a loved one during the pandemic, to those who are surviving in its wake, and especially to those that keep imagining better worlds and actively working towards them.

Contents

Contents

Figures

Tables

Illustrations

Notes on Contributors

Editors

Masaya Llavaneras Blanco is an Executive Committee Member at DAWN. She is an Assistant Professor of development studies at Huron University College at Western University in Canada. Her research focuses on global social policy, human mobilities and social reproduction in the global South. Her work has been published both as part of DAWN's collective work and independently in *Global Social Policy, Environment and Planning C,* and *Political Geography* among other academic publications.

Damien P. Gock is a DAWN Associate and a Board Member of the Alliance for Future Generations, AFG Fiji. He is currently a PhD candidate at Western Sydney University. His research focuses on migration, women and care regimes in Australia and Fiji.

Authors

Dr. Daniele Bobb is a Lecturer at the University of the West Indies. Her research interests include gender and development, social policies, mothering, and women and work. She co-authored the book *Marginalized Groups in the Caribbean: Gender, Policy, and Society.* She is Secretary of the Association of Caribbean Women Writers and Scholars.

Crystal Brizan is an Attorney-at-Law with over fifteen years of experience, particularly in occupational safety and health, industrial relations, legal research, and legislative drafting and review. She holds a master's degree in gender and development studies, and has extensive experience in conducting research and managing projects on cross-cutting themes such as human rights, gender justice and health. She has worked with and is a member of several non-governmental organizations in Trinidad and Tobago. Currently, she is Chair of the Caribbean Association for Feminist Research and Action Trinidad and Tobago (CAFRA TT).

Roi Burnett is currently the Research Program Coordinator for a Pacific climate-related (im)mobilities project. She has a Bachelor of Arts (Hons) in geography and politics from the University of Otago and a Master of Arts in Pacific studies from the University of Auckland. Her research interests are in gender and labour mobility. Roi is of I-Kiribati and European descent.

Ayesha Constable pairs activism with research on gender, feminism and climate change as part of her doctoral studies at the University of the West Indies, Mona. The research combines her interests in agriculture, youth and gender. She has served as a member of several regional and global youth and gender networks, including the Commonwealth Youth Climate Network and the Sustainable Development Solutions Youth Network. She is the Technical Director for climate justice at the Global Fund for Women and a Global Advisor to FRIDA The Young Feminist Fund. She is also founder of the Young People for Action on Climate Change Jamaica (YPACCJa) and GirlsCARE - Girls for Climate Action for Resilience and Empowerment.

Prof. Ritu Dewan is President of the 64th Conference of Indian Society of Labour Economics, Visiting Professor at the Institute of Human Development, co-founder of the Feminist Policy Collective, Trustee of the Centre for Budget and Governance Accountability, Trustee of the India Forum and Director of the Leaflet. Previously, she was Vice President of the Indian Society of Agricultural Economics (2019–22) and President of the Indian Association for Women's Studies (2014–17). She was the first-ever woman director of the Department of Economics, University of Mumbai, and founder of the first Centre for Gender Economics in Asia.

Silvia Amparo Fernández Cervantes is a feminist activist and social worker. She has a master's in sustainable human development, a diploma in gender sensitive budgets from the Latin American Faculty of Social Sciences in Ecuador and a diploma in higher education. Fernández Cervantes is a member of the Colectivo Cabildeo Foundation, where she developed the categories and indicators for the orientation and measurement of public investment in gender equality. She provides technical assistance in gender sensitive budgets and costing in Bolivia and other countries. She is also is an international consultant for AECID, OXFAM and UN Women for planning, costing of violence and gender sensitive budgets.

Cecilia Fraga is a feminist researcher and sociologist at the University of Buenos Aires, Argentina. She is currently a Postdoctoral Fellow at the Interdisciplinary Center for the Study of Public Policies (CIEPP), Argentina. Fraga teaches social research methodology at the Universidad Metropolitana para la Educación y el Trabajo (UMET). She has a master's degree in gender studies and a PhD in social sciences from the El Colegio de México.

Nanette Liberona Concha is an academic in the Department of Anthropology and the Postgraduate Doctorate in Social Sciences programme at the Universidad de Tarapacá. She has a doctorate in anthropology and sociology from the University of Paris 7. Her research interests are borders, racism, corporeality and migrant health.

Yen Ne Foo is an independent consultant specializing in labour rights, human trafficking and migrant smuggling. She has a Master of Science in international relations and affairs from the Nanyang Technological University in Singapore. Her work aims to promote the understanding that unity, mutual dependence and collective action are the foundations of decent work.

Sylvia Ohene Marfo is a Research and Program Manager at the Union for African Population Studies at the University of Ghana. She is interested in the sociology and anthropology of food and agriculture, especially constructing ethnic identity through foodways, girls' education, gender and labour studies.

Corina Rodríguez Enríquez is a feminist economist based in Buenos Aires, Argentina. She is part of DAWN's Executive Committee and a researcher at the National Scientific and Technical Research Council (CONICET) and CIEPP in Argentina. She is also co-Director of the PhD programme on political economy at Escuela IDEAS, University of San Martin.

Dr. Karen A. Roopnarine has a PhD in economics from the University of Nottingham. She has two decades of professional experience as an economist. Her areas of expertise encompass econometrics, gender equality, central banking and labour market dynamics. She is presently a Senior Economist with the Central Bank of Barbados.

Zhihong Sa is an Associate Professor at the Beijing Normal University. Her research interests include the social determinants of health, care work and gender with a focus on older adults, rural-urban migrants and adolescents. She has published in the *Journal of Chinese Women's Studies, Sex Roles* and *BMC Geriatrics.*

Sius-geng Salinas Pérez is a psychologist with a master's degree in international relations and cross-border studies. She is currently pursuing a PhD in social sciences at the Universidad de Tarapacá. Salinas Pérez has worked as an assistant on several research projects on migration and gender, gender-based violence in migrant smuggling and irregular migration of women analysed from the perspective of social reproduction.

Busi Sibeko is an economist and researcher. She holds a Bachelor of Science in economics from Duke University and a Master of Science in the political economy of development from SOAS, University of London. She was previously at the Institute for Economic Justice, where her research focus was macroeconomic policy, including participatory feminist budgeting. She was co-Chair of the Budget Justice Coalition and has provided research support to the labour constituency. In 2020, she was featured in the roundtable series of renowned economists on Rebirthing the Global Economy to Deliver Sustainable Development by the United Nations Secretary-General.

Liva Sreedharan is currently the Head of Strategy, Policymaking and Data Analytics at NEOM. She is a dedicated labour rights specialist who shapes policy and strategic decisions by placing rights holders at the core of legislative and policy discussions. Advocating justice, unity, human nobility, gender equality and moderation, she is committed to setting high labour standards that reflect her principles and values.

Carolina Stefoni is the Director of the Postgraduate Doctorate in Social Sciences programme at the Universidad de Tarapacá, a Professor at Universidad de Tarapacá and an Associate Researcher at the Centre for Social Conflict and Cohesion Studies (COES). She is also a consultant in the area of migration with organizations such as ECLAC/CELADE, ILO, IOM, UNESCO and UNHCR. Stefoni is a sociologist from Pontificia Universidad Católica de Chile. She has a master's degree in cultural studies from the University of Birmingham and a PhD in sociology from Universidad Alberto Hurtado. Her research interests include migration policy, intercultural education, and labor and gender migration.

Gertrude Dzifa Torvikey is a Research Fellow at the Institute of Statistical, Social and Economic Research (ISSER), University of Ghana. She also works with *Feminist Africa Journal* at the same university. Her research interests include agrarian livelihoods, migration, labour and gender.

Leigh-Ann Worrell is the Project Coordinator at the Institute for Gender and Development Studies, Nita Barrow Unit. She holds a Master of Arts in women's and gender studies from Carleton University and a master's in social policy from Beijing Normal University. Leigh-Ann has a bachelor's degree in media and communication and began her career in journalism before moving on to gender and development.

Foreword

In 2020, less than half a year into the Covid-19 pandemic, we at DAWN had begun to see that, while the virus was no respecter of persons, neither was it the great equalizer that some had initially believed it might be. Lack of access to vaccines, severe illness, struggles for hospital beds, oxygen and survival, collapsing livelihoods and extreme hardships were the fate of some, while others with greater wealth and resources got off more lightly despite lockdowns and infection surges. A growing question for us as a feminist network from the global South was whether and how our governments were responding to the biggest pandemic of our lifetimes and what this might mean for feminist resistance and collective struggles.

The pandemic happened in the midst of multiple economic, ecological, social and political crises and the worsening inequalities that have marked recent decades. We were already seeing that the unwillingness of the wealthy and powerful to seriously tackle climate change has worse consequences for those with the least resources or capacity to adapt or mitigate. The economic inequality unleashed by neoliberal globalization – a system built on weak social protection, attacks on hard-won labour rights and with austerity as its policing mechanism – was complemented by border closures and mobility restrictions affecting the livelihoods and rights of migrant workers and refugees. Weak socialization of care arrangements meant increased pressure on poorly paid or unpaid domestic and care work, most often the responsibility of women and girls. States were increasingly beginning to manage these challenges by turning to draconian surveillance and privacy violations while dithering on the provision of health care and other public services. Anti-gender ideologies and the promotion of social divisions among people on such bases as religion, gender, ethnicity/race and caste were spreading like wildfire.

These pressures were already being felt by many people in the global South and also in the North by the time the pandemic broke out. And then came the pandemic. How did governments react to the outbreak of Covid-19 in the midst of existing crises?

This question was first raised for us by DAWN's former general coordinator, Peggy Antrobus, who was deeply concerned about whether the governments in her native Caribbean region were responding in ways that would protect poor and marginalized people, especially women. In the course of our discussions with Peggy and among ourselves, and through the stimulating discussions in a series of 'DAWN Talks' webinars,[1] we realized that delving into state responses to Covid-19 would help us understand whether the pandemic was indeed a 'portal' (Roy 2020) to more equitable policy changes and progressive transformation or would be a story of missteps and missed opportunities. We expected different governments to respond differently. The important question was why. What factors would shape their responses? We hoped through a series of case studies to tease out possible answers to that question, to sort out the elements of more progressive versus retrograde policies as governments designed and implemented them.

It isn't often that one has a vantage point on policy responses as they are happening on a scale as large and as widespread as Covid-19. Or in the context of a crisis whose appearance was as sudden and unexpected, and whose progression was as unpredictable as that of the pandemic. It meant that as feminist analysts and activists, DAWN had to scramble to develop the conceptual framework and to set up the process for the development of the case studies in rapidly shifting and fluid environments.

This book is one of the outcomes of this effort. Coordinated with superb efficiency by its co-editors with strong support from DAWN's General Co-coordinator María Graciela Cuervo and the DAWN Secretariat team, it is a testimony to the ability of feminist researchers and activists to respond rapidly to crises as they emerge. DAWN has always prioritized building a solid evidence base, of which the book is an able illustration.

The book's chapters have as their background the uneven and unequal structure of global power relations affecting different regions and countries differently, and encapsulated in colonial history and neocolonial economic paradigms. Not all countries or governments were taking off from the same block when the Covid-19 starter gun was fired. But governments' own predilections towards progressive social change, towards gender equality and women's human rights, towards worker protection and larger social protections, towards neoliberal versus equalizing economic agendas also had much influence on how they responded to the pandemic.

Spanning twelve countries from across the global South, the case studies provide insights not only into policies but also into the growing digitality of life, the ongoing centrality of care, rising authoritarianism and the role of corporate power on the one side and counter-responses from social movements and civil society on the other. This project's companion is the advocacy campaign Feminists for a People's Vaccine[2] that DAWN coordinated together with Third World Network to improve access to Covid-19 vaccines, diagnostics, therapeutics and equipment in the global South. In both projects, corporate power and its crushing effect on public policies affecting people's health and, more broadly, their livelihoods and survival have emerged as issues of great concern for feminist advocates and activists.

This book goes into publication when the Covid-19 pandemic has been declared over even though variant strains of the virus keep emerging. But its deep dive into the policy arena during the pandemic leaves us with many lessons. Central among these is the pervasive influence of corporate power on the policy space and on specific policies, a subject on which DAWN has been working in recent times (Rodríguez Enríquez and Llavaneras Blanco 2023). This power does not only take the form of crony capitalism through which corporate chieftains get special access to and favours from high levels of the state. Our studies show that was certainly the case during the pandemic. But corporate power has also been baked hard into the macroeconomic policy environment through four decades plus of neoliberal globalization's capture of state policies under the aegis of the Bretton Woods institutions. Nowhere did this become clearer than when austerity policies were insisted upon by the International Monetary Fund at the height of the pandemic in over a hundred countries reeling from economic recession even as governments were being advised to invest in health system infrastructure (Ortiz and Cummins 2021). Corporate influence on public policy has also twisted meso-policies in ways that have made it harder for governments to invest in health, education or other social infrastructure, protect workers' rights, ensure social protection, or promote gender equality and women's human rights. Without such investments, the intrinsic disequalizing effects of austerity policies have been worsened. And it has left states poorly prepared to handle Covid-19 type crises effectively.

Nonetheless, social movements don't give up easily, as this book shows. Values of solidarity, fairness, justice and a sense of our common humanity still hold in the darkest times. Creative ideas and actions emerge, bringing new possibilities and hope. This book is an effort to document some of those actions so that we can learn from them and prepare more effectively for the challenges to come. We hope in this way that we can continue our tradition of supporting fresh thinking that cuts through analytical confusions, breaks new ground in understanding emerging realities, foregrounds the lives of women and other oppressed groups and helps create renewed bases for feminist advocacy and activism.

Gita Sen
DAWN General Co-Coordinator 2014-2024

Notes

1   See: https://dawnnet.org/2020/06/youre-invited-to-dawntalks/; https://www.youtube.com/watch?v=XLw4ztKLx98&t=1121s.
2   See: https://feminists4peoplesvaccine.org/

References

Ortiz, I. and Cummins, M. (2021), 'Global Austerity Alert: Looming Budget Cuts in 2021–25 and Alternative Pathways', SSRN. Available at: https://doi.org/10.2139/ssrn.3856299 (accessed 23 June 2023).

Rodríguez Enríquez, C. and Llavaneras Blanco, M. (2023), 'Conclusion: Corporate Capture of Development in Times of Exacerbated Crises: Implications for Democratic Governance, Rights and Global Inequality', in C. Rodríguez Enríquez, C. and M. Llavaneras Blanco (eds), *Corporate Capture of Development*, 279–291, London: Bloomsbury Publishing.

Roy, A. (2020), 'The Pandemic is a Portal', *Financial Times*, 3 April. Available at: https://www.ft.com/content/10d8f5e8-74eb-11ea-95fe-fcd274e920ca (accessed 11 January 2024).

Acknowledgements

This book is the culmination of three years of hard work and was borne out of the imagination of Southern feminists, researchers, activists and academics who envisioned a renewed world of equity and justice. The initial conceptualization of this project would not have been possible without DAWN's Executive Committee, its global Board and the conversations held by Peggy Antrobus and Gita Sen as the pandemic became part of our lives everywhere. It is on the basis of this collaboration that the analytical framework used for this volume was created.

Our deepest gratitude to the contributors to this volume who, despite being in the midst of a pandemic, took time away from their multiple responsibilities, friends and families to develop these case studies. Many thanks to Crystal Brizan, Daniele Bobb, Roi Burnett, Nanette Liberona Concha, Ayesha Constable, Ritu Dewan, Corina Rodríguez Enríquez, Silvia Fernández, Yen Ne Foo, Cecilia Fraga, Sylvia Ohene Marfo, Sius-geng Salinas Pérez, Karen Roopnarine, Zhihong Sa, Carolina Stefoni, Busi Sibeko, Liva Sreedharan, Gertrude Dzifa Torvikey and Leigh-Ann Worrell.

We would like to thank the DAWN co-coordinators Gita Sen, María Graciela Cuervo and Kamala Chandrakirana for their invaluable support throughout this process, both in terms of the care work of sustaining feminist collaboration across the world and the intellectual work of imagining it with us. Our appreciation to Sharan Sindhu and the DAWN Secretariat for their administrative and communications assistance. We would like to give a special thank you to Sohel Sarkar, who worked rigorously on copyediting this volume. Thank you to Dr Tracey Wagner-Rizvi for her generous availability to support us when this book was about to go to print. We would also like to acknowledge the invaluable contributions of the individuals and organizations that supported the process that led to this book through their labour and participation in collective discussions: Yálani Zamora, Carol Barton (WIMN), Soledad Salvador, Bhumika Muchhala, Rachel Moussié (WIEGO), Lena Lavinas, Fish Ip (IDWF), Sakshi Rai (CESR), Kate Donald (CESR), Roberta Clark, Judith Wedderburn, Gabrielle Hosein, Catalina Valencia (Cooperativa de Economía Feminista Desbordada), Amparo Bravo Arias (Cooperativa de Economía Feminista Desbordada) and

Paola Cyment (WIMN). We would also like to acknowledge the Wellspring Philanthropic Fund for setting this project in motion and for their support at every stage of the development of the case studies.

Finally, we acknowledge all our relations and the labour that sustained everyone involved in making this edited volume. ¡Gracias! Vinaka!

Masaya Llavaneras Blanco and Damien P. Gock

Abbreviations

AAFP	Adopt A Family Programme (later renamed Adopt Our Families Programme)
AIDWA	All India Democratic Women's Association
AMMPO	Association of Nationalist Overseas Filipino Workers in Malaysia
AMPRO	Open Assembly of Migrants and Promigrants of Tarapacá (Asamblea Abierta de Migrantes y Promigrantes de Tarapacá)
APU	Azim Premji University
BBD	Barbados Dollar
BERT	Barbados Economic Recovery and Transformation
BIG	Basic Income Grant
CAADP	Comprehensive Africa Agricultural Development Programme
CAF	Development Bank of Latin America
CAFRA TT	Caribbean Association for Feminist Research and Action Trinidad and Tobago
CAP	Coronavirus Alleviation Programme
CARE	Covid Allocation of Resources for Employees
CASEN	National Socioeconomic Characterization Survey (Caracterizacion Socioeconomica Nacional)
CBGA	Centre for Budget and Governance Accountability
CCTP	Conditional Cash Transfer Programme
CDB	Caribbean Development Bank
CDG	Care Dependency Grant
CII	Confederation of Indian Industry
CMIE	Centre for Monitoring Indian Economy
CNY	Chinese Yuan
CPS	Cash Paymaster Services
CSG	Child Support Grant
CSO	Civil Society Organization
DG	Disability Grant
DIA	Department of Internal Affairs
DS	Supreme Decree (Decreto Supremo)

ECLAC	Economic Commission for Latin America and the Caribbean
EFF	Extended Fund Facility
EMCO	Enhanced Movement Control Order
ENES	National Survey on Social Structure (La Encuesta Nacional sobre la Estructura Social)
EO	Emergency (Essential Powers) Ordinance
FAO	Food and Agriculture Organization
FCG	Foster Care Grant
FLFP	Female Labour Force Participation
FWPR	Female Work Participation Rate
GBV	Gender-Based Violence
GDP	Gross Domestic Product
GES	Ghana Education Service
GH¢	Ghanaian Cedi
GoRTT	Government of the Republic of Trinidad and Tobago
GSF	Ghana Stabilisation Fund
GSFP	Ghana School Feeding Programme
GSS	Ghana Statistical Service
GST	Goods and Services Tax
HIPC	Heavily Indebted Poor Countries
HIV-AIDS	Human Immunodeficiency Virus-Acquired Immunodeficiency Syndrome
HSF	Heritage and Stabilisation Fund
ICT	Information and Communication Technology
IDB	Inter-American Development Bank
IDWF	International Domestic Workers Federation
IEJ	Institute for Economic Justice
IFAD	International Fund for Agricultural Development
IGAE	Global Economic Activity Index
ILO	International Labour Organization
IMF	International Monetary Fund
INDEC	National Institute of Statistics and Censuses (Instituto Nacional de Estadística y Censos)
INE	National Statistics Institute (Instituto Nacional de Estadística)
INR	Indian Rupee
IOM	International Organization for Migration
IP	Intellectual Property
ISST	Institute for Social Studies Trust

IT	Information Technology
IWWAGE	Initiative for What Works to Advance Women and Girls in the Economy
JHS	Junior High School
JHWU	Jamaica Household Workers Union
KIT	Kiribati Institute of Technology
LLRC	Labour Law Reform Coalition
MAF	Malaysia Armed Forces
MAS	Movement Towards Socialism
MCO	Movement Control Order
MDW	Migrant Domestic Worker
MESCP	Productive Community Social Economic Model (Modelo Económico Social Comunitario Productivo)
MFAT	Ministry of Foreign Affairs and Trade
MGCSP	Ministry of Gender, Children and Social Protection
MGNREGS	Mahatma Gandhi National Rural Employment Guarantee Scheme
MLSS	Ministry of Labour and Social Security
MMGD	Ministry of Women, Gender and Diversity
MOHR	Ministry of Human Resources
MSD	Ministry of Social Development
MSDFS	Ministry of Social Development and Family Services
MSME	Medium, Small and Micro Enterprise
MTC	Marine Training Centre
MWCD	Ministry of Women and Child Development
NFSA	National Food Security Act
NGO	Non-Governmental Organization
NIDS-CRAM	National Income Dynamics Study-Coronavirus Rapid Mobile Survey
NIF	National Insurance Fund
NIS	National Insurance System (Trinidad)
NIS	National Insurance Scheme (Barbados, Jamaica)
NSO	National Statistical Office (India)
NSO	National Statistics Office (Kiribati)
OAP	Old Age Pension
OBC	Other Backward Caste
OSC	One Stop Centre
OSF	Open Society Foundations

PALM	Pacific Australia Labour Mobility
PCR	Polymerase Chain Reaction Test
PDI	Investigative Police (Policía de Investigaciones de Chile)
PDS	Public Distribution System
PERTIMIG	Indonesian Migrant Domestic Workers Association (Persatuan Pekerja Rumah Tangga Indonesia Migran)
PESA	Panchayats (Extension to Scheduled Areas) Act
PIC	Pacific Island Country
PLM	Pacific Labour Mobility
PLMAM	Pacific Labour Mobility Annual Meeting
PLS	Pacific Labour Scheme
PMJDY	Pradhan Mantri Jan Dhan Yojana
PPE	Personal Protective Equipment
PTC	Territorial Parliaments of Care (Parlamentos Territoriales del Cuidado)
RMP	Royal Malaysia Police
RSE	Recognised Seasonal Employer Scheme
RSF	Resilience and Sustainability Fund
RTC	Reverse Tax Credit
SALDRU	Southern African Labour and Development Research Unit
SC	Scheduled Caste
SDG	Sustainable Development Goal
SIDS	Small Island Developing State
SINCA	Integral System of Care Policies in Argentina (Sistema Integral de Políticas de Cuidados en la Argentina)
SJM	Jesuit Migrant Service (Servicio Jesuita a Migrantes)
SOCSO	Social Security Organization
SPII	Studies in Poverty and Inequality Institute
SRD	Social Relief of Distress (Grant)
SRHR	Sexual and Reproductive Health Rights
ST	Scheduled Tribe
STATIN	Statistical Institute
SWAN	Stranded Workers' Action Network
SWP	Seasonal Worker Programme
TCCTP	Targeted Conditional Cash Transfer Programme
TT	Trinidad and Tobago Dollar
TTPS	Trinidad and Tobago Police Service
TVET	Technical and Vocational Education and Training

UBIG	Universal Basic Income Grant
UNCTAD	United Nations Conference on Trade and Development
UNDP	United Nations Development Programme
UNGA	United Nations General Assembly
UNHCR	United Nations High Commissioner for Refugees
UNICEF	United Nations Children's Fund
UNRISD	United Nations Research Institute for Social Development
UPACP	Domestic Helpers' Union (Unión del Personal Auxiliar de Casas Particulares)
UWU	United Workers Union
VAT	Value Added Tax
WFP	World Food Programme
WHO	World Health Organization

Lather, Rinse, Repeat? Women and Intersectional Inequalities in the Pandemic Conjuncture

Masaya Llavaneras Blanco and Damien P. Gock

March 2020 marked a defining moment. The Covid-19 crisis became a global phenomenon that shook, even if temporarily, the prevailing status quo. Writer Arundhati Roy (2020) described the pandemic as a portal, an opportunity to enter a stage of transformative potential. The global crisis opened up space to reconfigure power relations and institutions. It was an opportunity for global governance bodies to reshape the rules of international trade, financial architecture and the terms of access to knowledge and technology. It was also an opportunity for national governments to take bold decisions and experiment with transformative policies that could address the longstanding structural gendered, racialized and class-based inequalities accentuated by the pandemic. Not all governments had the same resources at their disposal or were at the same starting point. However, how they reacted to this shock was telling of long-term policy trajectories, their disposition towards redistributive justice and their commitment to democratic practices, both domestically and transnationally. Furthermore, their policy responses reflected the uneven leeway available to different governments based on their financial liquidity and the unequal power dynamics that characterize the global sphere.

The reality on the ground was complicated. Production chains and global trade halted (Esper 2021, Gurbuz et al. 2023). Businesses shut down, reduced wages and working hours, and laid off workers (Apedo-Amah et al. 2020). In the G20 countries, industrial production fell 28 per cent on average between February and April 2020 (ILO 2020a). Between December 2019 and April 2020, labour markets in the G20 countries saw a 40 per cent decline in the number of people working (ibid.). Globally, 94 per cent of workers were living in countries where workplaces had closed (ILO 2020b). In tandem, people on the move found themselves stranded due to border closures. In 2020, the International Labour Organization (ILO) estimated that there were 164 million migrant workers, who constituted 4.7 per cent of the global workforce. Nearly half of this number were women (ILO 2020c). Migrants and asylum seekers were often excluded from health systems and emergency social protection measures in their countries of residence (ibid.).

As this situation unfolded, activists, advocates and researchers were caught in multiple crises that affected their everyday lives and subsistence. Their safety was also under threat, especially in contexts where social mobilization and political organizing became increasingly challenging and risky. Social movements struggled to understand the implications of the pandemic while their members tried to find their footing and survive. As governments across the globe sought to stem the spread of the Covid-19 virus, strict measures such as lockdowns, lock-ins, curfews and social distancing became normalized. Social mobilization strategies had to adapt to these measures by limiting social gatherings and navigating new forms of control and criminalization of people's mobility. Large swaths of society ground to a halt, exposing groups of people who either could not afford to stay at home or for whom staying at home implied exposure to increased domestic violence.

Social movements were often the first to attend to the needs of those who were falling through the cracks of policy responses that ignored the lived realities of informal workers, migrants and other marginalized communities. At the intersection of care provision and activism, movements collected and distributed food and personal protective equipment (PPE), facilitated access to emergency programmes and advocated for the expansion of social protection and mutual aid. They also understood this as a political moment in which collective organizing strategies were affected by increased political control. At the same time, social movements recognized that the halt in economic and political systems offered an opportunity to foster structural change.

DAWN was convinced of the urgent need to understand the complex political potential of this moment, and out of this endeavour emerged the research and discussions that led to this book. The key question that we were looking to address is as follows: Did the pandemic usher in a feminist and democratic transformation or did it become an alibi to double down on existing systems of oppression? The answer, of course, was not a simple either-or, but rather lay in the complexities of domestic and transnational contexts and power relations that defined the Covid-19 moment.

1. Was the pandemic a portal after all?

Much of the global narrative on the transformative potential of the pandemic revolved around the buzzword 'essential workers', used to refer to those employed in the labour- and economy-specific sectors and services that were deemed vital for the functioning of society during the global halt (Stevano, Ali and Jamieson 2021). This narrative lauded workers who were on the front lines of critical service provisions, such as nurses, physicians and garbage collectors. Social media was replete with video footage of people clapping and banging pans in support of workers in places as far apart as India, Spain and China. For the most part though, the clapping and praising did not translate into improved labour conditions and labour protection in a context of acute risks (Chen et al. 2021).

Social distancing, which was key to managing the spread of Covid-19, also brought its own challenges, especially for those already facing socioeconomic and political barriers. Informal workers, internal and transnational migrants, racialized folks and people living in poverty were especially affected by lockdowns and the reduction in or prohibition of in-person activities. Globally, the ability to abide by social distancing was the purview of the privileged, namely those who were able to continue working or studying from home, had enough savings or were receiving sufficient government support in the form of cash or in-kind transfers that enabled them to remain in some degree of isolation. However, these options were either unviable or insufficient for informal workers who relied on daily earnings. Domestic workers, in particular, found themselves in impossible situations. Belonging to one of the least protected labour sectors worldwide, they were among the first to be exposed to the virus. Those who lived in with their employers saw their workloads intensify and mobility curtailed, with little or no opportunity to visit their families. Others were laid off, often without compensation. Stuck between a rock and a hard place, domestic workers were among the communities with the least access to government cash transfers and other social protection measures (see the chapters by Constable, Sa, and Sreedharan and Ne Foo in this volume).

Other instances where social isolation measures exacerbated socioeconomic inequalities were school closures and the transition to alternative teaching formats (online, via texting or by phone calls). About 1.5 billion learners were impacted, and those in already vulnerable situations were the worst affected (UNESCO 2023, Betthäuser, Bach-Mortensen and Engzell 2023). Learners in households with access to the internet and enough devices for all family members could continue their education remotely while those with limited or no access to technology and data could no longer realize their right to education.

Perhaps the starkest inequalities emerged in relation to health. Against a backdrop of corporate capture of the production and distribution of vaccines, diagnostics, therapeutics and other necessary medical products, the health sector struggled to confront the novel coronavirus. These challenges were not experienced uniformly across countries and sectors of society. For example, by the end of July 2023, only 27 per cent of the eligible population in low-income countries had been vaccinated compared with 72 per cent in the European Union (Our World in Data 2023). Inequalities shaped access to not only vaccines but also other related therapeutics, which had been stockpiled by the global North, leaving substantial parts of the South scrambling. The hoarding of vaccines and therapeutics was matched by an unforgiving international intellectual property (IP) system. In its current form, the IP system favours the concentration of knowledge and manufacturing of vaccines and therapeutics in the hands of private multinational pharmaceutical corporations 'even when taxpayers finance a significant part, sometimes more than 90%, of product research and development' (FPV 2023: 7). The ongoing struggle over the flexibilization of the IP regime has concrete everyday implications. Existing and new patent applications render these products unaffordable for low- and middle-income countries and leave them unable to produce these goods even when they have the necessary infrastructure to do so.

The corporate capture of the medical industry and, indirectly, of the global pandemic response is a product of the sustained defunding of the public sector around the world (Chancel et al. 2022). Shaped by austerity, both public policy and transnational solidarity developed in ways that privileged profit over the common good. Central to the pandemic of austerity was the global South's external debt, which was at the core of the international economic system in the 1980s and '90s, when these countries underwent strict restructuring processes, and is now making a comeback in global policy circles and everyday lived experiences.

Even though indebtedness is endemic to most governments, it is experienced differently. The International Monetary Fund (IMF) has observed a steady increase in the global debt-to-GDP ratio since 2005. Well before 2020, the debt-to-GDP ratio of the United States and other advanced economies had surpassed 100 per cent; China is projected to get there by 2027.[1] In contrast, the so-called emerging markets, excluding China, and low-income countries maintained public debt-to-GDP ratios well below 50–60 per cent even at the height of the pandemic. What these numbers tell us is that fiscal tightening is an expectation placed on the global South while the North continues to have room for expansionary fiscal policies. This discrepancy was most evident in the first responses to the Covid-19 crisis. Global North governments responded by injecting significant amounts of liquidity into their economies in the form of cash transfers and private sector bailouts. In 2020, high-income countries on average assigned 20.3 per cent of their GDP to wage subsidies and liquidity support (which included health expenditures) while the corresponding figures for middle- and low-income countries stood at 6 per cent and 1.8 per cent, respectively (IMF 2020). The World Health Organization (WHO) estimates that 'per capita health spending on COVID-19 [. . .] in 2020 averaged US\$ 212 in 16 high income countries and US\$ 14 in 21 low- and middle- income countries with comprehensive data' (2022: vii).

It is unsurprising that public expenditure on health and social protection varied drastically between high-, middle- and low-income countries. Austerity cuts, nonetheless, were widespread. According to Ortiz and Cummins (2021), such measures likely affected 85 per cent of the world population in 2022. Austerity politics has direct implications for what governments do (or do not do) for their people. A common government practice in times of fiscal constraint is to defund certain (often vital) social policies to fund emergency packages. This was often the case during the pandemic when funds were redirected towards cash transfers and away from other social policies such as shelters for domestic violence survivors and school meal programmes, thus neglecting vulnerable sectors of the population (see, for example, the chapters by Sibeko, and Torvikey and Marfo in this volume).

2. Making sense of the pandemic through an interlinkages approach and an intersectional lens

Against this backdrop, understanding the pandemic as a period that held transformative potential, this book analyses the changes that took place beyond global policy prescriptions. We prioritize Southern feminist analyses of local and national policies in the global South. We devise four potential interconnected scenarios to help us make sense of the policies and political processes that different governments were embarking upon as they responded to the crisis (Llavaneras Blanco and Cuervo 2021). These scenarios include policy and political responses that i) carried on with existing trajectories, following established paths; ii) increased the influence of corporations in the political sphere, expanding private sector control over policies and biopolitics; iii) intensified state control through biopolitics, reinforcing authoritarian trends; or iv) were transformative and progressive, leading to feminist policies that promoted democracy and redistributive justice. These scenarios are not mutually exclusive, but we use them as reference points to zero in on key actors and policy trajectories.

By working with an interlinkages approach, we seek to examine how broad policy areas influence each other and affect gender, class and other power relations in ways that are relevant to effecting change. As Sen and Durano (2014: 21) argue, different 'forces of political economy such as globalization, military conflict and ecology are a significant influence on the environment for power relations such as gender, and thereby give them shape'. At the same time, gender relations also influence these broader processes. In this book, we focus on four main policy areas, namely labour, care and social protection, macroeconomics, and migration and human mobility, recognizing that they are interlinked in important ways. We understand, for example, that care provision is deeply intertwined with macroeconomic policy, such that the economic value of unpaid care labour, mostly done by women, sustains much of the existing market economy. Similarly, we understand that the interface between human mobility and labour shapes labour and migration policies. These policy areas affect everyday lives and are not implemented and experienced in 'airtight compartments' (ibid.), but rather in interlinked ways. These interlinkages are in no way obvious or ever present but are critical in the process of forming coalitions and advocating for structural change.

Just as we understand that policy areas do not exist in isolation from each other, we also acknowledge that individual and collective experiences are embedded in sets of complex intersectional power relations. The analyses presented in this book prioritize an intersectional lens that situates gender within a larger set of categories of oppression and privilege. This was an important lens to bring in because there is no homogeneity of experience based on a universal category of womanhood or, more generally, gender. Rather, gender intersects with class, sexuality, ethnicity, race and caste, location, citizenship and migratory status, age and other categories of difference. These intersectionalities do not emerge homogeneously or in every political, social and economic structure. Rather, different combinations of these and other categories of difference produce complex social positionings, lived experiences and forms of oppression (Lorde 1984, Hill Collins 2002). Oppressions based on racialized, nationalist, ableist and patriarchal logics do not simply manifest in personal attitudes and individual experiences but have collective and political implications: 'they are typically built into policy packages with significant distributive consequences' (Folbre 2020: 225).

The case studies presented in this book examine the collective and political implications of policies adopted during the pandemic. The twelve chapters have been penned by feminist activists and researchers from twelve countries of the global South: Argentina, Bolivia, Chile, Barbados, Jamaica, Trinidad and Tobago, Ghana, South Africa, India, Malaysia, China and Kiribati. The result is a set of complex and situated analyses that centre the experiences of women, workers, migrants, racialized folks and social movements. The chapters highlight people's lived experiences vis-à-vis weakened labour protection and forced mobility and immobility in the context of a global emergency. They shed light on how social protection policies and care systems were either stagnant or emerged amidst deep-seated austerity, thus intensifying the corporate capture of development. By attending to both interlinkages and intersectionalities, the chapters capture the complexity of a historical moment in which ongoing multidimensional crises were exacerbated in ways that have significant implications for global inequalities and political organizing. They offer a window into how Southern feminisms articulate across movements and issues, contributing to building broad sociopolitical coalitions amid growing global authoritarianism and austerity politics.

The twelve chapters of the book are grouped into three parts. The first section examines countries in which policy responses to the pandemic were marked by austerity and path dependence as governments continued or doubled down on pre-existing trajectories. The second section looks at countries where governments introduced some policies and innovations that attempted to change path dependence, with varying degrees of success. Finally, the third section focuses on instances of resistance and transformation led by social movements.

2.1 Examining austerity and path dependence

Austerity is generally defined as a group of policies that aim to reduce public spending and steady government debt, often accompanied by an increase in indirect taxes. It creates the conditions for increased corporate power, limits state capacity and reduces the sphere of the public. It is also a principle that places fiscal constraint at the centre of economic, social and political thought.

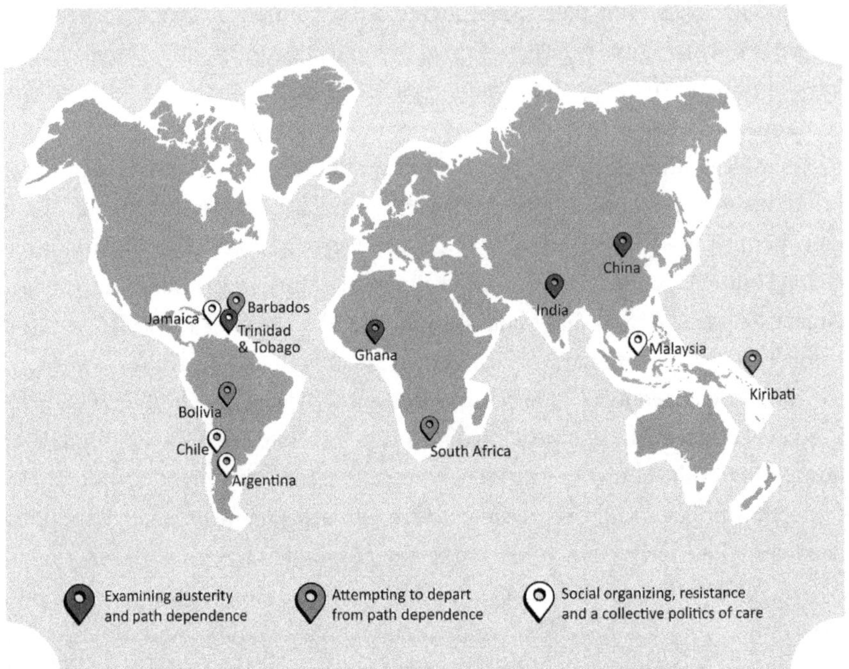

Illustration 0.1 World map indicating the case studies covered by this volume, per section. *By Marla Rabelo on behalf of DAWN.*

The current mode of austerity experienced globally is an ideological extension of the fiscal tightening and structural adjustment programmes promoted by the IMF and the World Bank in the 1980s and '90s, and their new iterations (Clarke and Newman 2012, Rodríguez Enríquez and Llavaneras Blanco 2023). Prescribed by external actors or brewed nationally, austerity is often the guiding principle behind many of the policies we currently witness in the global South. For the most part, these are path dependent, meaning that they are built around the weight of past outcomes (Murphy 2010). Path-dependency literature suggests that even under the gravity of a pandemic, certain modes of problem solving prevail because they have been developed under an existing system of policy choices (Marsden and Docherty 2021).

Despite the technical jargon that often surrounds it, austerity is not an abstraction, but rather manifests in concrete ways in people's everyday lives. It shapes labour dynamics, creating the conditions for further exploitation. Costs cut at the public level are ultimately borne by private households and, within them, by women and girls. In 'Macro-Patriarchal Pandemic Policy: The India

Case', Ritu Dewan assesses the interlinkages between labour policies, workers' rights, internal mobility and migration, social protection and macroeconomic policies. Dewan characterizes India's federal policy response as uncompassionate amid an already harsh and deteriorating socioeconomic and political environment. This was evident in the food subsidy cuts at the height of the pandemic and the massive forced return of internal migrants from urban to rural areas. A central focus of the chapter is the link between the government's pandemic response and the already deteriorating pre-pandemic economic and human and women's rights policies.

Focusing on the temporary discontinuation of the Ghana School Feeding Programme, Gertrude Dzifa Torvikey and Sylvia Ohene Marfo demonstrate how pandemic-related austerity measures undertaken by the Ghanaian government, compounded by an ongoing macroeconomic crisis, negatively affected the lives of women and children. Their chapter 'Food Curtailed: Austerity, Socioeconomic Crises and Ghana's School Feeding Programme' highlights the worrying rise in food insecurity among children and explains how the weight of austerity policies fell squarely on the shoulders of women. In this instance, women and food producers, who are mostly informally employed, bore the added burden of reproductive labour and heightened financial and food insecurities.

Accounting for unpaid care work in policy making remains one of the key pending mandates of the Beijing Platform for Action. As in Ghana, women's social reproductive labour absorbed part of the shock of the pandemic in Trinidad and Tobago. In 'Social Protection and Care Policies: Impact on Gendered Inequalities in Trinidad and Tobago', Karen Roopnarine and Crystal Brizan demonstrate how policies implemented by the government in response to the pandemic were essentially an extension of pre-pandemic trajectories. Most significantly, people faced challenges in accessing emergency cash transfers, which was made contingent on contributions to the country's National Insurance System. As such, the policy had built-in class and gender-based biases that excluded informal and unpaid workers, a majority of whom are women.

In China, policies related to domestic work were highly fragmented and compounded by path-dependent social protection mechanisms and a complex internal migration regime. In 'Impact of Covid-19 on Domestic Workers in China: Reflections on a Fragmented Policy Response', Zhihong Sa showcases how domestic workers had little or no access to social protection, with detrimental impacts on their terms of employment, working conditions and mental health during the pandemic. These policies were historically shaped by the informalization of care work during China's reform era, which prioritized economic growth and privatization of care provision with an urban bias. This resulted in the development of a domestic service industry that employed internal migrants from rural communities in urban centres while curtailing their mobility and offering them little or no access to social protection and welfare.

2.2 Attempting to depart from path dependence

Transformation is a messy process. One of the analytical challenges of this research was understanding how change comes about and what forms of transformation we, as Southern feminists, should work towards. Amid a global emergency, it was especially challenging to tease out the different actors, policy goals, and global and local political dynamics that shaped government responses. A close examination of policy processes in this section, especially by those that attempted to shift policy trajectories, sheds light on the complex power relations and historical tensions within and between states, organizations and institutions. These chapters address the transnational nature of policy change, especially in, but not limited to, the context of labour migration. They also zero in on questions such as how to implement distributive policies that reach marginalized groups against a backdrop of fiscal constraint. In particular, they reveal longstanding questions around the universality and focalization of distributive policies, exposing the limitations of both targeted and universal cash transfer mechanisms in addressing racialized, gendered and place-based income inequalities.

The chapter 'Who Really Wins? Kiribati Labour Mobility Schemes in the Post-Covid Era' illustrates the impact of mobility controls. Focusing on migrant I-Kiribati women workers and the Pacific Labour Mobility (PLM) schemes in New Zealand and Australia, author Roi Burnett explains how diaspora I-Kiribati communities and non-governmental organizations provided some social protection to stranded migrant workers in the absence of cohesive government policy responses. Burnett notes that historically, the PLM schemes have been wrought by human and labour rights violations, which were exacerbated during the pandemic by border closures, business shutdowns and reductions in working hours. The chapter reveals the cracks in labour mobility schemes and the gaps in visa regimes as many migrants, unable to return home, were left suspended in the grey area between legality and breach of visa conditionalities.

In 'Social Protection versus Orthodoxy in the Covid-19 Pandemic: Lessons from South Africa', Busi Sibeko analyses the country's Social Relief of Distress

Grant and Caregiver Allowance, which invigorated calls for a Universal Basic Income Grant. Sibeko assesses these two social protection policies vis-à-vis the residual effects of Apartheid and the country's macroeconomic structures. The chapter shows that the South African government moved to raise the social protection floors enshrined in its Constitution but did so under conditions of self-imposed austerity, which translated into divestment in other social policies. While the move to raise social protection floors was laudable, these measures fell short of meeting the needs of women, youth and others living in poverty.

Another noteworthy effort at changing policy trajectories was seen in Barbados. In 'Barbados: Pandemic, Economic Restructuring and the Social Organization of Care', Daniele Bobb and Leigh-Ann Worrell explore the country's social policy response during the tail end of a structural adjustment programme. While implementing the Barbados Economic Recovery and Transformation Plan, the government introduced two expansionary policies, namely the Adopt Our Families Programme and an increase in and expansion of the minimum wage. While the expansionary nature of these policies at a time of fiscal restructuring was praiseworthy, women's unpaid care labour did not receive attention in their formulation. Bobb and Worrell argue that in order for these policies to realize their transformative potential, there should be a shift towards a Universal Basic Income.

In 'Conditional Cash Transfer Programmes in Bolivia during the Covid-19 Crisis: A Thwarted Redistributive Potential', Silvia Amparo Fernández Cervantes brings to the fore the relevance of context in policy making and implementation. The chapter analyses how the four Conditional Cash Transfer Programmes implemented by the Bolivian government during the pandemic reproduced gendered, racialized and class-based inequalities. Fernández Cervantes points out that despite its expansionary nature, the Bolivian policy response preserved the economic status quo and favoured the middle and upper classes while excluding rural and indigenous communities, especially women. In contrast to the arguments put forth by Sibeko, and Bobb and Worrell, Fernández Cervantes problematizes the principle of universality for its tendency to homogenize different social and political subjects. This chapter argues that such homogenization reproduces colonial logics and forms of exclusion.

2.3 Social organizing, resistance and a collective politics of care

Governments and policymakers were not the only actors responding to the global crisis. Social movements were essential in addressing the consequences of insufficient or exclusionary government policy responses that left segments of the population in acute precarity. One such instance of resistance entailed supporting the livelihoods of marginalized groups followed by creating alternative ways of collective organizing. The struggles covered by the chapters in this section lie in the interlinkage between collective care and political organizing. This interface creates the conditions for an expansive and transformative politics in a global context of growing authoritarianism and austerity. In these chapters, collective care and organizing push against exclusions based on labour, location and country of citizenship. They are generative of a transformative politics that entitles internal and transnational migrants to social and political rights irrespective of their place of residence, delinks workers' rights and belonging from participation in formal labour, and attaches economic and political value to care and unpaid work. These political practices and projects take the form of labour organizing, inter-movement solidarities and movement-state interactions.

In 'Building a Care System in Argentina: Transformative Potential and Persistent Challenges' Corina Rodríguez Enríquez and Cecilia Fraga explore how care was placed at the centre of social policy discussions in Argentina. Their chapter focuses on the country's national care system and highlights opportunities for feminist policy transformation through processes such as the creation of the new Ministry of Women, Gender and Diversity, and the Territorial Parliaments of Care. Rooted in years of collective mobilization by feminist movements, these policy processes were catalysed and shaped by the pandemic. In highlighting the historical overload of care placed on women and LGBTI+ people, Rodríguez Enríquez and Fraga shed light on the contextual and community dynamics of care as a rich aspect of political and social organizing. The chapter also includes an epilogue that accounts for the drastic government change that followed.

The chapter 'Grassroots Feminist Organizing in Jamaica: Fostering Transformative Change for Domestic Workers during Covid-19' focuses on the labour precarity and policy exclusion experienced by domestic workers, which were exacerbated by the pandemic. Author Ayesha Constable examines how the government's decision to link access to emergency cash transfers to contributions to the country's National Insurance Scheme excluded domestic and other informal workers whose marginalization was worsened by mobility controls and social isolation measures. The chapter explores how the Jamaica Household Workers Union (JHWU) supported workers despite these structural challenges. It identifies the main challenges in JHWU's mobilization and puts this struggle in historical context.

Political mobilization is often linked to the right to nationality and citizenship. Migrants and other subjects on the move often experience profound political exclusions due to their limited access to nationality and documentation such as visas. Such exclusions were worsened by the pandemic. In Chile, the pandemic coincided with significant changes in migration legislation in the form of border closures and heightened criminalization of migration. In 'Collective Care to Confront the Pandemic: Migrant and Pro-migrant Activism in Chile', Nanette Liberona Concha, Carolina Stefoni and Sius-geng Salinas Pérez analyse the centrality of mutual aid and social reproduction in navigating an increasingly exclusionary context in solidarity with migrants.

Political mobilization in contexts of deep-seated exclusion is also at the heart of the chapter titled 'Organizing from the Heart: Migrant Domestic Workers' Resistance in Malaysia during the Covid-19 Pandemic'. In it, Liva Sreedharan and Yen Ne Foo illustrate how migrant domestic workers (MDWs) successfully entered into dialogue with the Malaysian state to demand their right to social protection despite prevailing anti-migrant conditions, which were intensified by the pandemic. Amid rising authoritarianism and growing criminalization of migration, MDWs collaborated with civil society organizations and trade unions in innovative ways, relying on digital access and organizing. As a result, their organizations grew despite the global crisis. Most significantly, even though their labour conditions continue to be precarious, MDWs successfully mobilized for inclusion into the national social security scheme for the first time in its history. This victory opens the door to regulation of Malaysia's labour sector and demonstrates that there is transformative potential in new and hands-on forms of political mobilization.

3. Emerging issues

While the twelve case studies differ in the policy and political trajectories pursued by their governments, people and social movements, two common themes emerged across most of them. The first is the growing digitality of social policy and political organizing and the second is the centrality of care provision, solidarity and mutual aid. Information technology (IT) shaped significant aspects of government policy responses, including social protection measures and increased surveillance. In tandem, IT turned into a powerful tool for political and social organizing in a context of acute mobility restrictions. Relatedly, a radical politics of care emerged as a palpable site of resistance, sustaining communities and facilitating the mobilization for collective political action.

3.1 Feminist digital justice

The digital sphere permeated most facets of daily life during the pandemic, with government leaders rethinking, reshaping and integrating it into policies on mobility, education, work and communication (Kuah and Dillon 2022). Access to emergency social protection measures was mostly structured through digital technologies. In several cases, potential beneficiaries were expected to register in online systems to apply for state support or provide documentation to demonstrate and validate their presence in the country.

The transition to digital government services made sense given the social distancing measures in place and the expected expediency of digital processes. However, the digitalization of access to social and political rights, such as the right to social security and the right to identity, often heightened structural exclusion. Suddenly, access to computers and mobile phones and the ability to interact with digital interfaces determined who could (or could not) access social protection. Intersecting inequalities based on class, gender, able-bodiedness, location and racialization were exacerbated. Rural and racialized women, informal workers and poor folks struggled to find devices through which to access social services. When devices were available, they struggled to navigate the new forms of digital bureaucracy due to limited digital literacy. As Constable and Sibeko document in their respective chapters, this was the experience of domestic workers in Jamaica as well as poor and rural South Africans trying to access emergency support.

To be sure, the growing digitalization of welfare services in the global South predates the Covid-19 pandemic. The notion of the digital welfare state has been circulating in global policy circles since the last decade. In 2019, the Special Rapporteur on extreme poverty and human rights had warned the United Nations Secretary-General that the digitalization of welfare ran the risk of shifting the understanding of individuals from rights holders to applicants. The weakening of rights has also been exacerbated by increased digital surveillance as access to basic social rights is made contingent on the surrender of personal data. The use of digital technologies was essential to the 'governmentality of health' that characterized the first years of the pandemic, illustrating how different power apparatuses were deployed to govern bodies (Horton 2020). As Dewan explains in her chapter, the brunt of such policies was acutely felt by internal migrant workers in India, where access to identity and social protection is dependent on inclusion in a centralized biometric identification system. Similarly, digital inequalities shaped how and to what extent migrants were able to partake of regularization processes, leading to documented cases of mass deportation in Chile.

Notwithstanding the significant problems thrown up by the digital sphere in government responses to the pandemic, IT was central to social and political mobilization. Many organizations supported marginalized communities in accessing their rights by providing them with data, devices and/or guidance on how to navigate digitalized bureaucratic processes. In the case of migrant domestic workers in Malaysia, access to data and digital platforms proved to be a fundamental step towards labour organizing, as Sreedharan and Ne Foo highlight in their chapter. Digital organizing enabled them to expand their membership and successfully advocate for their right to social protection in ways that they had never managed before. In Argentina, digital platforms became crucial to organizing the Territorial Parliaments of Care, the participatory mechanism at the heart of the country's national care system, in a context of social distancing.

The cases explored in this volume indicate that the digitalization of life is here to stay, but the terms under which it happens are now a significant site of struggle. Feminist digital justice thus becomes a strategic issue for feminisms rooted in the global South. As proposed by Gurumurthy (2020), a feminist digital economy should necessarily centre sustaining the material conditions of living, putting livelihoods and access to social services at the heart of the digital sphere. This vision, further developed by the Feminist Digital Justice Working Group (2023), fosters public investment in digital infrastructure, turns internet access into a right and provides poor women with free data allowances. As exemplified by the digital mobilization of MDWs in Malaysia, translocal solidarity between and across movements is already a vital part of feminist mobilization. The construction of a truly public sphere in digitality thus becomes essential for a feminist digital future.

3.2 A radical politics of care

Historically, social reproductive labour has been at the heart of Southern feminisms. It is unsurprising then that all twelve case studies explored in this book address care in some form, especially considering how the social organization of care was drastically shaken by the pandemic the world over. This volume sees the invisibility of unpaid social reproductive labour as a buffer on which austerity politics relies to cut public spending. It argues that the reduced cost to the public treasury resulting from the implementation of austerity measures is, in reality, a reproductive labour burden transferred to households and, within households, to women and girls. This was evident in Ghana, for example, where the temporary suspension of a school feeding programme translated into increased unpaid care work for women in households with school-aged children.

In turn, the invisibility and devaluation of care labour results in distributive problems as, following a neoliberal logic, care provision is turned into an individual problem. Due to the intersections of gender with class, racialization, ethnicity and migration status, these distributive problems particularly affect poor, migrant, rural and indigenous women who remain at the margins of social protection measures. As subsequent chapters show, this was the case in India and Bolivia. Relatedly, in Jamaica, China and Malaysia, paid care workers, and particularly domestic workers, experienced heightened precarity, either losing their jobs or facing greater exploitation and isolation.

Alongside the multiple material manifestations of the central role of care in sustaining life, care also emerged as a form of translocal political action. In many contexts, political organizing began as collective cross-movement solidarity actions meant to guarantee that those most at risk of marginalization had access to nourishment and support. The successful organizing by migrant domestic workers in Malaysia and the building of broad coalitions between migrants and non-migrant groups in Chile began with the distribution of care packages to those whose livelihoods were most at risk. These forms of solidarity took place at the local level regardless of migration or citizenship status. They also took place transnationally, as experienced by I-Kiribati seasonal workers stranded in Australia and New Zealand. Care was thus a significant political action that included, but was not limited to, conventional forms of political organizing such as advocacy for policy change. Rather, forming translocal relations of solidarity among workers, migrants and activists was both a means and an end. It was a means in that solidarity and relationship building were part of collective action and political organizing. It was an end in that care labour created and sustained these relationships. Francisco-Menchavez refers to this significant part of transnational solidarity as 'communities of care' that 'function like immigrant social networks through mutual assistance in practical issues of migrant life' (2018: 24), and are embedded in shared identities and experiences beyond simply transactional arrangements. The diasporic solidarities that sustained I-Kiribati workers were based on kinship, reciprocity and communal obligation, and acted as subaltern social protection mechanisms in a context of structural constraint and crisis (Ratuva 2014).

Care is at the heart of political mobilization (Tungohan 2023). Inasmuch as it can act as a form of *doing* politics, how care is practised, experienced and defined is at the heart of political struggle (Llavaneras Blanco 2024). The attempt at creating a national care system in Argentina offered the possibility of incorporating territorially-based care practices in the national policy process through participatory deliberative spaces. In this way, the pandemic period served as an opportunity to rethink care beyond the neoliberal rationale, to expand policy imagination and envision care provision as a collective responsibility. This volume is thus interested not only in policy changes measured through the successes of movements (ibid.) but also the political doings of women, queer, poor, migrant and other diverse and subaltern folk navigating constantly shifting policy and political contexts. Equally, this volume is concerned with the potential expansion of Southern feminist political imaginations that coexist with path-dependent policy environments, increased corporate capture and authoritarianism in the name of development.

4. Where are we headed?

This anthology is a collective attempt to grapple with the structural and multidimensional crisis catalysed by the Covid-19 pandemic. Our use of the word catalysed is deliberate because we believe that this complex crisis was triggered, but not caused, by the pandemic. In examining the crisis through the lenses of interlinkages and intersectionality, we understand that diverse and context-specific positionings shaped how individuals and collectives experienced it. Similarly, different aspects of our everyday lives, such as the right to move back home in times of crises or the access to vaccines in the midst of a pandemic, were closely interlinked with labour, social protection, care and macroeconomic policies. As the chapters in this book demonstrate, the Covid-19 crisis exposed these complexities for us to see.

In engaging with an interlinked and intersectional analysis of policy and political responses to the pandemic, this book cuts through mainstream narratives such as 'we are in this together' and critically examines a period of exception that will shape the years to come. By privileging a Southern feminist lens and centring social movements, the anthology contributes to a people-based and truly global analysis of the social, political and economic implications of the Covid-19 pandemic. It is an exercise in bearing witness to a growing wave of authoritarianisms that coexists with global and local efforts to sustain livelihoods and transform relations of power.

In so doing, this volume also flags worrying political trends and longstanding tensions that urgently demand our attention. The decommissioning of rights via extraordinary powers, the criminalization of internal and transnational migrants and the defunding of the public sphere are concerning processes that need to be addressed as we imagine and contribute to desirable futures. At the same time, in creating this partial register, we identified social organizing practices that hold potential for mobilizations to come: solidarity, care and mutual aid across movements, among citizens and non-citizens as well as among formal and informal workers were essential to building broad coalitions, changing policy discussions and creating political opportunities for social justice.

Finally, this book asks questions about the future to come. What have we learnt about collective organizing in a context in which the state does not guarantee our rights? How do states navigate path dependence and create new policy and political pathways towards social justice? How does care emerge despite the expansion of austerity? What drives and sustains collective care politics in a context of global corporate capture and growing authoritarianism? Part of the answers to some of these questions emerge from the following chapters.

Notes

1   See: https://www.imf.org/external/datamapper/GGXWDG_NGDP@WEO/
    OEMDC/ADVEC/WEOWORLD

References

Apedo-Amah, M. C., Avdiu, B., Cirera, X., Cruz, M., Davies, E., Grover, A., Iancovone, L., Kilinc, U., Medvedev, D., Maduko, F. O., Poupakis, S., Torres, J. and Tran, T. T. (2020), 'Unmasking the Impacts of COVID-19 on Businesses. Firm Level Evidence from Across the World', World Bank Group, Finance, Competitiveness and Innovation Global Practice, Policy Research Working Paper 9434. Available at: https://documents1.worldbank.org/curated/en/399751602248069405/pdf/Unmasking-the-Impact-of-COVID-19-on-Businesses-Firm-Level-Evidence-from-Across-the-World.pdf (accessed 4 July 2023).

Betthäuser, B.A., Bach-Mortensen, A.M. and Engzell, P. (2023), 'A Systematic Review and Meta-analysis of the Evidence on Learning during the COVID-19 Pandemic', *Nat Hum Behav*, 7: 375–385. Available at: https://doi.org/10.1038/s41562-022-01506-4 (accessed 20 February 2024).

Chancel, L., Piketty, T., Saez, E., and Zucman, G. (2022), 'World Inequality Report 2022', World Inequality Lab. Available at: https://wir2022.wid.world/www-site/uploads /2021/12/WorldInequalityReport2022_Full_Report.pdf (accessed 13 February 2024).

Chen, M., Grapsa, E., Ismail, G., Rogan, M., Valdivia, M., Alfers, L., Harvey, J., Ogando, A.C., Reed, S.O. and Roever, S. (2021), 'COVID-19 and Informal Work: Distinct Pathways of Impact and Recovery in 11 Cities Around the World', WIEGO Working Paper No. 42. Available at: https://www.wiego.org/sites/default/files/publications/file/ WIEGO_Working%20Paper%20No%2042%20May%202021.pdf (accessed 18 December 2023).

Clarke, J. and Newman, J. (2012), 'The Alchemy of Austerity', *Critical Social Policy*, 32(3): 299–319. Available at: https://doi.org/10.1177/0261018312444405 (accessed 26 October 2023).

Esper, T. L. (2021), 'Supply Chain Management Amid the Coronavirus Pandemic', *Journal of Public Policy & Marketing*, 40(1): 101–102. Available at: https://doi. org/10.1177/0743915620932150 ((accessed 26 October 2023).

Feminist Digital Justice Working Group (2023), 'Background Paper – Feminist Digital Justice'. Available at: https://feministdigitaljustice.net/background-paper/ (accessed 16 November 2023).

Folbre, N. (2020), *The Rise and Decline of Patriarchal Systems: An Intersectional Political Economy*, London: Verso.

FPV (2023), '"The End is Not Yet in Sight! Long-term Public Health Action is Critically Needed": Germany's Obligation to Support a Global Public Good Approach to COVID-19 Diagnostics, Vaccines and Therapeutics', A Shadow Report to 85th Session of the CEDAW. Available at: https://feminists4peoplesvaccine.org/wp-content/uploads/2023/05/Shadow-Report-CEDAW-2023-Germany.pdf (accessed in 4 August 2023).

Francisco-Menchavez, V. (2018), *The Labor of Care: Filipina Migrants and Transnational Families in the Digital Age*, Urbana: University of Illinois Press.

Gurbuz M. C, Yurt, O., Ozdemir, S., Sena, V. and Yu, W. (2023), 'Global Supply Chains Risks and COVID-19: Supply Chain Structure as a Mitigating Strategy for Small and Medium-sized Enterprises', *Journal of Business Research*, 155, Part B. Available at: https://doi.org/10.1016/j.jbusres.2022.113407 (accessed 13 February 2024).

Gurumurthy, A. (2020), 'A Feminist Future of Work in the Post-Pandemic Moment: A New Social Contract as if Women Matter', IT For Change and DAWN. Available at: https://itforchange.net/sites/default/files/1620/Feminist%20Digital%20Justice%20 Issue%20Paper%203_%20updated%20name%20and%20logo_0.pdf (accessed 20 February 2024).

Hill Collins, P. (2002), *Black Feminist Thought: Knowledge, Consciousness, and the Politics of Empowerment*, London, United States: Taylor & Francis Group.

Horton, R. (2020), 'Offline: COVID-19 – A Crisis of Power. Comment', *The Lancet*, 396. Available at: https://doi.org/10.1016/S0140-6736(20)32262-5 (accessed 13 February 2024).

ILO (2020a), 'The Impact of the COVID-19 Pandemic on Jobs and Incomes in G20 Countries', ILO-OECD paper prepared at the request of G20 leaders, Saudi Arabia's G20 Presidency 2020. Available at: https://www.ilo.org/wcmsp5/groups/public/---dgreports/---cabinet/documents/publication/wcms_756331.pdf (accessed 4 July 2023).

ILO (2020b), 'ILO Monitor: COVID-19 and the World of Work. Sixth Edition', Briefing Note. Available at: https://www.ilo.org/wcmsp5/groups/public/---dgreports/---dcomm/documents/briefingnote/wcms_755910.pdf (accessed 4 July 2023).

ILO (2020c), 'Protecting Migrant Workers During the COVID-19 Pandemic: Recommendations for Policy-makers and Constituents', Policy Brief. Available at: https://www.ilo.org/wcmsp5/groups/public/---ed_protect/---protrav/---migrant/documents/publication/wcms_743268.pdf (accessed 1 August 2023).

IMF (2020), 'Fiscal Monitor: Policies for the Recovery'. Available at: https://www.imf.org/en/Publications/FM/Issues/2020/09/30/october-2020-fiscal-monitor (accessed 18 December 2023).

Kuah, A. T. H. and Dillon, R. (2022), 'Introduction: Standing on the Shoulders of Giants: Sustainable Innovation, Disruption, and Change', in Adrian T. H. Kuah, Roberto Dillon (eds), *Digital Transformation in a Post-Covid World Sustainable Innovation, Disruption, and Change*, Boca Raton, Abingdon: CRC Press.

Llavaneras Blanco, M. and Cuervo, M.G. (2021), 'The Pandemic as a Portal: Policy Transformations Disputing the New Normal', DAWN. Available at: https://dawnnet.org/wp-content/uploads/2021/07/DAWNTalks_01_2021_AnalyticalFramework-1-1.pdf (accessed 18 December 2023).

Llavaneras Blanco, M. (2024) '"Do You Really Want to Know About This?": Critical Feminist Ethics of Care as a Project of Unsettling', in Bourgault, S., FitzGerald, M, and Robinson, F. (eds), *Decentering Epistemologies and Challenging Privilege: Critical Care Ethics Perspectives*, Rutgers University Press.

Lorde, A. (1984), *Sister Outsider: Essays and Speeches, Rev. ed (electronic), Crossing Press Feminist Series*, Berkeley, Calif.: Crossing Pres.

Marsden, G. and Docherty, I. (2021), 'Mega-disruptions and Policy Change: Lessons from the Mobility Sector in Response to the Covid-19 Pandemic in the UK', *Transport Policy*, 110: 86–97. Available at: https://doi.org/10.1016/j.tranpol.2021.05.015 (accessed 18 December 2023).

Murphy, J. (2010), 'Path Dependence and the Stagnation of Australian Social Policy Between the Wars', *Journal of Policy History*, 22(4): 450–473. doi:10.1017/S0898030610000229 (accessed 18 December 2023).

Ortiz, I. and Cummins, M. (2021), 'Global Austerity Alert: Looming Budget Cuts in 2021-25 and Alternative Pathways', SSRN. Available at: https://doi.org/10.2139/ssrn.3856299 (accessed 23 June 2023).

Our World in Data (2023), Coronavirus Pandemic (COVID-19). Available at: https://ourworldindata.org/covid-vaccinations (accessed 25 July 2023).

Ratuva, S. (2014), 'Failed' or Resilient Subaltern Communities? Pacific Indigenous Social Protection Systems in a Neoliberal World', *Pacific Journalism Review*, 20(2): 40–58. Available at: https://doi.org/10.24135/pjr.v20i2.165 (accessed 13 February 2024).

Rodríguez Enríquez, C. and Llavaneras Blanco, M. (2023), 'Conclusion: Corporate Capture of Development in Times of Exacerbated Crises: Implications for Democratic Governance, Rights and Global Inequality', in C. Rodríguez Enríquez, C. and M. Llavaneras Blanco (eds), *Corporate Capture of Development*, 279–291, London: Bloomsbury Publishing.

Roy, A. (2020), 'The Pandemic is a Portal', *Financial Times*, 3 April. Available at: https://www.ft.com/content/10d8f5e8-74eb-11ea-95fe-fcd274e920ca (accessed 11 January 2024).

Sen, G. and Durano, M. (2014), *The Remaking of Social Contracts: Feminists in a Fierce New World*, London: Zed Books.

Special Rapporteur on Extreme Poverty and Human Rights (2019), 'A/74/493: Digital Welfare States and Human Rights – Report of the Special Rapporteur on Extreme Poverty and Human Rights', OHCHR. Available at: https://www.ohchr.org/en/documents/thematic-reports/a74493-digital-welfare-states-and-human-rights-report-special-rapporteur (accessed 17 November 2023).

Stevano, S., Ali, R. and Jamieson, M. (2021), 'Essential for What? A Global Social Reproduction View on the Re-organisation of Work during the COVID-19 Pandemic', *Canadian Journal of Development Studies / Revue canadienne d'études du développement*, 42(1–2): 178–199. Available at: https://doi.org/10.1080/02255189.2020.1834362 (accessed 13 February 2024).

Tungohan, E. (2023), *Care Activism: Migrant Domestic Workers, Communities of Care and Movement-Building*, Champaign: Illinois: University of Illinois Press.

UNESCO (2023), 'UNESCO's Education Response to COVID-19'. Available at: https://www.unesco.org/en/covid-19/education-response/initiatives (accessed 13 January 2024).

WHO (2022), 'Global Spending on Health: Rising to the Pandemic's Challenges', Geneva: World Health Organization. Available at: https://apps.who.int/iris/bitstream/handle/10665/365133/9789240064911-eng.pdf (accessed 25 July 2023).

Section I

Examining Austerity and Path Dependence

1

Macro-Patriarchal Pandemic Policy: The India Case

Ritu Dewan

1. Introduction

India was among the countries most negatively impacted by the Covid-19 pandemic. The reasons are several, not least being an already collapsing economy and an uncompassionate policy response. The fundamental purpose of this chapter is to examine the impact of state responses during the pandemic, locating the analysis within four major spheres that are simultaneously independent and interconnected: labour policy and workers' rights, mobility and migration, social protection and macroeconomic structures (Llavaneras Blanco and Cuervo 2021). Dealing with these four spheres in isolation would result in an incomplete, partial and possibly truncated understanding of the issues and their impacts in the short and long term. This chapter equates labour structures with livelihoods rather than employment and work, extending further into sustainability, both of production and reproduction as well as in relation to the environment and ecology. It understands social protection as societal rights, thus eschewing the emphasis on protection, which is paternalistic and implies that the state *may* grant some handouts rather than implementing its mandate to fulfil the economic and extra-economic rights of the current and future labour force.

The chapter analyses the short- and long-term impacts of the lockdowns and the pandemic policies of the macro-patriarchal state on the gendered labour, livelihood and mobility rights of the working population through the framework of what I term feminist finance (Dewan 2019). That means I use a gender lens to study the relevant 'relief' measures, revenue raising and expenditure allocation, such as subsidies that affect both paid and unpaid work, enacted under the cover of the pandemic. I also examine the intersectional impacts of pandemic policies, or the lack of them, on the gendered economic and extra-economic realities of the poor, with a special focus on single women and transgender persons. Based on this analysis, I argue that the pandemic and the state response to it not only increased poverty, food insecurity and indebtedness but also produced what I call collateral inequalities: child marriage, domestic violence, and Covid widows and orphans.

Little macroeconomic data, let alone sex-disaggregated statistical information, exists on the pandemic's impact on informal workers and internal migrants. To address this gap, I gathered information from surveys and studies conducted by institutions and non-governmental organizations (NGOs) focusing on vulnerable sections who are being increasingly marginalized in the ongoing struggles between profits and wages, and between an uncaring state and its citizens.

2. Contextualizing India's gendered pandemic policy response

The pandemic struck in India at a time when the process of de-development and de-equalization had been gathering momentum for several years. Few, if any, serious rectification measures had been undertaken, with virtually all growth and development indicators declining sharply. The country's gross domestic product (GDP) had witnessed a secular fall since the third quarter of 2016–17, reaching a 42-year low of 4 per cent in the financial year 2019–20 (Mint 2022). Other indicators, too, declined, especially after demonetization in 2016 (Dewan and Sehgal 2018) and the flawed and hastily implemented goods and services tax (GST) (The Economic Times 2017). Weakening growth metrics were coupled with an unresponsive fiscal architecture, a sharp rise in the debt-to-GDP ratio (Mishra 2021), reduced public provisioning, a spike in inflation to nearly 13 per cent and industries functioning at less than 40 per cent capacity (Chauhan and Jaffrelot 2022, Sarkar and Bhowmik 2021).

This led to a massive rise in income inequality, with the top 1 per cent holding more than four times the wealth owned by the bottom 70 per cent (Chaudhuri and Ghosh 2021). Unemployment rose to a 45-year high of over 7 per cent (NSO 2021) and India recorded the lowest monthly minimum wage in South Asia at 4,300 Indian rupees (INR) (US$58) (Trading Economics 2023).

In terms of gender parity, India stood at 140 out of 156 countries on the World Economic Forum's Global Gender Gap Index 2021, and was ranked 151st in economic participation and opportunities (WEF 2021). India's female labour force participation (FLFP)[1] rate, historically among the lowest in the world, fell from 29.6 per cent in 1983 to 21.9 per cent in 2011–12 and 16.5 per cent in 2017–18 (Sundari 2020). The urban female workforce participation rate (FWPR)[2] witnessed a gradual decline, especially over the past two decades, to an all-time low of 14.2 per cent in 2018–19 (ibid.) while the gender wage gap rose 7 per cent between 2018–19 and 2020–21 (ILO 2022), exacerbating an ongoing process of gender de-equalization. In general, a low FWPR disproportionately impacts the most vulnerable sections, including Scheduled Tribes (STs), Scheduled Castes (SCs), Other Backward Castes (OBCs) and minorities.[3]

Given the desperate economic situation of a majority of India's citizens, one would have expected budgetary allocations for the financial year 2020–21 to not only be fully utilized but also expanded beyond revised estimates. The opposite was true, with the government using the 25 per cent fall in central revenue between April–September 2019 and April–September 2020, primarily due to the slashing of corporate tax rates, as an excuse. As of October 2020, central expenditure was less than 48 per cent of the 2020–21 target compared with nearly 60 per cent in the same period in the previous financial year. In tandem, expenditure by states rose INR0.20 trillion (US$2.7 billion) (CBGA 2021, Ministry of Finance 2020–21). It is important to note that the sharp decrease in disbursement of the due share of GST collections to the states, at a time when they needed it the most, was a crucial constitutional issue. It translated into decreased development expenditure, hindering the attainment of the Sustainable Development Goals (SDGs).

What is also disquieting is the fall in spending by crucial ministries and departments between April–September 2019 and April–September 2020. Major subsidies, which primarily benefit the working poor, fell 26 per cent. Allocations to ministries and departments, crucial to ameliorating economic distress, declined sharply: statistics and programme implementation by 72 per cent, medium, small and micro enterprises (MSMEs) by 59 per cent, textiles by 58 per cent, skill development and entrepreneurship by 51 per cent, tribal affairs by 51 per cent and commerce and industry by 47 per cent.

The pandemic 'relief' packages focused on supply-side factors, easing credit to businesses rather than creating demand, even though the latter is essential to addressing massive unemployment and a deepening wage crisis. The first set of relief measures, introduced on 26 March 2020, was worth INR170,000 crore (US$22.97 billion). This was followed on 12 May 2020 by packages worth INR20 trillion (US$307.60 billion). More than 60 per cent of this cumulative amount was meant to extend credit rather than revive consumption.

The disastrous consequences of these policies for India's marginalized sections have to be viewed within the context of three essential processes that gained ascendency over the past decade: the growing centralization of political power, the concentration of capital and appropriation of public assets, and the shrinking space for economic and political dissent, as seen in the imprisonment of activists without trial. India's ranking in the Global Democracy Index fell from twenty-seven in 2014 to fifty-one in 2019 due to significant *democratic backsliding*: it is now categorized as a *flawed democracy* and has been downgraded from *free* to *partly free* (Economist Intelligence Unit 2022). India's current global rankings across several indicators are the lowest in its entire history: 122/166 across all SDGs (Sustainable Development Report 2023), 107/121 on the Global Hunger Index (von Grebmer et al. 2022), 127/146 on the Global Gender Gap Index (WEF 2023) and 123/161 on Oxfam's Commitment to Reducing Inequality (Walker et al. 2022).

2.1 Morphology of labour, livelihoods and mobility

Despite repeated warnings, the state did not respond for several weeks after the first Covid-19 case was reported in December 2019. The first policy response, if it can be called that, was the imposition of a brutal three-week complete nationwide lockdown on 25 March 2020, which began with a mere four-hour notice to the population. That left 200 million people, primarily workers and internal migrants, stranded and compelled to walk thousands of kilometres back to their villages with their families and whatever little they could carry. Almost a thousand people died on the way (Gaon Connection 2022). There was no state support in the form of food, shelter or transportation. While free flights flew back those stranded abroad, trains for migrants were permitted only six weeks later and available to only those who could pay their own fares. The images of these desperate citizens in the world's largest democracy will haunt the nation for eternity. While rights groups, unions, organizations, institutions, NGOs and individuals stepped in to assist in whatever way possible, they could fill the huge vacuum left by the state only partially.

The impact on the economy was immediate. By April 2020, at least 100 million men and 19 million women lost their jobs (CII and APU 2021, Deshpande 2020a). Subsequent recovery was tempered by a lack of preparedness for the second wave (APU 2021). A year later, employment rates stood at 94 per cent of pre-pandemic levels for men and 73 per cent for women (Abraham 2021), with urban unemployment at 18 per cent (TNN 2021). Although men lost more jobs in absolute terms, employment declined more sharply for women at 43 per cent compared with 30 per cent for men. This was true for women in all categories of employment and across sectors (CII and APU 2021, APU 2021). Women also benefitted less from any subsequent recovery in the employment market. Fewer women than men reported actively looking for work (ActionAid 2020, IWWAGE 2020). Women were seven times more likely than men to lose employment and eleven times more likely to not return to work (Abraham et al. 2021b). Major reasons included severe contraction in women-friendly sectors such as health, education, garment and textiles, construction and MSMEs, and the loss of fallback options (Abraham et al. 2021a, 2021b; APU 2021; IWWAGE 2020).

Job losses were accompanied by declines in work intensity and wages, with informal and migrant women workers more severely impacted and often forced to accept exploitative terms for fear of being unemployed (AIDWA 2020a, 2020b; Mohan et al. 2021). Home workers in Ahmedabad, for instance, were paid INR10–15 (14–20 cents) for eight hours of work (Thomas and Sundaram 2020) while sex workers in Uttar Pradesh and Bihar charged INR5 (7 cents) per encounter. Further, 52 per cent more women than men did not receive due wages (ActionAid 2020).

A large proportion of those who lost jobs were internal migrants, as the lockdowns triggered huge waves of reverse migration from urban to rural areas (SWAN 2020). While there are no numbers for how many women migrated back during the pandemic, census figures show a spurt in female rural-to-urban migration from 4.1 million in 2001 to 8.5 million in 2011 in response to agrarian distress (Mazumdar and Neetha 2020). Coming from socioeconomically marginalized communities with little education, female migrants work at the bottom of the informal labour pyramid, mostly as cane cutters, brick kiln workers, construction labour, street vendors, waste pickers, home-based workers for textile and garment factories, and domestic workers (Neetha 2021, Mukerjee and Naryanan 2020, Xavier 2020). Facing disproportionate job losses during the pandemic (AIDWA 2020a, Agnihotri and Hans 2021, ISST 2021, Jan Sahas 2020) and having limited or no access to social protections, many were forced to return to their villages.

Despite this massive reverse migration, the 2020–21 Union Budget reduced allocations to agriculture and allied activities by 13 per cent. It also cut allocation for the PM Kisan Saman Nidhi (Farmer Fund) from INR75,000 crore (US$9.02 billion) to INR65,000 crore (US$7.82 billion) (Ramakumar 2021). Similarly, allocations to MSMEs were drastically cut from INR69,800 crore (US$8.39 billion) to INR15,699 crore (US$2.12 billion), even though they account for 40 per cent of industrial production and employ 120 million workers (Tambe 2023). This came amid supply disruptions, domestic demand shocks and a decline in external demand.

Illustration 1.1 Migrant workers and their family members walk with their belongings on a highway towards Uttar Pradesh as they leave for their villages during a government-imposed nationwide lockdown as a preventive measure against the COVID-19 coronavirus, in Faridabad on March 27, 2020. *Photo by Money SHARMA / AFP via Getty Images.*

Those who had remained in the villages were unable to sell their produce (MAKAAM 2020), withdraw money without Aadhaar (digital identity) cards or get jobs under the Mahatma Gandhi National Rural Employment Guarantee Scheme (MGNREGS), India's largest employment guarantee scheme,[4] due to increased competition from returning migrants (Centre for Equity Studies et al. 2020, Sharma 2020). By 2021, fewer women were migrating from rural to urban areas (Jan Sahas 2021). Yet, the 2020–21 Budget reduced allocation to the MGNREGS by 13 per cent from the previous year (The Economic Times 2020b). Only 2.7–2.8 million individual workdays were possible through this policy in 2020–21 compared with 3.4 million in the earlier year (Dewan 2023).

Under the Pradhan Mantri Jan Dhan Yojana (PMJDY), INR500 (US$6.8) was to be given to women account holders each month between April and June 2020.

While 75 per cent of those eligible received the transfers (APU 2020, Totapally et al. 2020), only 32 per cent got all three tranches (MAKAAM 2020, Kejriwal 2020, Kesar et al. 2020, Patel et al. 2020). This was in large part because beneficiaries had to travel three times to receive the transfers rather than availing of the total amount of INR1,500 (US$20.3) at one go. This at a time when public transport was suspended.

2.2 Household income, poverty and inequality

The sudden and adverse changes in the labour market translated into collapsed incomes, eroded savings and rising household debt. Per capita average monthly real income declined 30 per cent from pre-pandemic levels; for the lowest decile, the fall was 42 per cent (APU 2021). The result was a greater rise in poverty. The number of people earning below the national minimum wage threshold rose 15 per cent in rural India and 20 per cent in urban areas (ibid.). The bottom 20 per cent of households reported a 71 per cent income loss compared with 51 per cent for the top quintile (Totapally et al. 2020). In 2021, India accounted for 57.3 per cent of the global rise in pandemic-induced poverty; for the middle-income category, poverty rose 59.3 per cent (Kochhar 2021). The Pew Research Center estimated that the Indian middle class would shrink by 32 million in 2020 and over 75 million people would join the ranks of the poor (ibid.).

The immediate outcome of the collapse of livelihood structures, coupled with inadequate state-sponsored cash and food transfers, was a massive increase in food insecurity. Despite the Right to Food being enshrined in the Constitution, 76 per cent of rural households could not afford a nutritious diet even in the pre-pandemic period (Neetha 2021). Following the first national lockdown, about 70 per cent of households in the lower income deciles had to reduce consumption, with 60 per cent continuing to remain hungry six months later (Kumar and Kumar 2021).

Especially in a crisis, the stress of inadequate food falls disproportionately on women, who eat the last and the least. This gender gap in nutrition is wider for socioeconomically vulnerable groups, including migrants (Puskur and Mohan 2020). During the pandemic, the monthly allotment of five kilograms of free grains and one kilogram of pulses between April and June 2020, which was later extended to November 2021, was made available only to those who could produce ration cards[5] and met Aadhaar card conditionalities.[6] That left out migrants, who are not covered under the National Food Security Act (NFSA) (Bhat 2021), and single women, who typically do not possess independent cards.

Seventy million poor women were excluded from free food support in 2020 due to the lack of ration cards (IWWAGE 2020). As seen with the cessation of the Ghana School Feeding Programme (Torvikey and Marfo, this volume), the suspension of food provisions through child care centres and school mid-day meals increased child undernutrition (Madhavan 2020). Yet, the first post-pandemic Budget reduced the overall food subsidy by a third, nutrition allocations by 16 per cent and allocation to the Mid-Day Meal Scheme by INR500 crore (US$67.6 million).

Meanwhile, the drastic fall in incomes compelled the poor, especially single women, to cut consumption, draw upon meagre savings, sell assets and borrow to meet daily consumption and health needs. Households with land, livestock, bicycles, watches, mobile phones and even cooking vessels sold or pawned them. The main assets thus disposed of included jewellery (35 per cent) and livestock (25 per cent), both of which typically belong to women (APU 2020). With banks and cooperatives providing little credit in both rural and urban areas, people borrowed from informal institutions and networks. The median loan amount ranged from two to six times the monthly income (APU 2021). Not only were asset-less households more likely to borrow, the amount borrowed was a higher multiple of their pre-pandemic incomes (APU 2020). ActionAid (2020) reported that the incidence of debt was greater among migrants than non-migrants.

By the time the second wave of the pandemic hit, most households had depleted their resources and/or were in debt, leaving them with little protection against future shocks and delaying their exit from poverty. Between March and December 2020, household debt ballooned from INR68.9 trillion (US$930 billion) to INR73.1 trillion (US$990 billion). Savings in the form of bank deposits crashed from INR3.6 trillion (US$49 billion) in the July–September quarter of 2020 to INR1.7 trillion (US$23 billion) in the following quarter (Varma 2021).

2.3 Unpaid work burden

Globally, India has among the highest percentages of people engaged in unpaid work, with a bulk of it done by women. The potential annual addition to India's GDP from raising women's paid employment is estimated between INR518 trillion (US$7 trillion) and INR2,146 trillion (US$29 trillion); about 70 per cent of the increase could come from a mere 10 per cent rise in the FLFP (Mckinsey Global Institute 2016).

India's first time use survey (2019) reveals that women spend four hours and fifty-nine minutes per day on unpaid domestic work compared with one hour and thirty-nine minutes spent by men (Shaik 2020). In times of crises, women's unpaid work intensifies to ensure the survival of households and communities, especially when the state defaults on its responsibilities such as the provision of food security and public health (Dewan et al. 2017). The Covid-19 lockdown, too, intensified women's unpaid work burden by increasing the number of members present in the house and shifting the burden of public services such as schools, crèches, anganwadis,[7] clinics and hospitals on to women (IMPRI 2021). Interestingly, although the time spent by men on unpaid work increased during the lockdown, it subsequently declined but remained above the pre-pandemic level (Deshpande 2020b).

Despite the rising burden of unpaid work, subsidies on cooking energy were withdrawn during the pandemic year. The gas subsidy, opted for by poor women in particular, was stopped without notice in April 2020; the free gas cylinder scheme Ujjwala ceased to function on 30 September 2020 although the 2021–22 Budget assured its extension to 10 million households. The refill price more than doubled, making clean cooking energy unaffordable for even the lower middle class, especially in a context of declining incomes. Direct Benefit Transfer of kerosene, sold under the public distribution system (PDS) to those who do not have a gas connection, was withdrawn in February 2020. This subsidy allocation had been halved in the 2019–20 Budget even as fuel retailers were permitted to raise prices fortnightly.

3. Collateral inequalities

The apathetic state response resulted in what I term collateral inequalities, namely an increase in violence, child marriage, new widows and orphans. In addition to the risks faced by all migrants, women were particularly prone to assault, rape and other types of violence, including police brutality (Sen, A. 2020, Thapliyal 2020). With priority given to the pandemic, few medical services were available to persons with disabilities, pregnant women, post-natal women and infants. Menstrual health and hygiene were ignored because sanitary products are not defined as essential goods (Kakar 2020). With babies born on the roads, in auto rickshaws and at hospital gates, deaths of mothers and newborn babies increased (AIDWA 2020a).

Women in returnee migrant households faced domestic violence due to financial and mental stress (Kumar and Anand 2020). Migrant women who stayed back in cities in search of jobs suffered police high-handedness, and physical and sexual violence (ISST 2020). The National Commission for Women reported a 2.5-fold increase in domestic violence cases registered between 27 February and 31 May 2020 (Chandra 2020). Kolkata-based feminist organization Swayam reported a 55 per cent increase in domestic violence during the lockdown in April–May 2020, escalating to 171 per cent post the lockdown in June–July 2020 (Kapoor 2021). This included cases of domestic violence against married women by husbands and in-laws, including marital rape (Sen, A. 2020); against unmarried or single young women by fathers, brothers, boyfriends, neighbours and others; and against women with disabilities by partners and personal attendants. Caregivers' inability to reach their dependents and reduced access to medicine, groceries, therapy and rehabilitation emerged as major challenges (Bhandare 2020). No state agency collected disaggregated data on domestic violence against women with disabilities (Sen, R. 2020).

Despite an April 2020 Delhi High Court order to take appropriate measures to curb domestic violence (The Economic Times 2020a), state response in the form of One Stop Centres (OSC) and a national helpline failed to translate into real services on the ground (Kapoor 2021). Although women's rights and transgender and sexuality rights organizations stepped in, they were impeded by movement restrictions and the lack of transport (Kumar and Kumar 2021). The absence of a comprehensive policy led to the invisibilization of domestic violence, especially against women with disabilities, those with HIV-AIDS, sex workers, prisoners and transgender persons.

The transgender community is among the most exploited in India, facing high levels of stigma, discrimination, violence and rights violations. A majority are in informal jobs and the lack of a transgender-sensitive pandemic policy response exacerbated their extant marginalization, precarity and susceptibility to violence. Most became unemployed, especially as sex work was drastically affected due to the fear of infection and physical distancing requirements. With existing laws criminalizing transgender people, policing during lockdowns became an added source of threat (Vee and Salelkar 2021). The loss of income robbed them of respect, increased their chances of facing domestic violence from fathers and brothers, and cut off their access to specialized health treatments such as HIV-AIDS medication, hormone treatments and support groups. Even as some states introduced welfare packages, disbursement was delayed and access required some form of official certification (Queer Relief 2020).

New forms of collateral inequality included women widowed by the Covid-related deaths of their husbands and children orphaned after losing both parents.

While no official data has been collected on the numbers of those derogatorily termed 'Covid widows', the National Commission for Protection of Child Rights reported 30,071 'Covid orphans' between April 2020 and June 2021, which is likely a vast underestimation. Testimonies reveal the manifold vulnerabilities of such women and children: health problems due to Covid and other conditions; social isolation; ostracization; homelessness; job losses; financial stress; domestic violence; sexual and other kinds of harassment by family members, neighbours and strangers; uncertainty regarding children's education and future; and high levels of mental and emotional stress. Orphan girls in particular faced a host of problems, including hunger, starvation, eviction, discontinuation of education, child labour, early marriage and trafficking (Gupta 2021).

When alerted by NGOs, the Ministry of Women and Child Development (MWCD) issued a public warning against social media messages discussing adoption of these children and outlined steps that could be followed by district welfare committees and other organizations to track such messages (Roy 2021). Several states, including Kerala, Delhi, Punjab, Madhya Pradesh, Uttarakhand, Karnataka and Andhra Pradesh, announced schemes for financial assistance and free education, which can potentially be converted into permanent policies, but none made provisions for claims to natal and marital property (Kad 2021). At the national level, the first post-pandemic Budget cut allocation to education by INR6,000 crore (US$810 million) in a context where 22 per cent of ST and 18 per cent of SC children had dropped out of school due to lack of money for fees.

Among the most disastrous consequences was the rise in child marriages. The United Nations Children's Fund (UNICEF) (2021) predicted that financial distress caused by Covid-19 could push an additional 10 million girls into child marriage by the end of the current decade. Before the pandemic struck, India was progressing towards achieving SDG Target 5.3 to end child marriage by 2030. The proportion of women aged twenty to twenty-four who were married off before they were eighteen declined to 27 per cent in 2015–16 from 47 per cent in 2006–07 (Jejeebhoy 2021). However, the lack of a child- and gender-sensitive pandemic policy led to a spurt in child and teenage marriages, heightening the risk of domestic slavery, spousal violence and poor health. Childline, a nodal agency of the MWCD for assisting children in distress, received 5,584 calls relating to child marriage between May and July 2020, a 33 per cent increase from pre-pandemic levels (ibid.). Several NGOs reported increased child marriages, with more cases involving girls than boys (Bahl et al. 2021, Chakraborty 2021, Thomas 2021).

4. Demissioning democratic rights

During the pandemic, the executive power introduced three major legal and policy changes in an authoritarian manner with little democratic space for discussion and debate. These included the replacement of existing labour laws with Labour Codes, the promulgation of the Farm Acts and the reduction of access to common property resources, which curtailed tribal and forest rights.

In a situation which urgently called for safeguarding, if not expanding, labour, livelihood and mobility rights, the state did the opposite, repealing all thirty-five existing labour laws and replacing them with Labour Codes that it claimed were needed for the 'ease of doing business'. These included the Code on Wages, which was officially announced in the Gazette on 7 July 2020; the Code on Occupational Safety, Health and Working Conditions, which was promulgated outside Parliament on 29 September 2020; the Code on Social Security, which was finalized in December 2020; and the Code on Industrial Relations, which was circulated in December 2020. The last three Bills were passed after less than two hours of discussion amid a boycott of Parliament by Opposition parties over the passage of the Farm Bills (The Hindu 2020).

All four Labour Codes eliminated labour protections and workers' rights and reinforced gender stereotypes. They restricted the definition of employee/worker to establishment/industry; derecognized home-based workers, domestic workers and apprentices by precluding work in private households; extended the workday from eight to twelve hours; delinked sexual harassment from safe working conditions; invisibilized female- and child-headed households; allowed self-certification of compliance by employers; reduced women's representation on boards and committees; and extended the ban on strikes and other forms of democratic protest to all sectors (Dewan 2020).

The three Farm Acts passed in September 2020, namely the Farmers (Empowerment and Protection) Agreement on Price Assurance and Farm Services Act, 2020; the Farmers' Produce Trade and Commerce (Promotion and Facilitation) Act, 2020; and the Essential Commodities (Amendment) Act, 2020, faced severe criticism nationally and internationally, both for their provisions and the undemocratic haste with which they were pushed through. The provisions compelled farmers to directly trade with large corporations, allowed companies to dictate crop choices and cultivation practices that ignore agro-climatic concerns, emphasized online trading, bypassed state-run and regulated Agricultural Produce Market Committees, denied fixed minimum selling prices, deregulated prices of products of mass consumption, impacted PDS availability and transferred powers of arbitration and redressal from the judiciary to the executive (MAKAAM 2020, Premkumar 2020). As such, they were against the interests and lived realities of small and marginal farmers, including women. The farmers' agitation against these laws became the largest ever in world history, with at least 250 million people participating across the country (Pahwa 2020). The massive mobilization eventually forced the central government to repeal the laws in November 2021 (PRS n.d.).

Despite the farmer mobilization's success, the demissioning of democratic rights under the pandemic camouflage continued with the draft Environment Impact Assessment Policy released in 2020, which specifically affected tribal communities. The dilution of the Forest Rights Act, 2006; curtailed powers of the state under the Forest Conservation Act, 1980; and the recent mining reforms, including the privatization of coal, violate the provisions of the Panchayats (Extension to Scheduled Areas) (PESA) Act, 1996.[8] These policies made it easier for the government and the private sector to implement projects without environmental scrutiny and led to the denial of historical and constitutional rights that guaranteed the protection of tribal communities and natural resources.

5. In lieu of a conclusion

The unethical, uncompassionate, people-insensitive and gender-blind pandemic policy response has long-term generational consequences, exacerbating the de-equalization of gendered labour, livelihood and mobility rights. Such consequences include the loss of potential for improving employment and employability; intensification of labour precarity and horizontal and vertical migration; reinforcement of patriarchal divides; widening of the gender wage gap; expansion and deepening of poverty; intensification of economic and extra-economic inequalities; and a decline in nutritional, health and educational access, thereby negatively affecting the quality of not only the present but also the future workforce.

Despite the depth of the crisis, a few state governments, often at the behest of NGOs, especially women's and civil rights organizations, took several gender-sensitive measures that can be refined and replicated going forward. These include measures related to food availability, identity proof, digitalization, cash transfers to families where the main earner has died and financial support to sex workers and transgender persons. The case of the state of Kerala stands out as a best practice from which much can be learnt about gender sensitivity, an effective public health system, a strong database, and welfare orientation combined with a decentralized system of governance and a culture of mass participation. Kerala's pandemic relief package of 19 March 2020 was prompt, generous, pro-poor and pro-migrant: nearly 400,000 ready cooked meals were distributed every day from community kitchens; every family received a food kit; 5.5 million elderly/disadvantaged persons were given INR8,500 (US$115) each as welfare payments and an equal number of workers were paid INR1,000–3,000 (US$13.5–41) each. Local governments, strengthened by devolution of administrative and financial powers, set up camps for migrant workers, ensuring provision of food and medicine (Isaac 2020). The state's 600,000 self-help groups, state-institutionalized and financially supported women neighbourhood groups (Kudumbashree), and civil society organizations also played crucial roles (Roy and Dave 2020).

Also inspiring were the sparks of feminist progressive practices that offer learning opportunities for transformative policy, advocacy and action. Every corner of the country witnessed the unprecedented coming together of a massive number of social organizations. Women's groups, human and civil rights groups, trade unions, NGOs, donor organizations, housing societies, teachers and students' organizations, etc., stepped forward to provide support, especially to the labouring poor, and create a baseline of social statistics. Although these efforts could not fill the vast vacuum left by an uncaring state, they led to greater awareness of democratic, constitutional and human rights, and new forms of solidarity, association and organizing that cut across class, community, sectoral and often political divides. The challenges thrown up by the lack of mobility and physical protest were turned into opportunities through social media and by using the long periods of compulsory isolation for introspection and research. The result was a creative process of decentralization and deepening of feminist transformative change combined with a strengthening of the interconnections between macro, meso and micro movements. In addition, there was a renewed recognition that the struggles of marginalized sections must unite in terms of issues, tactics and strategies. All this despite extensive rollback of democratic freedoms and the right to dissent and protest as well as attacks on funding opportunities. The struggle is long and difficult, but the sparks are many and multiple.

Notes

1 Labour force participation refers to the sum of employed and unemployed people.

2   The workforce participation rate refers to the percentage of people in the working age population that are in the labour force.

3   STs, SCs and OBCs are groups recognized by India's Constitution as deserving of positive discrimination in education and public sector employment. ST and SC groups constitute 9 per cent and 17 per cent of the population, respectively (2011 Census). While no precise numbers are available for OBCs, they comprise a sizeable section as well.

4   MGNREGS is a nationwide rural workforce programme where each registered family is assured, on demand, 100 days of unskilled wage work in a year at wages fixed by the government.

5   The ration card is an official document issued to the head of the household, which entitles them to purchase of essentials such as wheat, rice, sugar and oil at subsidized prices from the PDS under the NFSA.

6   Every resident of India has to compulsorily have an Aadhaar card with a twelve-digit unique identity number based on biometric and demographic data. This digital identity is essential for availing of any scheme and benefit, including wages.

7   Anganwadis, which translates into courtyard shelters, are rural child care centres started by the government in 1975 as part of the Integrated Child Development Services programme to combat child hunger and malnutrition. As part of India's public health system, they provide a diverse bundle of basic health services.

8   Panchayats are the basic components local self-government in rural areas mandated under the 73rd Constitutional Amendment (the Panchayati Raj Act,1992). The Act exempted from its provisions predominantly tribal areas identified as Scheduled Areas. The PESA Act provides these areas with a system that takes into consideration customary resources, minor forest produce, minor minerals, minor water bodies, selection of beneficiaries, sanction of projects and control over local institutions. The Act has been viewed as a panacea for tribal populations who have suffered from rampant land acquisition and displacement due to modern development processes and statutes unfair to their communities.

References

Abraham, R. (2021), '1 Year of Covid and the Way Forward', *Hindustan Times*, 5 May. Available at: https://www.hindustantimes.com/india-news/1-year-of-covid-and-the-way-forward-101620160471649.html (accessed 12 June 2021).

Abraham, R., Basole, A. and Kesar, S. (2021a), 'Younger Workers and Women Were Hit Most by Covid-19 – and They're Still Struggling to Recover', *Scroll*, 21 January. Available at: https://scroll.in/article/984591/younger-workers-and-women-were-hit-most-by-covid-19-and-theyre-still-struggling-to-recover (accessed 14 June 2022).

Abraham, R., Basole, A. and Kesar, S. (2021b), 'Down and Out? The Gendered Impact of the Covid-19 Pandemic on India's Labour Market', CSE Working Paper No. 40, Centre for Sustainable Employment, Azim Premji University. Available at: https://cse.azimpremjiuniversity.edu.in/wp-content/uploads/2021/02/Abraham_Basole_Kesar_Gender_Covid_Feb_2021.pdf (accessed 5 November 2023).

ActionAid (2020), *Workers in the Time of Covid-19: Round 1 of the National Study on Informal Sector*, New Delhi: ActionAid Association India. Available at: https://www.actionaidindia.org/wp-content/uploads/2020/08/Workers-in-the-time-of-Covid-19_ebook1.pdf.

Agnihotri, I. and Hans, A. (2021), 'The "New Normal": Making Sense of Women Migrants' Encounter with Covid-19 in India', in A. Hans, K. Kannabiran, M. Mohanty and Pushpendra (eds), *Migration, Workers and Fundamental Freedoms: Pandemic Vulnerabilities and States of Exception in India*, 53–69, New York: Routledge.

AIDWA (2020a), 'Covid-19 Pandemic and the Modi Regime: The Invisible Despair of Women', All India Democratic Women's Association. Available at: https://www.aidwaonline.org/sites/default/files/2020-08/AIDWA%20Booklet%20PDF%20FInal.pdf (accessed 5 November 2023).

AIDWA (2020b), 'Impact of Covid-19 Lockdown on Domestic Workers in India', All India Democratic Women's Association. Available at: https://aidwaonline.org/sites/default/files/2020-10/AIDWA%20DOMESTIC%20WORKERS%27%20SURVEY%20REPORT.pdf (accessed 5 November 2023).

APU (2020), 'Covid-19 Livelihood Survey: Compilation of Findings', Azim Premji University. Available at: https://ruralindiaonline.org/en/library/resource/covid-19-livelihood-survey-compilation-of-findings/ (accessed 5 November 2023).

APU (2021), 'State of Working India', Azim Premji University. Available at: https://cse.azimpremjiuniversity.edu.in/state-of-working-india/swi-2021/ (accessed 5 November 2023).

Bahl, D., Bassi, S., and Arora, M. (2021), 'The Impact of Covid-19 on Children and Adolescents: Early Evidence in India', Issue Brief No. 448, Observer Research Foundation. Available at: https://www.orfonline.org/wp-content/uploads/2021/03/ORF_IssueBrief_448_Covid-Children-Adolescents.pdf (accessed 5 November 2023).

Bhandare, N. (2021), 'The Lockdown is Hard for Women with Disability', *Hindustan Times*, 1 May. Available at: https://www.hindustantimes.com/columns/the-lockdown-is-hard-for-women-with-disability/story-4uOVBLxLOoukdlcqWvP1vJ.html (accessed 24 June 2021).

Bhat, R. M. (2022), 'Poor Hungry During Covid Despite PM's Garib Kalyan Anna Yojna', *NewsClick*, 22 May. Available at: https://www.newsclick.in/poor-hungry-during-covid-despite-PM-garib-kalyan-ana-yojna (accessed 30 June 2021).

CBGA (2021), 'Budget in the Time of the Pandemic: An Analysis of Union Budget 2021-22', Centre for Budget and Governance Accountability. Available at: https://

www.cbgaindia.org/wp-content/uploads/2021/02/Budget-in-the-Time-of-Pandemic-An-Analysis-of-Union-Budget-2021-22.pdf (accessed 26 October 2023).

Centre for Equity Studies, Delhi Research Group and Karwan-E-Mohabbat (2020), 'Labouring Lives: Hunger, Precarity and Despair Amid Lockdown'. Available at: http://centreforequitystudies.org/wp-content/uploads/2020/06/Labouring-Lives-_Final-Report.pdf (accessed 19 June 2021).

Chakraborty, R. (2021), 'What India Can Learn from Community Efforts in Patna to Prevent Child Marriages during Lockdown', *Scroll*, 19 April. Available at: https://scroll.in/article/991227/what-india-can-learn-from-community-efforts-in-patna-to-prevent-child-marriages-during-lockdown (accessed 19 June 2021).

Chandra, J. (2021), 'NCW Records Sharp Spike in Domestic Violence Amid Lockdown', *The Hindu*, 15 June. Available at: https://www.thehindu.com/news/national/ncw-records-sharp-spike-in-domestic-violence-amid-lockdown/article31835105.ece (accessed 24 June 2021).

Chaudhuri, D. and Ghosh, P. (2021), 'Why Inequality is India's Worst Enemy?', *Down to Earth*, 5 March. Available at: https://www.downtoearth.org.in/blog/economy/why-inequality-is-india-s-worst-enemy-75778 (accessed 24 June 2021).

Chauhan. T and Jaffrelot, C. (2022), 'Upsurge Affects Poor the Most, Govt Must Retool Policy to Ensure that Inequalities Do Not Deepen', *The Indian Express*, 16 June. Available at: https://indianexpress.com/article/opinion/columns/inflation-income-inequality-economic-policies-7972236/ (accessed 26 October 2023).

CII and APU (2021), 'Reviving Employment and Livelihoods in India: Covid-19 and After'. Available at: https://cse.azimpremjiuniversity.edu.in/wp-content/uploads/2021/03/CII-Report-Employment-Livelihoods-1.pdf (accessed 5 November 2023).

Deshpande, A. (2020a), 'The Covid-19 Pandemic and Gendered Division of Paid and Unpaid Work: Evidence from India', Discussion Paper 13815, Bonn: IZA Institute of Labour Economics. Available at: https://docs.iza.org/dp13815.pdf (accessed 5 November 2023).

Deshpande, A. (2020b), 'The Covid-19 Pandemic and Lockdown: First Order Effects on Gender Gaps in Employment and Domestic Time Use in India', GLO Discussion Paper Series 607, Global Labour Organisation. Available at: https://ideas.repec.org/p/zbw/glodps/607.html (accessed 5 November 2023).

Dewan, R., Sehgal, R., Kanchi, A. and Raju, S. (2017), *Invisible Work, Invisible Workers: The Sub-Economics of Unpaid Work and Paid Work*, New Delhi: UN Women.

Dewan, R. and Sehgal, R. (2018), *Demonetisation: from Desperation to Destitution*, Mumbai: Himalaya Publishing House.

Dewan, R. (2019), 'Gender Equalisation through Feminist Finance', in *Economic & Political Weekly*, 54(17): 17–21. Available at: https://www.epw.in/journal/2019/17/commentary/gender-equalisation-through-feminist-finance.html (accessed 5 November 2023).

Dewan, R. (2020), 'Gender De-equalisation via Labour Codes. In Tamil Nadu', *National Law University Law Review*, 3(1): 1–8.

Dewan, R. (2023), "Resilient' Women, 'Resilient' Agriculture', *Indian Journal of Agricultural Economics*, 78(1): 71–78. Available at: https://isaeindia.org/wp-content/uploads/2023/04/3-Ritu-Dewan-keynote-address.pdf (accessed 5 November 2023).

Economist Intelligence Unit (2022), Democracy Index 2022. Available at: https://www.eiu.com/n/campaigns/democracy-index-2022/ (accessed 5 November 2023).

Gaon Connection (2022), 'The Lockdown Story: The Road to Hell and Back', 25 March. Available at: https://www.gaonconnection.com/read/lockdown-anniversary-coronavirus-covid19-migrant-labourers-deaths-hunger-disease-poverty-reverse-migration-jobs-development-50556#:~:text—eanwhile%2C%20a%20private,standing%20in%20lines (accessed 5 November 2023).

Gupta, V. (2021), 'Second Wave Ruins Families and Orphans Children in Punjab', *NewsClick*, 10 June, Available at: https://www.newsclick.in/second-wave-ruins-families-and-orphans-children-punjab (accessed 27 June 2021).

ILO (2022), 'OpEd: The Gender Pay Gap, Hard Truths and Actions Needed', 19 September. Available at: https://www.ilo.org/newdelhi/info/public/fs/WCMS_857392/lang--en/index.htm (accessed 5 November 2023).

IMPRI (2021), 'Release of Study Findings Rural Telephonic Time Use Survey Study in Bihar - Life in the Era of COVID-19: Impact on Village Makers of Bihar and Future Prospects'. Available at: https://www.impriindia.com/event-report/life-in-the-era-of-covid-19-impact-on-villagemakers/ (accessed 5 November 2023).

Isaac, T. D. (2020), 'What Nation Can Learn from Kerala: Lockdown is Not Enough. Preparedness, Decentralisation, Are Key', *The Indian Express*, 17 April. Available at: https://indianexpress.com/article/opinion/columns/coronavirus-covid-19-kerala-curve-6365935 (accessed 4 July 2021).

ISST (2021), 'Women in the Indian Informal Economy'. Available at: https://www.indiaspend.com/uploads/2021/03/26/file_upload-446784.pdf (accessed 5 November 2023).

IWWAGE (2020), 'Women and Work: How India Fared in 2020'. Available at: https://iwwage.org/wp-content/uploads/2021/01/Women-and-Work.pdf (accessed 5 November 2023).

Jan Sahas (2020), 'Voices of the Invisible Citizens: A Rapid Assessment on the Impact of COVID-19 Lockdown on Internal Migrant Workers. Recommendations for the State, Industry & Philanthropies'. Available at: https://jan-sahas-website.s3.ap-south-1.amazonaws.com/publications/Voices+of+the+invisible+citizens_April_2020_JS.pdf (accessed 5 November 2023).

Jan Sahas (2021), 'Voices of Invisible Citizens II: One Year of COVID-19 - Are We Seeing Shifts in Internal Migration Patterns in India?', Migrants Resilience Collaborative. Available at: https://jan-sahas-website.s3.ap-south-1.amazonaws.com/publications/upload-1624283517.9970686.ONE_YEAR_OF_COVID-19.pdf (accessed 5 November 2023).

Jejeebhoy, S. (2021), 'Child Marriages During the Pandemic', *The India Forum*, 18 June. Available at: https://www.theindiaforum.in/article/child-marriages-during-pandemic (accessed 19 June 2021).

Kad, R. (2021), 'Plight of COVID Widows in the Absence of Support System', *NewsClick*, 27 June. Available at: https://www.newsclick.in/Plight-Covid-Widows-Worsens-Absence-Support-System (accessed 28 June 2021).

Kakar, V. (2020), 'Differently-abled Migrant Women Workers Grapple with the Pandemic', *The Leaflet*, 21 July. Available at: https://theleaflet.in/differently-abled-migrant-women-workers-grapple-with-the-pandemic/ (accessed 27 June 2021).

Kapoor, A. (2021), 'An Ongoing Pandemic: Domestic Violence during COVID-19', *Economic & Political Weekly*, 56 (17): 73–79. Available at: https://www.epw.in/journal/2021/17/review-womens-studies/ongoing-pandemic.html (accessed 5 November 2023).

Kejriwal, S. (2020), 'Is Jan Dhan Money Actually Reaching People', *IDR Online*, 6 May. Available at: https://idronline.org/is-jan-dhan-money-actually-reaching-people/# (accessed 30 June 2021).

Kesar, S., Abraham, R., Lahoti, R., Nath, P. and Basole, A. (2020), 'Pandemic, Informality, and Vulnerability: Impact of COVID-19 on Livelihoods in India', CSE Working Paper 2020-21, Azim Premji University. Available at: https://cse.azimpremjiuniversity.edu.in/wp-content/uploads/2020/10/Kesar_et_al_Pandemic_Informality_Vulnerability_June_2020.pdf (accessed 5 November 2023).

Kochhar, R. (2021), 'In the Pandemic, India's Middle Class Shrinks and Poverty Spreads while China Sees Smaller Changes', Pew Research Center. Available at: https://www.pewresearch.org/short-reads/2021/03/18/in-the-pandemic-indias-middle-class-shrinks-and-poverty-spreads-while-china-sees-smaller-changes/ (accessed 5 November 2023).

Kumar, A. and Kumar, N. (2021), 'Incomes and Coping Strategies among Informal Sector Workers', in State of Working India 2021, Background Paper 03, Azim Premji University. Available at: https://cse.azimpremjiuniversity.edu.in/wp-content/uploads/2021/05/SWI2021_Background_Paper3_Kumar_Kumar.pdf (accessed 5 November 2023).

Llavaneras Blanco, M. and Cuervo, M.G. (2021), 'The Pandemic as a Portal: Policy Transformations Disputing the New Normal', DAWN Discussion Paper No. 32. Available at: https://dawnnet.org/wp-content/uploads/2021/04/DAWN-Discussion-Paper-32_The-Pandemic-as-a-Portal.pdf (accessed 30 June 2021).

Madhavan, R. (2020), 'Corona Virus Fans Child Starvation Epidemic in Karnataka?', *New Indian Express*, 23 November. Available at: https://www.newindianexpress.com/states/karnataka/2020/nov/23/coronavirus-fans-child-starvation-epidemic-in-karnataka-2226820.html (accessed 30 June 2021).

MAKAAM (2020), 'Unlocking the Crisis: Understanding the Impact of Covid-19 and Subsequent Lockdown on Single Women Farmers of Maharashtra', SOPPECOM. Available at: https://drive.google.com/

file/d/1hKfTny7DZbmK952whfEwecQyhJ819p6P/view (accessed 5 November 2023).

Mazumdar, I. and Neetha, N. (2020), 'Crossroads and Boundaries: Labour Migration, Trafficking and Gender', *Economic & Political Weekly*, 55(20). Available at: https://www.epw.in/journal/2020/20/review-womens-studies/crossroads-and-boundaries.html (accessed 5 November 2023).

Mckinsey Global Institute (2016), 'The Power of Parity: Advancing Women's Equality in India'. Available at: https://www.mckinsey.com/~/media/mckinsey/featured%20insights/employment%20and%20growth/the%20power%20of%20parity%20advancing%20womens%20equality%20in%20india/mgi%20india%20parity_full%20report_november%202015.pdf (accessed 5 November 2023).

Ministry of Finance (2020–21), 'Statement on Half Yearly Review of the Trends in Receipts and Expenditure in Relation to the Budget at the End of the Financial Year'. Available at: https://dea.gov.in/sites/default/files/H2%202020-21%20FRBM%20English.pdf (accessed 26 October 2023).

Mint (2022), 'India's GDP Contracts by 6.6% in 2020-21: First Revised Estimates', 31 January. Available at: https://www.livemint.com/economy/indias-gdp-contracts-by-6-6-in-2020-21-first-revised-estimates-11643631759648.html (accessed 5 November 2023).

Mishra, A.R. (2021), 'India's Debt to GDP Ratio is Now at a 14-Year High', 28 June, *Mint*. Available at: https://www.livemint.com/economy/debt-at-58-8-of-gdp-as-economy-shrinks-11624818421328.html#:~:text–EW%20DELHI%20%3A%20The%20Union%20government%27s,to%20raise%20concerns%20over%20debt (accessed 26 October 2023).

Mohan, D., Mistry, J., Singh, A. and Sreedhar, S. (2021), 'How Daily Wage Workers in India Suffered in the Lockdown – and Continue to Struggle Months Later', *Scroll*, 26 March, Available at: https://scroll.in/article/989258/how-daily-wage-workers-in-india-suffered-in-the-lockdown-and-continue-to-struggle-months-later#:~:text=Our%20data%20from%20Lucknow%20indicated,a%2054.5%25%20decline%20per%20month (accessed 27 June 2021).

Mukerjee, A. S. and Naryanan, P. (2020), 'From Hardship to Hope: Women Migrant Workers in the Indian Ready-made Garment Industry', *Open Global Rights*, 23 December, Available at: https://www.openglobalrights.org/hardship-to-hope-women-migrant-workers-in-the-indian-ready-made-garment-industry/ (accessed 27 June 2021).

Neetha, N. (2021), 'Crisis After Crisis: The Pandemic and Women's Work', *The Indian Economic Journal*, 69(3), 1–16. Available at: https://doi.org/10.1177/00194662211013234 (accessed 5 November 2023).

NSO (2021), 'Periodic Labour Force Survey (PLFS), July 2020 – June 2021'. Available at: https://dge.gov.in/dge/sites/default/files/2022-07/Annual_Report_PLFS_2020-21_0_0.pdf (accessed 24 December 2023).

Pahwa, N. (2020), 'India Just Had The Biggest Protest In World History. Will It Make a Difference?', *Slate*, 9 December. Available at: https://slate.com/news-and-politics/2020/12/india-farmer-protests-modi.html (accessed 18 October 2023).

Patel, A., Divakar, P. and Prabhakar, R. (2020), '40% Of Jan Dhan Account Holders Could Not Access Govt's COVID-19 Relief', *IndiaSpend*, 29 June. Available at: https://www.indiaspend.com/40-of-jan-dhan-account-holders-could-not-access-govts-covid-19-relief-survey/ (accessed 30 June 2021).

Premkumar, A. (2020), 'How Farm Acts Affect Women In Agriculture', *BehanBox*, 1 November. Available at: https://behanbox.com/2020/11/01/how-the-new-farm-acts-will-impact-womens-work-in-agriculture/ (5 November 2023).

PRS (n.d.), The Farm Laws Repeal Bill. Available at: https://prsindia.org/billtrack/the-farm-laws-repeal-bill-2021 (accessed 5 November 2023).

Puskur, R. and Ram, M. R. (2020), 'COVID -19 Opens Unknown Chapter on Rural Women's Plight in India's Migration Saga', *CGIAR*, 15 May. Available at: https://gender.cgiar.org (accessed 5 November 2023).

Queer Relief (2020), The Pink List. Queer Relief Active Fundraisers. Available at: https://www.pinklistindia.com/queerelief (accessed 5 November 2023).

Ramakumar, R. (2021), 'The Union Budget is Marked by an Overall Compression of Expenditures for Agriculture', *Frontline*, 11 February. Available at: https://frontline.thehindu.com/economy/union-budget-2021-22-penalises-farmers-by-showing-no-commitment-to-agricultural-growth-or-farmers-welfare-amid-farmers-protests-against-farm-laws-2020/article33775802.ece# (accessed 20 January 2024)

Roy, E. (2021), 'In Deluge of Covid Numbers, One Stands Out: 577 Children Orphaned in Second Wave of Pandemic', *New Indian Express*, 29 May. Available at: https://indianexpress.com/article/india/in-deluge-of-covid-numbers-one-stands-out-577-children-orphaned-in-second-wave-of-pandemic-7330279/ (accessed 5 November 2023).

Roy, A. and Dave, S. K. (2020), 'When People and Governments Come Together: Analysing Kerala's Response to COVID-19 Pandemic', *Economic & Political Weekly*, 55(18): 10–13. Available at: https://www.epw.in/journal/2020/18/commentary/when-people-and-governments-come-together.html (accessed 5 November 2023).

Sarkar, D. and Bhowmik. S. (2021), 'India's 2022: Capacity Utilisation and Economic Revival', *Observer Research Foundation*, 9 December. Available at: https://www.orfonline.org/expert-speak/indias-2022-capacity-utilisation-and-economic-revival/ (accessed 26 October 2023).

Sen, A. (2020), 'Pandemic Rape in India', *Eurozine*, 7 December. Available at: https://www.eurozine.com/pandemic-rape-in-india/ (accessed 5 November 2023).

Sen, R. (2020), 'Stay Home, Stay Safe: Interrogating Violence in the Domestic Sphere', *Economic & Political Weekly, Engage*, 55, 23 June. Available at: https://www.epw.in/engage/article/stay-home-stay-safe-interrogating-violence (accessed 5 November 2023).

Shaik, Z. (2020), 'How Indians Spend Time: Women Do the Unpaid Work; Lots of Socialising; Almost Zero Volunteering', *The Indian Express*, 5 October. Available at: https://indianexpress.com/article/explained/how-indians-spend-their-time-women-do-the-unpaid-work-lots-of-socialising-almost-no-volunteering-6647147 (accessed 5 November 2023).

Sharma, H. (2020), 'Migrants Back, Women's Share in NREGS Dips to 8-year Low', *The Indian Express*, 25 August. Available at: https://indianexpress.com/article/india/migrants-back-women-share-in-nregs-dips-to-8-year-low-6568476/ (accessed 5 November 2023).

Sundari S. (2020), 'Changes and Quality of Women's Labour in India', *The Indian Journal of Labour Economics*, 63(3): 689–717. Available at: https://doi.org/10.1007/s41027-020-00245-2 (accessed 5 November 2023).

Sustainable Development Report (2023), 'Rankings: The Overall Performance of all 193 UN Member States'. Available at: https://dashboards.sdgindex.org/rankings (accessed 5 November 2023).

SWAN (2020), 'To Leave or Not to Leave? Lockdown, Migrant Workers, and Their Journeys Home'. Available at: https://ruralindiaonline.org/en/library/resource/to-leave-or-not-to-leave-lockdown-migrant-workers-and-their-journeys-home/ (accessed 5 November 2023).

Tambe, N. (2023), 'MSME Statistics of 2024', *Forbes Advisor*, 7 November. Available at: https://www.forbes.com/advisor/in/business/msme-statistics/#:~:text—SMEs%20created%20120%20million%20jobs,and%20MSMEs%20for%20over%2090%25 (accessed 20 January 2024).

Thapliyal, N. (2020), 'Migrant Women Workers On The Road: Largely Invisible And Already Forgotten', *Feminism in India*, 26 June. Available at: https://feminisminindia.com/2020/06/26/migrant-women-workers-covid-19-impact/ (accessed 5 November 2023).

The Economic Times (2020a), 'Implement Steps to Curb Domestic Violence During Covid-19 Lockdown: High Court to Centre, Delhi Government', 20 April. Available at: https://economictimes.indiatimes.com/news/politics-and-nation/implement-steps-to-curb-domestic-violence-during-covid-19-lockdown-high-court-to-centre-delhi-govt/articleshow/75249397.cms?from=mdr (accessed 5 November 2023).

The Economic Times (2020b), 'Budget 2020: MGNREGA Funds Down by 13%, Marginal Dip in Other Rural Development Schemes', 31 December. Available at: https://economictimes.indiatimes.com/news/economy/policy/budget-2020-mgnrega-funds-down-by-13-marginal-dip-in-other-rural-development-schemes/articleshow/73847723.cms?utm_source=contentofinterest&utm_medium=text&utm_campaign=cppst (accessed 5 November 2023).

The Economic Times (2017), 'Manmohan Singh Takes Potshots at Note Ban, 'Hasty' Rollout of GST', 18 September. Available at: https://economictimes.indiatimes.com/news/politics-and-nation/manmohan-singh-takes-potshots-at-note-ban-hasty-rollout-of-gst/articleshow/60733652.cms?utm_source=contentofinterest&utm_medium=text&utm_campaign=cppst (accessed 5 November 2023).

The Hindu (2020), 'Parliament Passes Labour Bills Amid Boycott', 23 September. Available at: https://www.thehindu.com/news/national/parliament-passes-three-key-labour-reform-bills/article61723536.ece (accessed 5 November 2023).

Thomas, C. and Sundaram, N. (2020), 'Pandemic Crisis: 'Migrant Home-Based Women Workers Work 8 Hours/Day For Rs 10-15', *IndiaSpend*, 23 July. Available at: https://www.indiaspend.com/pandemic-crisis-migrant-home-based-women-workers-work-8-hours-day-for-rs-10-15/ (accessed 5 November 2023).

Thomas, M. (2021), 'Rise in Child Marriages in the Lockdown: How the Centre Ignored Data of its own Nodal Agency', *The Wire*, 8 April. Available at: https://thewire.in/rights/rise-in-child-marriages-in-the-lockdown-how-the-centre-ignored-data-of-its-own-nodal-agency (accessed 5 November 2023).

TNN (2021), '15 Million Lose Work in May, Urban Jobless Rate Hits 18%', *The Times of India*, 2 June. Available at: https://timesofindia.indiatimes.com/business/india-business/15-million-lose-work-in-may-urban-jobless-rate-hits-18/articleshow/83163687.cms (accessed 5 November 2023).

Totapally, S., Sonderegger, P., Rao, P. and Gupta, G. (2020), 'Efficacy of Government Entitlements for Low-income Families during Covid-19', Dalberg. Available at: https://policyinsights.in/wp-content/uploads/2021/12/20.07.27_Efficacy-of-government-entitlements-for-low-income-families-during-Covid-19.pdf (accessed 5 November 2023).

Trading Economics (2023), India National Floor Level Minimum Wage. Available at: https://tradingeconomics.com/india/minimum-wages (accessed 5 November 2023).

UNICEF (2021), '10 Million Additional Girls at Risk of Child Marriage due to COVID-19', UNICEF Press Release, 7 March. Available at: https://www.unicef.org/press-releases/10-million-additional-girls-risk-child-marriage-due-covid-19#:~:text–EW%20YORK%2C%208%20March%202021,analysis%20released%20by%20UNICEF%20today (accessed 5 November 2023).

Varma, S. (2021), 'Desperate Indians Used Savings, Took Loans to Survive COVID-19 Pandemic', *NewsClick*, 1 July. Available at: https://www.newsclick.in/Desperate-Indians-Used-Savings-Took-Loans-Survive-COVID-19-Pandemic (accessed 5 November 2023).

Vee, V. and Salelkar, A. (2021), 'Understanding the Experiences of Transgender Persons under Expanding Militarism: A Qualitative Study Based in Delhi and Lucknow, Uttar Pradesh', Asia Pacific Transgender Network. Available at: https://weareaptn.org/wp-content/uploads/2021/07/Understanding-experiences-of-Transgender-Persons-under-expanding-militarism.pdf (accessed 5 November 2023).

von Grebmer, K., J. Bernstein, D. Resnick, M. Wiemers, L. Reiner, M. Bachmeier, A. Hanano, O. Towey, R. Ní Chéilleachair, C. Foley, S. Gitter, G. Larocque, and H. Fritschel (2022), '2022 Global Hunger Index: Food Systems Transformation and

Local Governance', Bonn: Welthungerhilfe and Dublin: Concern Worldwide. Available at: https://www.globalhungerindex.org/pdf/en/2022.pdf (accessed 5 November 2023).

Walker, J., Martin, M., Seery, E., Abdo, N., Kamande, A., Lawson, M. (2022), 'The Commitment to Reducing Inequality Index 2022', Development Finance International and Oxfam International, Available at: https://oxfamilibrary. openrepository.com/bitstream/handle/10546/621419/rr-cri-2022-111022-en.pdf;jses sionid=7F37F2F21F99EFC73FD976654F8029FB?sequence=33 (accessed 5 November 2023).

WEF (2021), 'World Economic Forum Gender Gap Report 2021', March. Available at: https://www3.weforum.org/docs/WEF_GGGR_2021.pdf (accessed 5 November 2023).

WEF (2023), 'World Economic Forum Gender Gap Report 2023', June. Available at: https://www3.weforum.org/docs/WEF_GGGR_2023.pdf (accessed 5 November 2023).

Xavier, J. (2020), 'Walking with the Migrants Beyond COVID-19 Pandemic', Indian Social Institute, Caritas Global and Indo Global Social Service Society. Available at: https://www.caritasindia.org/wp-content/uploads/2020/08/Walking-with-the-migrants-beyond-COVID-19-pandemic.pdf (accessed 5 November 2023).

2

Food Curtailed: Austerity, Socioeconomic Crises and Ghana's School Feeding Programme

Gertrude Dzifa Torvikey and Sylvia Ohene Marfo

1. Introduction

Ghana has been reeling under a severe economic crisis characterized by debt default, debt restructuring and high inflation. In 2022, the Ghanaian cedi (GH¢) was the worst performing currency in the world, depreciating 53.8 per cent in that year alone.[1] The country defaulted on most of its external debt payments in the same year and, in 2023, entered into a debt restructuring programme led by the International Monetary Fund (IMF). This macroeconomic crisis converged with and was exacerbated by the Covid-19 pandemic unfolding around the same time as well as the Russia-Ukraine war.

The weakened macroeconomic conditions that resulted from these overlapping crises spilled over into households, affecting vulnerable populations in particular. Ghana ended 2022 with a year-on-year inflation rate of 54.1 per cent in December, which is a 22-year high. Such high inflation levels came against a backdrop of low social protection expenditure, which, in 2021, stood at 1.5 per cent of the gross domestic product (GDP), below the average in Sub-Saharan Africa (UNICEF Ghana 2023). These socioeconomic conditions reversed earlier gains made in poverty reduction, school enrolment and food security, among others, and increased gender-based violence and women's unpaid care work burden.

During periods of instability, social protection programmes are vital tools in building community resilience (Abdoul-Azize and El Gamil 2021, Kpessa-Whyte 2021, Tsikata 2021). However, such programmes are also likely to be derailed in the event of a crisis. The pandemic and the macroeconomic crisis hit

Ghana's existing social and economic programmes that provide relief to families. Most families that rely on these programmes work in the informal sector, which accounts for 90.1 per cent of all jobs in the country (ILO 2018). About 94 per cent of all working women in Ghana are in the informal sector (ibid.). Especially for such households, increasing inequalities and deepening deprivation converged with low social protection coverage and threatened to push many into poverty.

One social protection programme that offers relief to the country's low-income households is the Ghana School Feeding Programme (GSFP), which provides cooked meals to children who attend the public school system. By offering children school lunches, which otherwise would have to be provided by their families, the programme facilitates the redistribution of care work between the state and households. The programme is especially crucial given that, in Ghana, one in every five children under the age of five is stunted and one in every ten children is underweight (UNICEF 2019).

Ironically, the necessity of the GSFP was brought to the fore when the programme was temporarily suspended starting 16 March 2020, as the pandemic forced schools to shut down. It restarted only in January 2021 after schools reopened. This nine-month hiatus revealed vulnerabilities in beneficiary households as well as among farmers, traders and caterers (who are predominantly women) involved in the programme's supply chain. A joint report by the Food and Agriculture Organization (FAO), the International Fund for Agricultural Development (IFAD), the United Nations Children's Fund (UNICEF), the World Food Programme (WFP) and the World Health Organization (WHO) (2021) states that rising food prices and economic hardship in 2020 made healthy food unattainable for many poor people. The number of severely food-insecure people in Ghana increased from 5.1 per cent in 2014–16 to 5.6 per cent in 2019–21 while 4.1 per cent were declared undernourished. In 2020, 6.8 per cent and 14.2 per cent of children under the age of five showed signs of malnourishment and stunting, respectively, and about 61.2 per cent of the population was unable to afford a healthy diet (ibid.).

As such, the two crises, namely the pandemic and the debt default (and the subsequent IMF bailout), provide an opportunity to reflect on the GSFP's ability to advance its core objective of sharing the responsibility of social reproduction with the country's most vulnerable families, and especially women. At the same time, the programme's temporary suspension offers a lens through which to examine the policy and political directions taken by the Ghanaian government. This chapter uses the GSFP as a case study to reflect on critical questions about the Ghanaian government's approach to social policies against a backdrop of the two intersecting crises. It illustrates the shifts in the implementation of the GSFP during this period and reflects on how the government dealt with the conundrum of feeding its school children. We study the effects of the programme's discontinuation in 2020 on households, women and girls as well as the predominantly female farmers, vendors and caterers involved in the programme's supply chain. We argue that the government's responses exacerbated entrenched gender norms and class inequalities, affecting the well being of women and girls. Finally, we conclude that political actors used the health emergency to intensify austerity in the GSFP rather than making radical changes to address concerns pertaining to social justice, equity and women's social reproductive burden.

The study is based on a systematic review of the literature on social protection programmes in general and the GSFP in particular, with a special focus on how its implementation strategies changed in the context of the pandemic and the macroeconomic crisis. The study relies on relevant media reports, national Budget documents, newsletters of the programme and an interview with a district-level official in the Ghana Education Service (GES). In addition, in-depth interviews were conducted in eight households, including four female-headed households, in Accra, the national capital of Ghana and an epicentre of the Covid-19 pandemic, and Wa, the capital of the poorest region in the Upper Wester region of the country.[2]

2. Evolution of the Ghana School Feeding Programme

2.1 Context

Ghana registered its first two cases of Covid-19 on 12 March 2020, nine months before highly charged presidential and parliamentary elections. Thereafter, the onslaught of the pandemic and the macroeconomic instability meant that the country struggled to balance the livelihoods and health of its citizens. The measures and policies introduced to address these intersecting crises had deleterious effects on households with women and girls, leaving them to shoulder a heavier share of the social reproductive burden. The country imposed its strictest pandemic measures in April 2020, scoring 86.11 on the Covid-19 Stringency Index.[3] The restrictions were eased gradually and, in July 2020, the score dropped to 42.59.

Although Ghana's economy has held steady and its GDP has grown consistently for the past two decades, its economy carries significant structural problems.[4] The country has a longstanding history of high external debt, including a debt default in the 1980s, debt cancellation through the Heavily Indebted Poor Countries (HIPC) initiative[5] in the early 2000s and over fifteen IMF bailouts. In 2022, Ghana again defaulted on its debt and, thereafter, approached the IMF for relief, which was approved on 17 May 2023 (Savage and Miridzhanian 2023). In effect, the country's debt problem preceded but was exacerbated by the pandemic (Abotebuno Akolgo 2023).

While the terms of the 2023 IMF bailout deal called for sustaining and expanding the country's social protection programmes, there were concerns that the associated fiscal constraints would negatively affect such programmes. Social protection programmes are an important element in Ghanaians' livelihoods since a major part of the economy remains informal, with high unemployment and precarious labour conditions that specifically affect women. According to World Bank data from 2019, prior to the onset of the Covid-19 crisis, 76.6 per cent of working women faced precarious employment conditions compared with 58 per cent men. While there is no updated data on this, the pandemic is likely to have further worsened the vulnerability in employment conditions and increased the employment gap between women and men.[6] Generally, while official statistics indicate a steady reduction in monetary poverty over time, the decline is unevenly distributed among women and men, rural and urban areas, northern and southern regions, and different wealth quintiles (Ghana Statistical Service 2020).

Only 25.3 per cent of Ghana's population is currently covered by some social protection programme, according to ILO data from 2020.[7] This figure comprises pensioners (mostly men), poor households (mostly headed by women) and those covered under other social assistance programmes such as the school feeding programme. By failing to expand its social safety net, the Ghanaian state had ushered in a state of fiscal austerity long before the pandemic and the macroeconomic crisis. The existing structural conditions made women, rural dwellers, the urban poor, and households in the North, Upper East and Upper West regions of the country particularly vulnerable to the socioeconomic disruptions caused by the two intersecting crises.[8]

2.2 The origins of the GSFP

The GSFP is rooted in the Comprehensive Africa Agricultural Development Programme (CAADP); framed within the Sustainable Development Goals

(SDGs) on hunger, poverty, malnutrition and primary education; and anchored on SDG Pillar three, which prioritizes reduction of food insecurity and hunger (Government of Ghana 2015). It is part of the National Social Protection Policy, which the government frames as people centric. This intervention framework seeks to alleviate poverty by providing livelihood support and empowering the abject, the chronically poor as well as other categories of working poor who are vulnerable.

The GSFP provides children in primary school and kindergarten one hot nutritious meal a day, with the aim of increasing school enrolment and reducing short-term hunger and malnutrition among children.[9] It started in 2006 in ten regions with 64,775 beneficiaries (Acheampong 2022) and has since increased in scope and size, feeding 3.4 million school-aged children in over 10,832 schools across the country as of 2023 (Owusu 2023). Following its inception, the government expanded the project's goals by linking farmers to caterers and enhancing the consumption of locally produced foods. In that sense, the GSFP also seeks to boost agricultural production by creating a market for local foods.

2.3 A politicized programme

The implementation of the GSFP is a vexed and contested subject. Administered by the Ministry of Gender, Children and Social Protection (MGCSP), the programme is handled at the district level and overseen by regional and national coordinators. The selection of the GSFP caterers is politicized and based on party lines. As such, the selection process is susceptible to centralization even as the programme itself is localized in its implementation. Many Ghanaians consider the GSFP a vehicle to offer opportunities to ruling party supporters who cannot make it to critical positions in government (News Ghana 2017). Contracts to caterers are revoked upon change of government and new ones given mainly to party members, executives and their cronies. For this reason, the programme is at the centre of internal rifts between those who get contracts and others who do not. At the national level, the programme coordinator is usually an affiliate of the ruling political party, which furthers the politicized nature of the GSFP. Overall, the politicization of the programme affects its accountability, transparency, and the quality and quantity of meals served in schools, and allows the dismissal of questions about and criticism of the programme's implementation (Otchere 2021).

An instance of how deeply party politics influences the GSFP was seen when the supervisory minister from the MGCSP dismissed the programme's national coordinator only to revoke the dismissal within twenty-four hours, describing it as an 'administrative error' (The Ghana Report 2021). Similarly, in a recent stakeholder meeting in the Upper East region, municipal and district directors of education complained about the decline in the quality and quantity of food served to beneficiary school children. These complaints were mainly about meals not meeting the standards of a balanced diet.[10] However, the directors confessed that they were unable to complain openly for fear of victimization since the programme is managed by ruling party executives (News Ghana 2021).

2.4 Discontinuation and divestment of the GSFP

As schools shut down during the peak of Covid-19 in 2020, the GSFP was discontinued. However, its implementation strategy was temporarily repurposed and targeted at a different set of beneficiaries. Food was distributed during this period only in the two epicentres of the pandemic, namely Greater Accra and Kumasi. The directive to feed vulnerable groups came via a presidential address and was not specifically targeted at certain defined groups but instead treated as a universal measure for individuals residing in the two pandemic epicentres. Part of the funding for food distribution came from the Coronavirus Alleviation Programme (CAP) under the government's Ghana Stabilisation Fund (GSF), which had an allocation of GH¢1.25 billion (US$208.85 million).

Table 2.1 enumerates the prevailing food distribution programmes as outlined in the 2021 national Budget. All three categories of food distribution mentioned were short term and lasted three weeks, between April and May 2020. GSFP caterers delivered cooked food to 2,744,723 beneficiaries. The distribution did not specifically target children who benefitted from the GSFP in the past but

Table 2.1 Covid-19-Related Food Distribution Programmes in Ghana, 2020

Public provision	Beneficiaries	Implementing agency
Cooked meals	2,744,723 vulnerable persons (not gender disaggregated)*	MGCSP
Dry food	470,000 families	Faith-based organizations
Hot meals	584,000 (junior high school students) 146,000 (staff of public and private schools)	MGCSP

*Source: Compiled by authors based on data from the Ghana government's 2021 Budget statement and economic policy (Ministry of Finance 2021). *Note: Despite the lack of gender disaggregated data, it is known that female head porters in urban areas were among the key beneficiaries of the programme, given their labour precarity.*

simply assumed that they were part of the vulnerable persons and families that received government support, thus raising questions about accountability and transparency. Given the politicization of the programme, many Ghanaians doubted the figures offered in the 2021 Budget and an Opposition Member of Parliament asked for a probe (Modern Ghana 2020).

Like the undefined category of vulnerable persons, the feeding of junior high school (JHS) pupils and their teachers was directly implemented by the MGCSP between 24 August and 18 September 2020, until the completion of final school examinations. This group of beneficiaries was not part of the GSFP prior to Covid-19, but the pandemic and its social distancing requirements and health concerns, which necessitated the removal of food vendors from school premises, made it necessary to make arrangements to feed JHS students. The centralization of the food distribution programme during this time raised concerns among some GES officials. In addition, the quality and quantity of food was not adapted to JHS students' specific needs. Despite these shortcomings, the feeding of JHS pupils during the pandemic pointed to the need to expand the GSFP to cover such students in the long term.

The GES official interviewed for this study explained that many JHS children live alone in urban areas and work daily for food. During the lockdown, many did not get food to eat except through the repurposed food distribution programme. Some students called their school and teachers arranged food for them although classes were not in session. Because of the hardship, some children returned to their villages. In the urban areas, rape and teenage pregnancy became rampant. The GES official explained:

> Can you imagine that one of the girls in my district was nearly raped just because of a ball of *kenkey*?[11] She was hungry, and the boy offered to buy food for her in return for sex. Rape could have been prevented were the GSFP still sending food to these poor children. Teachers often used their monies to feed some children while schools were closed (Tema, 14 July 2021).

The GES official also reported that when schools reopened, there were six pregnant girls and two nursing adolescent mothers at the basic and junior high schools in her unit. She attributed it to hardship and poverty, which the feeding programme could have helped attenuate if it was properly implemented. Her assertion is in line with studies that associate adolescent pregnancy in Ghana with low economic status of households (Asare et al. 2019). At the same time, the GES official observed that school attendance and class participation improved and absenteeism reduced because of the feeding programme for JHS pupils.

However, when schools reopened and the earlier feeding programme resumed, benefitting only primary school children, the gains made during the short period were eroded – absenteeism increased and class participation dropped among JHS students.

The repurposed food distribution programme utilized the GSFP's budget as well as other sources without any transparency and accountability. It is unclear why the budget for the GSFP was repurposed to aid other beneficiaries while excluding the core group of kindergarten and primary school children. The burden of care provision for this section of the population was shifted to their households.

2.5 Covid-19 school closures and the consequent hunger crisis

Schools perform essential cross-sectoral functions. School feeding programmes in particular safeguard children, especially those belonging to low-income and female-headed households, against food insecurity and malnutrition (UNICEF 2021, Gelli et al. 2019). The GES official highlighted the case of nine-year-old Kofi[12] who was HIV positive and living with his father and stepmother in Tema. Kofi was regular at school, a brilliant student, and healthy and cheerful. Due to this parent's financial situation, he often went to bed hungry. Prior to the school closures, Kofi relied on meals from the GSFP for sustenance. When schools closed in March 2020, his teachers made attempts to reach him and referred his condition to the authorities in charge of the HIV-AIDS programme in the district to ensure that Kofi received his antiretroviral medication. However, by the time the officials got to him, two months after the school closures, Kofi had died from hunger and lack of medication. He was a healthy boy before Covid-19 since the school made sure he got his portion of the GSFP meal as well as his antiretroviral medication. An AIDS patient, Kofi needed to eat well to boost his immunity. 'To his parents, his death was a blessing because it was one less mouth to feed. The system killed little Kofi,' the GES official lamented.

The suspension of the programme affected many other beneficiary households. UNICEF (2021) estimates that more than 1.6 million children in the country's poorest and most deprived districts lost access to school meals during the pandemic. Households had to increase their food expenditure in order to plug the gap created by the discontinuation of the GSFP. Since more women than men tend to be single parents, the crisis exposed them to even greater difficulties (ibid.). In addition, the general economic hardship impacted small informal businesses that are primarily run by women, who rely on trading to feed their families. These households skipped meals or adjusted food consumption in other ways.

While the GSFP advances the goal of children's right to nutritious food and education, for some respondents, its importance is not in the nutrition per se, but rather in the 'food for thought' it provides (Aurino et al. 2018). As one research participant put it,

> The GSFP helps children get food to eat in school, which helps them concentrate and focus on their studies because one cannot learn on an empty stomach, especially when they do not eat before going to school (Dede, female trader, Wa, 18 June 2021).

Some women said the programme is useful since it supplements the bland food children belonging to poorer households often get at home by offering them greater dietary diversity. One interviewee explained:

> The school feeding programme is essential. My children used to eat in school before the Covid-19 pandemic broke and it helped me because sometimes I do not make enough daily sales to provide adequate food for them. So they relied on the GSFP. However, when they returned to school, they no longer got the food. So I gave them money for food, but it was difficult for me, as a single mother taking care of four children (Akorkor, onion trader, Accra, 21 June 2021).

The disruption in the programme during the pandemic meant that the state had abandoned its role of sharing care work and social reproduction with the target population. Households in locked-down regions and those headed by women and the poor experienced extreme forms of disruptions to their food security. These findings highlight the importance of food rations in the well being of vulnerable sections of the population and the need for more dignified and equitable alternatives in a crisis period.

2.6 Social provisioning and reproductive labour burden

When it started, the GSFP was an important state intervention in social provisioning, which otherwise fell squarely on women. After the programme was implemented and in full flight, women reported some relief in household food expenditure. However, the expenditure on food increased once the GSFP was discontinued during the pandemic. Amid a crisis, when livelihoods were badly affected and food prices were increasing, households had to provide what children would otherwise eat at school. Fatimah, a tomato seller from Wa, said,

'When schools were closed, I was struggling to feed the children at home. The closure of schools increased household expenditure in terms of food and utility bills.'

As is evident from the above testimony, school closures and the consequent discontinuation of the GSFP intensified women's social reproductive and provisioning burden. The experience of another respondent, Emelia, is illustrative. Emelia's husband, a driver in a private school, lost his job when schools closed due to Covid-19. Their three young children, who were enrolled in a government school, stayed home for the same reason. As a result, Emelia had to feed her family of five alone with the money she made from trading. The rise in food inflation in Ghana in 2020 compared with the previous year meant that Emelia spent more on food than before. With little support from her husband, the household was pushed into extreme financial vulnerability. In addition, her young children required Emelia's constant attention, increasing her social reproductive burden.

Households used different strategies to cope with the discontinuation of the GSFP. This included increasing food expenditure, consuming cheaper carbohydrates, putting children to work and increasing the social reproductive burden on other working children in the household. One example was the consumption of maize-based foods throughout the day due to the staple's affordability. As one interviewee said,

> My household missed the school feeding programme. Its absence put extreme pressure on me to get more food for my children at home. During the school closure period, I bought corn dough and, every morning, before I went out to sell, I would ask them [the children] to prepare porridge for breakfast and then use the remainder for *banku* for lunch and dinner. We did this often since maize was affordable. Honestly, the discontinuation of the school feeding programme was tough for me. There is no one to help me, no husband, and I take care of my mother who lives with us. I wish the children would not help me sell onions, but I have no option. So I make them sell in the market to get more money to feed the family (Akorkor, onion trader, Accra, 21 June 2021).

Like Akorkor, many households in Ghana put children to work to feed themselves and support the household income. According to Human Rights Watch (2021), when households are in economic turmoil, children's labour is used extensively to generate income and supplement adult earnings.

For some women, the provision of school lunches for children reduced the time and labour spent on cooking. The discontinuation of the GSFP meant that these women had to balance their economic activities with cooking for children who stayed at home. Confirming this point, Fatimah from Wa said, 'When the children go to school and eat, I don't cook lunch at home again. During the week, I don't cook lunch.'

That said, even prior to the pandemic, some households occasionally supplemented the food children received under the GSFP in various ways. Due to the inadequacy of the food served, some parents gave their children money to buy food from vendors in addition to what they received at school while others provided additional lunch when their children returned home. Some children stopped eating the food provided under the GSFP due to safety and nutritional concerns while others were demotivated by long queues at the serving tables. Sometimes, the amount of food provided to each school was inadequate and children at the end of the queue did not get their share. Despite these shortcomings, however, the GSFP was a crucial source of food security for children from extremely poor households. These households in particular became more vulnerable during school closures.

While not necessarily nutritious, the food provided under the GSFP was a crucial source of dietary diversity for many households. When the programme was suspended, children lost access to this source of diversity. Respondents to this study echoed concerns voiced by school managers about the lower nutritional standards of the food available to children in poorer households. During the pandemic, this was the only source of their daily food needs.

Households that were relatively better off reported not missing the GSFP after its discontinuation because of the inadequate food children received under the programme. Jenabu, a fish trader from Wa, said, 'The GSFP is of no importance to us now because the food they give children is not enough. The government is just implementing it for show.' Her testimony points to the state of many social protection programmes in Ghana, which are highly politicized, poorly implemented and yet popularized in public discourse.

3. Impact of austerity on food quality and livelihoods of farmers, caterers and vendors

Respondents to this study pointed out that the poor quality and quantity of food provided under the GSFP could be understood within the broader economic context of rising food prices coupled with the absence of any corresponding increments in the amount that the government pays per child. For a long time, caterers have raised the alarm about the poor funding provided by the state for implementation of the programme. The state pays GH¢1 (US$ 0.17) per child per meal (Peace FM Online 2021), an amount that has remained the same for a long time despite rising inflation. Caterers are required to cook meals with this paltry funding. It is little surprise then that the meals are reported to be poor in nutrition and quantity.

The reopening of schools in January 2021 should have come as a relief to parents with children in the GSFP schools. However, parents observed that while the programme was once again in operation, it was mired in far greater austerity than before. As one respondent put it,

> Upon resumption of school, the food served to the children was even lesser and of poorer quality. Before Covid-19 and the closure of schools, food staples were not that expensive. For example, maize was GH¢3.50 [US$ 0.58] per bowl but it's now GH¢7 [US$1.16] (Mansa, maize trader, Wa, 18 June 2021).

Caterers coped by lowering both the quality and quantity of school meals even further. Mama, a trader from Wa, said caterers often buy 'softened onions and tomatoes'. 'What used to be food for one child is now served to two children,' she added.

A major concern in the implementation of the GSFP was the government's indebtedness to suppliers, which was further exacerbated during the pandemic. Given that the programme is localized and requires the procurement of local food items, indebtedness impacts people across the supply chain. It affects the quality of the food as well as the livelihoods of suppliers, mainly market women who provide food items on credit to caterers. The discontinuation of the programme for nine months during Covid-19 meant that traders who had supply relations with caterers faced severe losses. 'Caterers buy on credit from the market women and do not pay on time. This affects everyone involved in the supply of food to the schools,' Mama explained.

By severely delaying payments to farmers, traders and caterers in an already inflationary context,[13] the government effectively derailed the programme's objective of enhancing local food production and consumption. Often, farmers, traders and caterers received their funds with a delay of nearly a year, even as the reasons for the delay remained unknown. As mentioned earlier, caterers are recruited from the ruling party rank and file, and their protests are not taken seriously.

The huge debt owed by the government to farmers, traders and caterers intensified the structural inequalities faced by them. In their paid roles as caterers and traders as well as unpaid role as household care providers, women bear the burden of feeding school children in public schools and in their own households. The problems of the school feeding programme came to a head in 2023 when caterers across the country undertook a series of actions, including laying down their cooking pots. The consequences were dire for many children who were denied food in the process. Caterers demanded that the government repay the huge debt owed to them and increase the amount allocated for feeding each child to GH¢3.5 (US$ 0.30). They refused to end their strike even after the government promised to increase the amount to GH¢1.20 (10 cents), calling it woefully inadequate (Citinewsroom 2023).

This was not the first time caterers went on strike since the pandemic started. In June 2022, the state honoured the arrears payment to caterers who went on strike in May that year. In July 2022, the Speaker of Ghana's Parliament tasked the education; finance; gender, children and social protection; health; and food and agriculture committees in Parliament with investigating the sustainability and challenges of the GSFP and the preparedness of the Ghana Buffer Stock Company in ensuring steady supply and food security (GBN 2022). The report produced by these committees was not accessible at the time of writing this chapter (December 2023).

4. School feeding: Looking forward

Despite concerns over declining social expenditure amid conditionalities imposed by the IMF bailout deal, Ghana's 2023 Budget reiterated the state's commitment to sustaining the school feeding programme. In recognition of the high inflation rates, particularly rising food and fuel costs, the Budget document stated that funding for the school grant would be increased in the same year to reflect the higher cost of living, but it stopped short of stating the precise number (Ministry of Finance 2022). Moreover, despite the growing poverty that many Ghanaians were facing in the aftermath of the pandemic and the debt default, the Budget did not expand the GSFP to include more beneficiaries. We, therefore, see the statement about sustaining and increasing the grant as tokenistic and the state's way of pacifying and placating civil society groups concerned about the sustainability of social protection programmes following the IMF bailout (B&FTOnline 2022). In any case, the already precarious condition of the programme raises doubts about the government's ability to protect the vulnerable (CDD-Ghana 2023).

5. Conclusion

Since its inception, the GSFP has been shaped by gradual austerity due to the lack of resources, politicization and the absence of political will to usher in transformative change. The pandemic and the macroeconomic crisis were perfect opportunities for the government to dedicate enough resources to the programme by increasing the funding per child in tandem with rising inflation and taxation. However, the state failed to rise to the occasion. Instead, the programme deteriorated as the government took a path-dependent approach to the macroeconomic crisis, which, in turn, deepened women's social reproductive burden and weakened the livelihoods of food producers and sellers. Traditionally responsible for social reproduction, women slipped further into precarity, increasing their exposure to violence, particularly in poorer regions, rural areas and urban slums. And while the use of the GSFP budget to feed older JHS students was novel, it was a short-term move and discontinued after their examinations.

Going forward, the government needs to effectively decentralize the implementation of the programme and end the cycle of indebtedness to caterers, which affects farmers and market traders further down the supply chain. Turning the GSFP around will also enable the state to meet its commitment of sharing social reproduction responsibilities with households.

From a feminist perspective, a transformative social policy should address longstanding gender- and class-based inequalities (Tsikata 2021). It should recognize care as an essential investment so that women and families are not left to meet such needs on their own. It should aim to eliminate structural inequalities that are reinforced and exacerbated by the current economic model. A transformative social policy must be multifunctional and sustainable and have comprehensive coverage. Episodic and ad hoc social protection measures do not go far in fostering solidarity, progressive development and structural change. The GSFP has done the reverse, as female caterers and traders are at the mercy of the government, increasing their burden of paid and unpaid work.

The Covid-19 crisis hit Ghana at a time when the country was already struggling with worsening inequality, agrarian distress, high unemployment and a looming debt crisis. During the pandemic, the government implemented temporary, untargeted and unsustainable programmes delivered with populist motives in an election year. The programmes were praised and critiqued in equal measure. Their supporters commended the government for offering social programmes and helping the poor while critics pointed to their unsustainability, politicization, corruption in implementation, targeting problems, etc. Despite the importance of the GSFP, it is going through a new phase of austerity, which means that many children and households will fall back into extreme poverty and food insecurity, as was observed when the programme came to a temporary halt during the pandemic. This form of austerity exacerbates women's already fragile livelihoods and creates a care and social reproduction crisis.

Notes

1 See: https://www.myjoyonline.com/cedi-depreciated-by-53-8-in-2022-ofori-atta/.

2 Due to movement restrictions during the pandemic, respondents were selected from samples drawn from the Covid-19 and African Food Systems Research Project conducted by researchers at the University of Ghana and women's rights group NETRIGHT, and funded by the International Development Research Centre (IDRC).

3 The Covid-19 Stringency Index is a composite measure of the strictness of policy responses, calculated as the mean score of nine policy measures, each taking a value between 0 and 100. For more, see: https://ourworldindata.org/coronavirus/country/ghana https://ourworldindata.org/grapher/covid-stringency-index?tab=chart®ion=Africa&country=~GHA.

4 See: https://data.worldbank.org/indicator/NY.GDP.MKTP.CD?locations=GH.

5 See more about the initiative here: https://www.imf.org/en/About/Factsheets/Sheets/2023/Debt-relief-under-the-heavily-indebted-poor-countries-initiative-HIPC.

6 See more at: https://data.worldbank.org/indicator/SL.EMP.VULN.FE.ZS?locations=GH.

7 See here: https://www.ilo.org/sesame/IFPSES.SocialDatabase.

8 See the Africa Covid-19 Community Vulnerability Index (CCVI) at: https://covid-static-assets.s3.amazonaws.com/Africa/CCVI+Index+Overview.pdf.

9 For more, see: https://schoolfeeding.gov.gh/major-themes/.

10 In Ghana, a balanced diet is referred to as a four-star diet and consists of cereals, starchy roots, tubers; legumes; fruits and vegetable sources; and animal protein sources like milk and eggs.

11 A corn dough-based staple dish.

12 Interviewees or people referenced have been given pseudonyms or are unnamed to protect their anonymity.

13 As of April 2020, the inflation rate was 10.6 per cent compared with 7.8 per cent in March. It continued to increase but reduced to 10.4 per cent in December. Inflation

increased to 11.8 per cent in January 2021, which was attributed to pressures from the pandemic. See: www.bog.gov.gh.

References

Abdoul-Azize, H.T., El Gamil, R. (2021), 'Social Protection as a Key Tool in Crisis Management: Learnt Lessons from the COVID-19 Pandemic', *Glob Soc Welf*, 8: 107–116. Available at: https://doi.org/10.1007/s40609-020-00190-4 (accessed 27 December 2023).

Abotebuno Akolgo, I. (n.d.), 'History Repeating Itself? Ghana, Financial Dependency and the Political Economy of Africa's Debt', *Development and Change*, 54(5): 1264–1295. Available at: https://doi.org/10.1111/dech.12791 (accessed 1 November 2023).

Acheampong, J.O. (2022), 'Stakeholders Perspective of the Ghana School Feeding Program: A Case of the Denkyembour District', *Interchange*, 53: 313–333. Available at: https://doi.org/10.1007/s10780-022-09461-9 (accessed 1 November 2023).

Asare, B.Y.A, Baafi, D., Dwumfour-Asare, B. and Adam, A.R. (2019), 'Factors Associated with Adolescent Pregnancy in the Sunyani Municipality of Ghana', *International Journal of Africa Nursing Sciences*, 10: 87–91. Available at: https://doi.org/10.1016/j.ijans.2019.02.001 (accessed 27 December 2023).

Aurino, E., Gelli, A., Adamba, C., Osei-Akoto, I., and Alderman, H. (2018), 'Food for Thought? Experimental Evidence on the Learning Impacts of a Large-scale School Feeding Program in Ghana', IFPRI Discussion Paper, International Food Policy Research Institute. Available at: https://doi.org/10.3368/jhr.58.3.1019-10515R1 (accessed 1 November 2023).

B&FTOnline (2022), 'A SEND Ghana Open Letter to IMF on 17th IMF Deal and Social Protection Delivery', 20 December. Available at: https://thebftonline. com/2022/12/20/a-send-ghana-open-letter-to-imf-on-17th-imf-deal-and-social-protection-delivery/ (accessed 18 November 2022).

CDD-Ghana (2023), 'The IMF Bail-out', 29 May. Available at: https://cddgh.org/the-imf-bailout/# (accessed 18 November 2022).

Citinewsroom (2023), 'School Feeding Caterers Reject GH¢1.20 Increment Per child; Vow to Continue Strike', 5 June. Available at: https://citinewsroom.com/2023/06/school-feeding-caterers-reject-gh%C2%A21-20-increment-per-child-vow-to-continue-strike/# (accessed 18 November 2022).

FAO, IFAD, UNICEF, WFP and WHO (2021), 'The State of Food Security and Nutrition in the World 2021: Transforming Food Systems for Food Security, Improved Nutrition, and Affordable Healthy Diets for All', Rome: FAO. Available at: https://doi.org/10.4060/cb4474en (accessed 15 July 2021).

GBN (2022), 'Parliament to Investigate Activities of School Feeding Programme and National Food Buffer Stock Company', 13 July. Available at: https://www.

ghanabusinessnews.com/2022/07/13/parliament-to-investigate-activities-of-school-feeding-programme-and-national-food-buffer-stock-company/ (accessed 1 November 2023).

Gelli, A., Aurino, E. Folson, G., Arhinful, D. K., Adamba, C., Osei-Akoto, I., and Alderman, H. (2019), 'A School Meals Program Implemented at Scale in Ghana Increases Height-for-age During Midchildhood in Girls and in Children from Poor Households: A Cluster Randomized Trial', *The Journal of Nutrition*, 149(8): 1434–1442. Available at: https://doi.org/10.1093/jn/nxz079 (accessed 1 November 2023).

Ghana Statistical Service (2020), 'Ghana's Multidimensional Poverty Index Report'. Available at: https://www.undp.org/sites/g/files/zskgke326/files/migration/gh/UNDP_GH_MPI_Report_2020.pdf (accessed 18 November 2023).

Government of Ghana (2015), Draft National School Feeding Policy. Available at: https://www.mogcsp.gov.gh/mdocs-posts/national-school-feeding-policy/ (accessed 18 November 2023).

Human Rights Watch (2021), '"I Must Work to Eat": Covid-19, Poverty, and Child Labor in Ghana, Nepal, and Uganda', 26 May. Available at: https://www.hrw.org/report/2021/05/26/i-must-work-eat/covid-19-poverty-and-child-labor-ghana-nepal-and-uganda (accessed 20 November 2023).

ILO (2018), 'Women and Men in the Informal Economy: A Statistical Picture', Geneva: ILO. Available at: https://www.ilo.org/wcmsp5/groups/public/---dgreports/---dcomm/documents/publication/wcms_626831.pdf (accessed 20 November 2023).

Llavaneras Blanco, M. and Cuervo, M.G. (2021), 'The Pandemic as a Portal: Policy Transformations Disputing the New Normal', DAWN Discussion Paper No. 32. Available at: https://dawnnet.org/wp-content/uploads/2021/04/DAWN-Discussion-Paper-32_The-Pandemic-as-a-Portal.pdf (accessed 20 November 2023).

Kpessa-Whyte, M. (2021), 'Social Policy in Times of Crises. CSPS Social Policy Brief 2021/02', Legon: Centre for Social Policy Studies, University of Ghana. Available at: https://csps.ug.edu.gh/sites/default/files/gbb-uploads/CSPS%20Social%20Policy%20Brief%202021_02_Social%20policy%20in%20times%20of%20crises.pdf (accessed 20 November 2023).

Ministry of Finance (2021), 'The Budget Statement and Economic Policy of the Government of Ghana for the 2022 Financial Year'. Available at: https://mofep.gov.gh/sites/default/files/news/2022-Budget-Statement.pdf (accessed 26 December 2023).

Ministry of Finance (2022), 'Draft 2023 Budget Speech'. Available at: https://mofep.gov.gh/sites/default/files/budget-statements/2023-Budget-Speech.pdf (accessed 26 December 2023).

Modern Ghana (2020), 'Probe Politicisation Of Food Distribution – Zanetor To Gov't', 16 April. Available at: https://www.modernghana.com/news/995965/probe-politicisation-of-food-distribution-zaneto.html (accessed 18 November 2023).

News Ghana (2017), 'NPP Caterers' Fight to Take Over School Feeding Program in Ashanti Region', 11 January. Available at: https://newsghana.com.gh/npp-caterers-fight-to-take-over-school-feeding-program-in-ashanti-region/ (accessed 18 November 2023).

News Ghana (2021), 'GES Directors Not Satisfied with Quality of Food Served Pupils', 3 July. Available at: https://newsghana.com.gh/ges-directors-not-satisfied-with-quality-of-food-served-pupils/ (accessed 18 November 2023).

Otchere, G. (2021), 'Confusion in C/R NPP as School Feeding Caterers Chase NPP Chairman for Cash,' *Adom Online*, 14 April. Available at: https://www.adomonline.com/confusion-in-c-r-npp-as-school-feeding-caterers-chase-npp-chairman-for-cash/# (accessed 18 November 2023).

Owusu, J. A. (2023), 'School Feeding Programme To Receive Payment Next Week', *Ghana News Agency*, 5 June. Available at: https://gna.org.gh/2023/06/school-feeding-caterers-to-receive-payment-next-week/ (accessed 18 October 2023).

Peace FM Online (2021), 'We Can't Cook With GHC0.97 Anymore – School Feeding Caterers Cry Out To Gov't', 13 July. Available at: https://www.peacefmonline.com/pages/local/news/202107/448383.php (accessed 18 November 2023).

Savage, R. and Miridzhanian, A. (2023), 'Fitch Upgrades Ghana's Currency Debt Rating After Domestic Debt Exchange', *Reuters*, 22 March. Available at: https://www.reuters.com/world/africa/fitch-upgrades-ghanas-long-term-local-currency-issuer-default-rating-ccc-2023-03-22/ (accessed 20 November 2023).

The Ghana Report (2021), 'Sacking School Feeding Boss An "Administrative Error" – Adwoa Safo', 20 May. Available at: https://www.theghanareport.com/sacking-school-feeding-boss-an-administrative-error-adwoa-safo/ (accessed 20 November 2023).

Tsikata, D. (2021), 'Gender Equitable and Transformative Social Policy Beyond COVID-19', CSPS Social Policy Brief 2021/02, Legon: Centre for Social Policy Studies, University of Ghana.

UNICEF (2019), 'The State of the World's Children 2019'. Available at: https://www.unicef.org/reports/state-of-worlds-children-2019 (accessed 20 November 2023).

UNICEF (2021), 'Preventing a Lost Decade: Urgent Action to Reverse the Devastating Impact of COVID-19 on Children and Young People'. Available at: https://www.unicef.org/media/112841/file/UNICEF%2075%20report.pdf (accessed 27 December 2023).

UNICEF Ghana (2023) '2023 UNICEF Ghana Budget Briefs'. Available at: https://www.unicef.org/ghana/reports/2023-unicef-ghana-budget-briefs (accessed 20 November 2023).

3

Social Protection and Care Policies: Impact on Gendered Inequalities in Trinidad and Tobago

Karen A. Roopnarine and Crystal Brizan

1. Introduction

Social protection measures and care policies are critical to addressing three threats to the well being of people and households. These include social assistance for those categorized as 'being poor', social insurance for those at risk of 'becoming poor' and social equity for those suffering from structural inequalities and abuses of power (Deveraux and Sabates-Wheeler 2004). To effectively respond to these threats, social protection must necessarily be redistributive, empowering and transformational. For women, social protection systems must be able to specifically address their location in the sexual division of labour and their responsibilities as mothers. Therefore, from a feminist standpoint, social protection must be understood as a mechanism for social inclusion and justice, social and economic redistribution, and the redress of intersecting gendered, social and economic inequalities.

In twenty-first-century Trinidad and Tobago, as in the rest of the Caribbean, the challenges of social protection and inclusion must be understood against a backdrop of colonial history and the legacies of the near decimation and marginalization of indigenous peoples, the forced transportation and enslavement of Africans, indentured labour migration of South Asians (Indians) and other migrations. African and Indian women entered the Caribbean not as wives but as enslaved persons and indentured workers labouring for long hours on plantations, leading to a tradition of women's wage work and involvement in family production. The legacies of these racialized systems of labour exploitation, colonial cultural hegemony and economic extraction continue to cast a shadow over the societies, polities and economies of the region.

Trinidad and Tobago's current social policy model combines a contributory pillar for social protection based on partial citizenry with access to social services in health and education. The latter includes a series of non-contributory cash transfer programmes for vulnerable groups such as people with disabilities, the poor, single parents, at-risk youth, children and the elderly (Robles and Vargas 2012). The main institution charged with implementing non-contributory social protection programmes is the Ministry of Social Development and Family Services (MSDFS), which offers four categories of social assistance grants: Senior Citizens' Pension, Public Assistance Grant, Disability Grant and General Assistance Grants. The fourth category includes assistance for housing, household items, medical equipment, domestic help, dietary needs, clothing and education, among others. Each of these grants have specific eligibility criteria and varying levels of benefits that are determined via means testing based on monthly income and the extent of vulnerability to poverty. Orphans, the elderly, persons with disabilities and victims of natural disasters are covered under the vulnerability to poverty parameter. The lack of detailed social statistics, especially on poverty and the impact of different reforms on the poor, is the biggest barrier in examining the overall performance of social protection policies in Trinidad and Tobago (ibid.). The dearth of reliable social statistics is even starker when looking for gender-disaggregated data. According to UN Women (n.d.), as of December 2020, Trinidad and Tobago had data on only 39.3 per cent of the indicators needed to monitor the Sustainable Development Goals (SDGs) from a gender perspective, with particular gaps in labour statistics.

This is the backdrop against which the Covid-19 pandemic swept across the country. The resulting crisis was in many ways unprecedented. The prolonged lockdowns brought to light and exacerbated many of the underlying problems, inequalities and structural inefficiencies of the current economic paradigm, including the over-reliance on unpaid care work. The government responded to the crisis not by strengthening social security systems and social services, but rather by focusing on monetary assistance to address the economic and social consequences of the pandemic and lockdowns. As in pre-pandemic times, targeted cash transfers and grants were the primary social protection measure implemented during this period, reaching over 220,000 households (GoRTT 2021b). The transfers co-existed with and relied on unpaid care activities that were predominantly performed by women and sustained everyday life.

This chapter examines the Trinidad and Tobago government's response to the pandemic, focusing mainly on its care and social protection policies. More specifically, it explores four main questions:

i)   What were the pandemic-related social protection and care policies implemented by the government of Trinidad and Tobago, and what was the broader social policy context in which they were introduced?;

ii) Were these policies stagnant and path dependent, that is, extensions of pre-existing policies, or were they innovative or progressive, creating some disjuncture with pre-Covid approaches?;

iii) What were the gendered implications of these policies and strategies?; and

iv) How did these strategies interface with other state or private sector-related strategies implemented during the pandemic, and did the Covid-19 social protection and care policies have a transformational effect on gendered social inequalities and macroeconomic policy?

The chapter is organized as follows: Section 2 offers a brief background on Trinidad and Tobago's social protection and care policy landscape prior to Covid-19; Section 3 analyses the pandemic-related cash transfer programmes and the impact of the closure of all learning institutions and non-essential businesses using a feminist lens; and Section 4 provides the main conclusions and findings of the case study.

2. Care and social protection in Trinidad and Tobago

Between 2004 and 2015, central government expenditure tripled while spending on social protection increased almost sixfold from $2,157 million Trinidad and Tobago dollars (TT$) (US$321.9 million) to TT$12,139 million (US$1,811.8 million). This increase coincided with a change in government in 2010, with a manifesto that focused on 'people-centred development' and poverty eradication (People's Partnership 2010). In 2013, the government introduced the Social Sector Investment Programme of 2014 as a component of the national Budget, identifying three main strategies:

i)   The extension of government grants to non-governmental organizations (NGOs) and civil society organizations (CSOs), including faith-based organizations, for service provisions (GoRTT 2014);

ii) The Targeted Conditional Cash Transfer Programme (TCCTP), which accounted for the largest component of the government's social expenditure and provided food assistance in the form of cash transfers; and

iii) The National Poverty Reduction and Eradication Programme, which
    focused on micro-enterprises as the key mechanism for social protection.

This approach, which continued but faced budgetary constraints under a
new administration that came to power in late 2015, effectively shifted the
responsibility of administering service provisions from the state to NGOs, and
emphasized cash transfers and micro-enterprise development as the main
poverty reduction mechanisms. Despite the overall expansion in social
expenditure, none of these individual strategies substantially reduced the
proportions of the working poor and the urban and rural underclasses.[1] The fact
that the social development portfolio was delinked from the gender portfolio
meant that the gender impact of these policies was seldom considered.

Today, Trinidad and Tobago's social protection strategy is a continuation of
the Social Sector Investment Programme implemented in 2013. It is guided by
the National Development Strategy (also known as Vision 2020, and later, Vision
2030), which advocates attaining developed country status by 2030 (earlier
2020). The Vision 2030 document states that, '. . .our citizens are central to our
development and, in fact, are our greatest assets. We must create a society in
which all the basic needs are met, and each individual is valued and given the
opportunity to contribute and to self-actualise' (GoRTT 2016: 45). However, it
also notes that despite the high expenditure on social protection, there has been
no significant improvement in the country's socioeconomic indicators,
suggesting that the issue may lie not in the level of expenditure, but rather in the
resource utilization approach.

3. Pandemic policy responses: Closure of child care centres and learning institutions, cash transfers and the invisibility of care

On 13 March 2020, Trinidad and Tobago recorded its first confirmed case of
Covid-19. In response, the state adopted a 'whole of government' approach,
which saw all ministries work with NGOs, the private sector and religious groups
as a core strategy to provide support and relief, and cushion the impact of
Covid-19 on the population (GoRTT 2021b). The underlying philosophy and
objective of the government's intervention, which it described as a 'set of policy
measures aimed at assisting the poor and vulnerable, protecting businesses, jobs,
and incomes, maintaining financial resilience, and sustaining economic activity',

was to balance containment efforts with the need to maintain livelihoods (GoRTT 2021c: 6).

The MSDFS spearheaded the implementation of social protection policies during the pandemic and collaborated with other ministries as well as civil society and non-governmental and faith-based organizations to provide support services to needy citizens. On 18 March 2020, the MSDFS introduced a targeted social safety net to protect the most vulnerable individuals and households, including the beneficiaries of existing cash transfer programmes such as the Food Support Programme, the Senior Citizens' Pension and the Disability Assistance Grant, and those that lost jobs and incomes due to virus-containment measures.

Notably, there was no explicit mention of unpaid domestic and care work in the government's Covid-19 support strategy. In fact, gender and care work may have been among the most significant blind spots of the government's policy response. The closure of service sector jobs deemed non-essential, which included paid domestic work, led to greater unemployment and underemployment among women. Middle-class women, too, found few or no employment opportunities. At the same time, care demands on women rose drastically due to social isolation, closure of child care centres and learning institutions, and an increase in the number of sick persons in the household (ECLAC 2021). Paradoxically, the relevance of paid and unpaid care work needed and provided at the household level was heightened at the very time when this work was deemed non-essential. The pandemic-related cash transfers excluded informal workers, leaving out a significant number of women, who benefitted the least from the emergency Covid-19 social protection measures even as their unpaid care workload increased.

The lack of attention to gender was also evident at other levels of the policy making process. For example, a committee set up by Prime Minister Keith Rowley and charged with examining and executing a post-pandemic recovery plan was constituted entirely by male members. As such, the committee's Roadmap to Recovery Post-Pandemic Report failed to address existing gender inequalities in a transformative way (Hosein 2021). To be sure, Trinidad and Tobago was not alone in this regard. The Covid-19 social protection programmes implemented by other Caribbean governments also failed to consider their gendered impacts. For example, two policies implemented in Barbados, namely the Adopt Our Families Programme and the increase in and expansion of the minimum wage, reproduced gender- and class-based inequalities because of the lack of attention to care and informal work (Bobb and Worrell, this volume).

3.1 Closure of child care centres, nurseries and learning institutions

One fallout of the absence of a gender lens in policy making was the failure to support families, and especially women, in dealing with the additional social reproductive responsibilities that cropped up due to the pandemic-induced stay-at-home orders.

Trinidad and Tobago has several categories of educational facilities operated by the state and private actors. These span early childhood, primary, secondary, technical and vocational training, and tertiary facilities. One of the immediate Covid-19 containment measures was the closure of all these teaching and learning institutions effective 13 March 2020, which resulted in children being out of school and at home for an extended period. Table 3.1 maps the number of school-age children and teachers affected by the closure of these facilities, which also impacted a wide cross-section of society.

In the months that followed, the distribution of domestic chores was highly disproportionate between women and men. Women bore a greater burden of the household chores, including homeschooling and entertaining children, caring for the elderly, cleaning and cooking. Seventy-one per cent of women reported being

Table 3.1 Number of Students and Teachers Impacted by School Closures in Trinidad and Tobago, 2020

Type of institution	Number of institutions	Number of students	Number of teachers
Early childhood care and education centres (public and private)	841	26,657	2,394
Primary schools (public)	557 (public and private)	120,455 (public)	6,978 (public)
Schools for children with disabilities, also known as special schools (public and private)	43	552	103
Secondary schools	189 (public and private)	83,554 (public)	6,928 (public)
Technical and vocational education and training (TVET)	148 (public and private)	37,661 (public)	2,049 (public)

Source: Compiled by authors based on data from the InterAmerican Development Bank in 2020. See https:// socialdigital.iadb.org/en/edu/covid-19/regional-response/6178.

responsible for coordinating or assisting with homeschooling compared with only 25 per cent of men (IDB 2020). Nearly 60 per cent of women were responsible for cooking and cleaning compared with less than 32 per cent of men (ibid.).

School closures also impacted the financial well being of women, as the teaching vocation, especially at the early childhood and day care levels, is predominated by them. While the higher level schools were able to switch to online learning platforms to hold classes and continue generating income to pay teaching and support staff, women who owned or were employed by private day care centres and pre-schools experienced income losses.

The closure of schools was accompanied by the shutdown of almost all sectors of the economy and simultaneous stay-at-home orders. This meant that most families were confined to the house, with few opportunities to step out unless they were essential workers. From the outset, there were fears that this would result in an increased incidence of gender-based violence (GBV). As one commentator predicted at the time, 'Girls' risk of sexual abuse is especially high now that uncles, step-fathers, cousins and other men are more present and difficult to escape' (Hosein 2020). These fears were well founded. Mere weeks into the lockdown, the then Commissioner of Police Gary Griffith reported a disturbing increase in the number of domestic violence cases reported to the Trinidad and Tobago Police Service (TTPS) from 232 in 2019 to 558 in the first three months of 2020, most of them concentrated in February and March (Alexander 2020). Further, these numbers only reflect reports lodged with the TTPS and do not account for domestic and sexual violence cases that went unreported. The pandemic thus exacerbated a situation in which women were already overworked and underpaid, and put their emotional well being and mental health on a razor's edge.

3.2 Cash transfers

According to a survey by the Inter-American Development Bank (IDB 2020),[2] the number of households in Trinidad and Tobago that reported incomes below the minimum wage[3] jumped in the immediate aftermath of the pandemic from 12 per cent in January 2020 to 47 per cent in April 2020. The report cited three main factors that led to this increase: business closures due to public health restrictions and the lack of demand for goods and services, employment loss, and the loss of rental income from real estate and vehicles. The employment shock was similar for women and men, with roughly 45 per cent of both groups reporting job losses.

The pandemic affected all households, but the magnitude of the impact varied depending on income levels (ibid.). About 67 per cent of households earning less than the minimum wage pre-pandemic were impacted by the loss of income and employment compared with 49 per cent of middle-income and 23 per cent of high-income households. Minimum wage households were also impacted far more severely than the rest. Fewer than 30 per cent of all households indicated having enough savings to cover an unexpected expense (ibid.).[4] Among households earning below the minimum wage, less than 20 per cent reported having enough savings for an emergency expense, and 43 per cent only had enough savings to cover one week or more of essential expenses. The latest publicly available poverty study for Trinidad and Tobago, the Survey of Living Conditions published in 2005, found that 28 per cent of all households and 38 per cent of the poorest households were headed by women (Kambon 2021). Indeed, we can expect that the pandemic had devastating effects on these households and further widened socioeconomic inequalities.

As mentioned earlier, the main government support programme during this time consisted of targeted cash transfers, including grants for food support, income support, senior citizens, public assistance, disability assistance and rental assistance, among others. In many ways, this support programme was a continuation of the pre-Covid-19 policy approach, which focused on cash transfers as opposed to strengthening social security systems and enhancing social services to address the causal factors contributing to economic and social inequalities, poor mental health and other social problems such as addiction, school dropouts, etc.

The emergency financial programmes included both new cash transfer policies as well as those adapted from pre-pandemic ones by redefining the terms of eligibility, access and coverage. Between March and September 2020, over 222,000 households were recipients of the Covid-19 social safety net measures and the interventions cost the government TT$482 million (US$71.9 million) (GoRTT 2021b).

The interface between the Covid-19 social protection programmes and the existing National Insurance System (NIS) was fraught with shortcomings and inefficacies. To be eligible for these grants, people needed to be registered with the NIS. However, the NIS is an insurance and pension scheme consisting of only formally employed people and registered businesses who make compulsory weekly contributions. As such, it leaves out large sections of the population, including self-employed individuals, informal workers, own-account workers and migrants. In the process, it also excludes a significant number of women, who constitute a disproportionate number of Trinidad and Tobago's informal workers.

The pandemic revealed how highly bureaucratic and inadequate the NIS was as a tool for identifying vulnerable persons in society, bringing to light the absence of direct links between poorer communities and the state's social development and support systems. Some people could not access the Covid-19-related cash transfers since they were not registered with the NIS and did not have bank accounts to receive financial grants. In certain cases, corrupt employers did not pay employee contributions to the NIS even though these were deducted from workers' salaries. As a result, the government was forced to lean on religious organizations that typically engage with communities at the grassroots level and were, therefore, able to assist with identifying vulnerable persons/households during the pandemic.[5] In 2020, the government provided cash transfers worth TT$30 million (US$4.5 million) to religious bodies to provide food hampers to the most vulnerable persons in their respective communities. Almost 50,000 food hampers were distributed this way, successfully assisting needy persons.

Another form of emergency cash transfer was the salary relief grant. As of September 2020, the MSDFS had received over 56,000 applications for the salary relief grant, of which 63 per cent were submitted by men and 33 per cent by women (4 per cent of the applications did not state the gender of the applicant) (GoRTT 2021b). Kambon (2021) notes that many women who were domestic workers or held other jobs in the informal economy had no contributions to the NIS prior to the pandemic, making them ineligible to apply for this grant. The gender gap was also reproduced in the lower acceptance rate of applications submitted by women: only 30 per cent of women applicants were approved to receive the salary relief grant compared with 58 per cent male applicants (GoRTT 2021b). The ministry did not share the reason(s) for the lower approval rate for female applicants. In addition to the inaccessible salary relief grant, some women could not apply for or receive the government's rental assistance grant as their rental contracts were informal and landlords would not, or could not, comply with the requirements necessary for the grant application.

In April 2021, the third wave of the pandemic hit the country and resulted in the reinstatement of several lockdown measures, closure of all non-essential businesses and the declaration of a state of emergency. In response, several of the emergency cash transfers introduced in 2020 were extended into 2021. By May 2021, over 86,000 salary relief grants were paid, and an additional 7,000 grants were approved, with payments pending due to issues with banking information (Julien 2021).[6] Each approved applicant received a grant worth TT$1,500

(US$223.9) per month for a maximum of three months. The bulk of applications came from people engaged in the food and restaurant as well as retail sectors, both feminized sectors of employment.[7]

Given that Trinidad and Tobago is an energy-exporting country, the economy was also adversely impacted by the collapse in oil prices in the first quarter of 2020. Amid a widening fiscal deficit and rising debts over the past decade, the expanded Covid-19 cash transfers were not fiscally sustainable. The government financed these expenditures through external borrowings from development banks like the IDB and the Development Bank of Latin America (CAF), and the World Bank as well as through withdrawals from the country's sovereign wealth fund, known as the Heritage and Stabilisation Fund (HSF). To finance the emergency social protection programmes, the government had to amend the HSF legislation to allow withdrawals to address dangerous infectious diseases as declared under the Public Health Ordinance (GoRTT 2021a). The country's public debt-to-GDP ratio rose from 62 per cent in 2019 to over 80 per cent in 2020 on the back of these borrowings and withdrawals. In 2022, public debt hovered around 70 per cent (Central Bank of Trinidad and Tobago n.d.).

3.3 Invisibility of care

The Covid-19 pandemic shed light on deep-seated inequalities in the existing social organization of care. These inequalities manifested in the form of lack of social protection for domestic workers and unequal distribution of care responsibilities and labour, especially between women and men within families and between families and the state. As discussed in Section 3.1, the overwhelming increase in unpaid care responsibilities brought on by the pandemic became the responsibility of women. In addition to working from home, women had to deal with the additional tasks of caring for the entire family, including school-age children attempting to learn from home, and ensuring household members' health and well being. These additional unpaid care responsibilities had significant negative implications for women's productivity and their physical and mental health. As stated by the Caribbean Association for Feminist Research and Action Trinidad and Tobago (CAFRA TT), 'the economic and social crisis is not merely due to the disease but to weak social sector structures, gender inequities, inadequate worker protection, food insufficiency, and inequitable access to educational resources' (2020). In effect, the over-reliance on women's unpaid care work was the result of impoverished social services.

As of December 2023, no comprehensive data existed in Trinidad and Tobago on the number of hours spent on unpaid care work or how this time was divided between women and men. Despite the Unremunerated Work Act of 1993 that mandates the Central Statistical Office to compile such information – one of the first legislations in the world to do so – the country has not conducted any recent full-scale time use surveys to quantify unpaid care work (ECLAC 2021).

While literacy rates are high for both women and men, the female labour force participation, at 48.6 per cent, is lower than the male participation rate of 63 per cent (World Bank 2022). In the pre-pandemic period, only half of all working-age women actively participated in the labour market (Roopnarine and Ramrattan 2012). However, a majority of people recorded as involved in home duties were women. This was not the case for men who were seldom recorded in this category. Many informal sector workers, who are predominantly women, were also not recorded in the labour force.

Against this backdrop, the country's increased reliance on women's unpaid care labour to absorb the shock of the pandemic may have pushed many more women out of the labour market. The closure of non-essential service sectors, including paid domestic work, led to increasing levels of female unemployment and underemployment. According to official labour statistics, the pre-pandemic female labour force participation rate stood at 49 per cent in the final quarter of 2019 compared with 45 per cent in the final quarter of 2021 (Central Statistical Office 2023). By the second quarter of 2023, the number hovered over 47 per cent, indicating a slight recovery (ibid.). However, there is a significant risk that the expulsion of women workers from the labour market becomes further normalized in the post-Covid-19 scenario. There is also the risk that the greater reliance on women's unpaid care labour becomes, directly or indirectly, a policy measure, thus further weakening publicly provided care services and externalizing the associated costs (Llavaneras Blanco and Cuervo 2021).

4. Conclusion and recommendations

Using a feminist interlinkages approach, this chapter sought to explore the transformative impacts, if any, of the Covid-19 social protection and care programmes implemented by the government of Trinidad and Tobago. In the pre-pandemic scenario, despite a relatively large fiscal spending on social protection, there was no significant improvement in socioeconomic indicators.

This suggests that the issue lay in how fiscal resources were used rather than the level of expenditure.

In the context of DAWN's analytical framework (ibid.), the emergency social protection measures put in place during the Covid-19 crisis were extensions of pre-existing policies. The government relied heavily on cash transfers and in-kind transfers (including fresh agricultural produce) to assist the most vulnerable (unemployed, children, elderly, etc.), which was in line with the social safety net programmes instituted almost a decade prior to the pandemic. These programmes were not fiscally sustainable and had to be financed, for the most part, by taking on additional public debt and development grants at a time when Trinidad and Tobago had limited fiscal space and an already high debt burden. In addition, the emphasis on cash transfers meant that there was little innovation in the delivery of care and social protection, which could have otherwise led to a positive transformation of the macroeconomy. As such, despite the new emergency cash transfers and other policy adaptations made during the pandemic, the overall social protection programme remained business as usual. In turn, this path-dependent approach exacerbated existing income and gender inequalities.

Even before the pandemic, Trinidad and Tobago's labour market had relatively high levels of informality.[8] During the Covid-19 crisis, this translated into weaker safeguards against the termination of employment and a lack of social protection, as the NIS did not cover informal workers. With a sharp rise in unemployment and a significant decline in household incomes, families relied on social security and social protection systems in the form of cash transfers and food programmes. The pandemic also exposed the limitations of the country's existing social insurance system, which is biased in favour of formal labour and excludes informal workers.

Moreover, the social protection measures applied in response to Covid-19 focused on social assistance and paid little or no attention to care services. Notably, there was no explicit mention of unpaid domestic and care work in the government's support strategy. This despite the fact that unpaid care labour, performed predominantly by women, acted as a countercyclical buffer, helping the country absorb the shock of the pandemic (Rodríguez Enríquez 2020). Some Covid-related policies, such as extended school closures and the shutdown of entire sectors of the economy, had a disproportionately negative impact on women. It not only increased their household work burden – cooking, cleaning, child care, supervision of online schools, caring for the sick and elderly, etc. – but also led to a rise in unemployment and underemployment among women, who are concentrated in the informal sectors of the economy.

Against this backdrop, a sustainable economic recovery will require urgently addressing the care economy to reduce the burden of unpaid care work on women. It would also require an overhaul of the existing sexual division of labour. In addition, the NIS should expand its coverage to include self-employed persons such as entrepreneurs and paid and unpaid domestic workers, a sizeable number of whom are women. Besides, social protection should not rely on formal labour data as its main source of information to identify people in need of state support.

A paradigm shift needs to occur in the way the government delivers social services, such that the underlying causes of social and gender-based inequalities are addressed. Social protection and care programmes need to become more efficient and effective, and ensure that children do not suffer because of the circumstances of their parents and women are not penalized for having children. The overarching aim of social protection and care programmes should be to address the underlying social challenges that negatively affect people's lives and their ability to fully participate as citizens in society.

With specific reference to the care economy, the state should actively engage in dismantling patriarchal gender norms by amplifying the message of 'share the care'; this could be facilitated through greater collaboration between the ministries of social development and gender and child affairs (CAFRA TT 2020). Moreover, the idea that men should participate equally in the care of their children, including as reliable providers of economic support, should be promoted through gender-sensitive parenting programmes, gender studies programmes in school and public education programmes. Failure to make the necessary transformational changes in the delivery of the country's social security and social protection services will undermine the nation's long-term socioeconomic goals, including that of social justice and gender equality.

Notes

1   The latest available official poverty statistics for Trinidad and Tobago date back to 2005. However, unofficial (and unpublished) data from the Survey of Living Conditions 2014 showed an increase in poverty from 16.5 per cent in 2005 to almost 25 per cent in 2014 (See Clyne 2016).
2   The online socioeconomic survey was conducted over a two-week period (16 April to 30 April 2020) and garnered over 4,700 responses.
3   The minimum hourly wage rate in the country is TT$ 17.50.

4   The survey defined an unexpected expense to be equivalent to a month's minimum
     wage of TT$ 2,800 (US$ 418).
5   The government relied on faith-based organizations to identify vulnerable persons/
     families at the community level largely because of the shift from community and
     family case management by the state to NGO provisions and cash transfers. This
     reduced direct links between the state and those living in poverty.
6   According to a public statement by the finance minister, debit cards were to be
     prepared and sent to people via post.
7   An innovative aspect of the Covid-19 relief programme was the Ministry of
     Agriculture's initiative where local farmers were paid to provide 25,000 fresh food
     baskets per month (in May, June, and July 2021) to be distributed to needy households.
8   An IDB (2022) study suggests that the size of the informal economy in Trinidad and
     Tobago is likely to range between 26 per cent and 33 per cent of GDP. Moreover,
     according to the World Economics Informal Economy Database (https://www.
     worldeconomics.com/Informal-Economy/Trinidad%20And%20Tobago.aspx), the
     current size of Trinidad and Tobago's informal economy is 31.6 per cent of GDP.

References

Alexander, G. (2020), 'CoP Warns Abusers Amid Spike During Stay Home', *Trinidad and
     Tobago Guardian*, 9 April. Available at: https://www.guardian.co.tt/news/cop-warns-
     abusers-amid-spike-during-stay-home-6.2.1095910.4f92b97b10 (accessed 22
     October 2021).
CAFRA TT (2020), 'Submission on the Road to Recovery', Input to the Roadmap to
     Recovery Committee Convened by the Government of Trinidad and Tobago to
     Mitigate the Fallout of the Pandemic, 3 May.
Central Bank of Trinidad and Tobago (n.d.), 'Public Sector Debt Outstanding (Per cent
     of GDP)'. Retrieved from: https://www.central-bank.org.tt/statistics/selected-
     aggregates/pub-sec-debt-outst-percentage-of-gdp (accessed 8 December 2023).
Central Statistical Office (2023), 'Continuous Sample Survey of Population'. Retrieved
     from: https://cso.gov.tt/subjects/continuous-sample-survey-of-population/ (accessed
     7 November 2023).
Clyne, K. (2016), 'Poor Working Just to Eat', *Trinidad and Tobago Guardian*, 29 May.
     Available at: https://www.guardian.co.tt/article-6.2.354558.f011d69452 (accessed 22
     October 2021).
Deveraux, S and Sabates-Wheeler, R. (2004), 'Transformative Social Protection', Institute
     of Development Studies, IDS Working Paper 232. Available at: https://www.ids.ac.uk/
     download.php?file=files/dmfile/Wp232.pdf (accessed 9 August 2021).
ECLAC (2021), 'The Burden of Unpaid Care Work on Caribbean Women in the Time of
     COVID-19', Background Note, Side Event for the 61st Meeting of the Presiding

Officers of the Regional Conference on Women in Latin America and the Caribbean. Available at: https://www.cepal.org/sites/default/files/events/files/background_note. pdf (accessed 9 August 2021).

GoRTT (2014), 'The Social Sector Investment Programme 2014: Sustaining Growth, Securing Prosperity'. Available at: https://www.finance.gov.tt/wp-content/ uploads/2014/02/Social-Sector-Investment-Programme-2014.pdf (accessed 9 August 2021).

GoRTT (2016), 'Vision 2030: The National Development Strategy of Trinidad and Tobago: 2016-2030'. Available at: https://www.planning.gov.tt/sites/default/files/ Vision%202030-%20The%20National%20Development%20Strategy%20of%20 Trinidad%20and%20Tobago%202016-2030.pdf (accessed 09 August 2021).

GoRTT (2021a), 'The Trinidad and Tobago Heritage and Stabilisation Fund: Annual Report 2021', Available at: https://www.finance.gov.tt/wp-content/uploads/2022/04/ HSF-AR-2021-web-1.pdf (accessed 21 November 2023).

GoRTT (2021b), 'Social Sector Investment Programme 2021: Resetting the Economy for Growth and Innovation'. Available at: https://www.finance.gov.tt/wp-content/ uploads/2020/10/Social-Sector-Investment-Programme-2021-1.pdf (accessed 22 October 2021).

GoRTT (2021c), 'Budget Statement 2021: Resetting the Economy for Growth and Innovation', 2021'. Available at: https://www.finance.gov.tt/wp-content/ uploads/2020/10/Budget-Statement-2021-1.pdf (accessed 22 October 2021).

Hosein, G. (2020), 'Emotional Pitfalls of Isolation', *Trinidad and Tobago Newsday*, 25 March. Available at: https://newsday.co.tt/2020/03/25/emotional-pitfalls-of-isolation/ (accessed 22 October 2021).

Hosein, G. (2021), 'Women Invisible – Again', *Trinidad and Tobago Newsday*, 6 October. Available at: https://newsday.co.tt/2021/10/06/women-invisible-again/ (accessed 22 October 2021).

IDB (2020), 'COVID-19: The Caribbean Crisis: Results from an Online Socioeconomic Survey'. Available at: https://publications.iadb.org/en/covid-19-the-caribbean-crisis-results-from-an-online-socioeconomic-survey (accessed 9 August 2021).

IDB (2022), 'Estimating the Size of the Informal Economy in Caribbean States', IDB Technical Note 1248. Available at: https://publications.iadb.org/en/estimating-size-informal-economy-caribbean-states (accessed 15 May 2022).

Julien, J. (2021), '14,000 Apply for Salary Relief Grants in Two Days', *Trinidad and Tobago Guardian*, 22 May. Available at: https://www.guardian.co.tt/news/14000-apply-for-salary-relief-grants-in-two-days-6.2.1331983.dbc44ffdfb (accessed 22 October 2021).

Kambon, A. (2021), Gender Impact Assessment of COVID-19 Pandemic in Trinidad and Tobago: Voices of Vulnerability And Resilience [Power Point Slides]. Government of Trinidad and Tobago.

Llavaneras Blanco, M. and Cuervo, M.G. (2021), 'The Pandemic as a Portal: Policy Transformations Disputing the New Normal', DAWN Discussion Paper No. 32.

Available at: https://dawnnet.org/wp-content/uploads/2021/04/DAWN-Discussion-Paper-32_The-Pandemic-as-a-Portal.pdf (accessed 22 October 2021).

People's Partnership (2010), 'Prosperity for All. Manifesto of the People's Partnership for a United People to Achieve Sustainable Development for Trinidad and Tobago'. Available at: https://unctt.org/wp-content/uploads/2013/02/peoples-manifesto-2010.pdf (accessed 22 October 2021).

Robles, C. and Vargas, L. H. (2012), *Social Protection Systems in Latin America and the Caribbean: Trinidad and Tobago*, s.l.: s.n.

Rodríguez Enríquez, C. (2020), 'RE-VALUE the Importance of Care in Society', in: Spotlight on Sustainable Development 2020: Shifting Policies for Systemic Change, 51–54. Available at: https://dawnnet.org/publication/spotlight-report-2020-shifting-policies-for-systemic-change/ (accessed 22 October 2021).

Roopnarine, K. and Ramrattan, D. (2012), 'Female Labour Force Participation: The Case of Trinidad and Tobago', *World Journal of Entrepreneurship, Management and Sustainable Development*, 8(2/3): 183–193. Available at: https://doi.org/10.1108/20425961211247789 (accessed 22 October 2021).

Roopnarine, K. (2018), 'Three-Fourths a Penny for Your Thoughts? Gender Pay Differentials in Trinidad and Tobago: An Empirical Analysis', PhD Thesis, University of Nottingham. Available at: https://eprints.nottingham.ac.uk/50401/ (accessed 22 October 2021).

Seguino, S. (2003), 'Why Are Women in the Caribbean So Much More Likely to Be Unemployed?', *Social and Economic Studies*, 52(4): 83–120, Available at: https://www.jstor.org/stable/27865354 (accessed 9 August 2021).

UN Women (n.d.). Trinidad and Tobago Country Fact Sheet, UN Women Data Hub. Available at: https://data.unwomen.org/country/trinidad-and-tobago (accessed 21 December 2023).

World Bank (2022). General Data Portal. Available at: https://genderdata.worldbank.org/countries/trinidad-and-tobago/#:~:text=In%20Trinidad%20and%20Tobago%2C%20the%20labor%20force%20participation%20rate%20among,males%20is%2063%25%20for%202022 (accessed 21 December 2023).

4

Impact of Covid-19 on Domestic Workers in China: Reflections on a Fragmented Policy Response

Zhihong Sa

1. Introduction

Demographically, China is contending with a rapidly ageing population, low fertility and small family size. At the same time, the burden of care responsibilities on the family, high labour force participation of women and a rapid rise in incomes have led to an increasing demand for domestic services among urban families. These trends, coupled with large-scale rural-to-urban internal migration, have resulted in the emergence of a fast-growing domestic service industry and a paid care workforce constituted mostly of women. According to an estimate by the International Labour Organization (ILO), China accounts for 22 million, or over 29 per cent, of all domestic workers in the world (2021). Of this, more than 90 per cent are women and around 80 per cent are rural-to-urban migrants (Wang and Wu 2016, Sa and Liu 2022).

While domestic workers in China play an increasingly important role in fulfilling the care needs of urban families, their labour rights and interests are largely neglected. Their vulnerability is closely linked to the state's development approach in the market reform era, which prioritized economic development and efficiency, retreating from its earlier role of supporting social reproduction and social welfare. Care provisions become privatized and marketized, and most domestic workers were informally employed (Tong 2018). This was a cause for concern since domestic workers' labour takes place in private households in complex and 'hidden' ways, and there is no supervision or regulation of employers who are considered consumers of care services under the current legal framework. Furthermore, under China's household registration system, known as the *hukou* system, rural-to-urban migrants have limited access to urban social security systems because they are not registered in that particular area or city. Introduced in 1958, the *hukou* system categorizes individuals as either urban or rural residents (Cheng and Selden 1994), which is then used to determine their eligibility to access government employment, affordable housing and social welfare (ibid). Since many domestic workers are rural-to-urban migrants, the *hukou* system ends up exacerbating their vulnerabilities. These workers face multiple social and economic exclusions, and are saddled with insecure jobs, poor working conditions and low levels of social protection (Liu 2017, Sa and Liu 2022).

Worldwide, domestic workers are over-represented in the informal labour market. They worked on the front lines of the Covid-19 crisis but were also hit the hardest by it (ILO 2021). Domestic workers in China were no exception. China was the first country to experience the outbreak of the novel coronavirus. While the government's strict restrictions brought the epidemic under control in a relatively short period, most domestic workers encountered job and/or income losses during the ensuing lockdown and many suffered employment insecurity (Beijing Hongyan Social Work Service Center 2020, Xing 2021, Yu et al. 2021).

Despite the central role they played during the pandemic, there is little policy analysis on domestic workers in China. This chapter attempts to fill that gap by investigating the impact of Covid-19 on the working conditions and livelihoods of domestic workers in China, and simultaneously assessing the domestic work-related policy changes introduced during and after the crisis. It uses a feminist interlinkages approach and an intersectional lens to study the intertwining effects of the state (more specifically, its labour and care policies), the market and gender on the multiple precarities that domestic workers faced even before Covid-19, and examines how the pandemic further exacerbated these vulnerabilities. The chapter then argues that China's pandemic policy responses were stagnant and path dependent in that they were an extension of pre-pandemic policies (Llavaneras Blanco and Cuervo 2021). Finally, based on this assessment, it offers recommendations for labour and social protection policies for domestic workers in China.[1]

The ILO (2021) defines domestic work as work performed in or for a household or households within a formal or informal employment relationship. Domestic workers in China typically undertake care work for children, the elderly, the sick and the disabled as well as cleaning, cooking and other household chores. To investigate how the Covid-19 crisis impacted them, we conducted semi-structured interviews with twelve domestic workers in Beijing in April

2020 and, following a new wave of outbreak, another four workers in Nanjing in July 2021. In the same month, we also interviewed four managers of domestic service companies and two representatives of non-governmental organizations (NGOs) that provide social support to domestic workers.[2]

2. Mapping the evolution of domestic work and care policies in China

To examine the pandemic's impact on domestic workers and the related policy changes, it is crucial to first review the institutional and cultural underpinnings of domestic workers' conditions in the pre-pandemic period and examine the shift in policies on paid care and rural-to-urban labour migration over time.

2.1 Dismantling state-led care provisions in China's reform era

As China transitioned from a planned to a market economy in the late 1970s, its national care policies underwent dramatic transformation. In the pre-reform era (1949–76), the state, urban employers (*danwei* in Chinese) and rural collectives played a role in care provisions along with families, with the ultimate goal of increasing women's labour force participation (Connelly et al. 2018). In the urban areas, women employees and their families enjoyed paid maternity leave and subsidized child care services provided through their *danwei*. Support for care of the elderly, the sick and people with disabilities was provided through pensions, public health care, subsidized housing and other services for retirees.

In contrast, the post-reform period witnessed a dismantling of social provisions and a shift in care responsibilities from the state to the household (Tong 2018). The state prioritized economic growth and efficiency while relegating the provision of welfare and care to households in order to keep expenditure on social welfare low (Connelly et al. 2018). Economic decentralization and privatization of state- and collective-owned enterprises brought an end to the era of cradle-to-grave socialism. Public sector restructuring led to a substantial decline in the support provided by the state and the *danwei* for child care and elder care. At the same time, the rapid expansion of private and informal sectors eroded the state's regulatory ability to protect women in their unpaid reproductive labour. As state-led child care services became more expensive and less accessible, a greater proportion of care responsibilities had to be shouldered by individual families. As a result of the family care deficit, paid care emerged in the early 1980s in the urban areas (Tong 2018). Employed women with young children increasingly sought the support of their extended families or paid care services. The privatization and commodification of care provisions were further bolstered by the rejuvenation of Confucian patriarchal values that emphasize traditional gender roles and consider care work as women's natural duty (Ji et al. 2017).

2.2 The state's role in developing China's domestic service industry

Over the past decade, China's domestic service industry has expanded rapidly. Its revenue increased from 203.4 billion Chinese yuan (CNY) (US$30.9 billion) in 2014 to CNY878.2 billion (US$127.3 billion) in 2020 and is expected to maintain an annual growth rate of 20 per cent going forward (Qianzhan Industry Research Institute 2021).

The state has been an important driver of the domestic service industry. In the early stages of its development, the main task of the state was to ease the double burden of work and family care on urban households and solve the problem of unemployment for urban female workers who were laid off (Tong 2018). In 1983, the Beijing Women's Federation established the Women Domestic Services Centre (Sanba jiazheng fuwu zhongxin), the first domestic service company in China. Thereafter, the All-China Women's Federation called for women's federations across the country to set up domestic service agencies. Since then, women's federations have collaborated with labour departments and domestic service companies to provide vocational training and facilitate labour export of rural migrant women into cities to provide urban families with paid care services (Liu 2017, Tong 2018).

In 2000, the Ministry of Labour and Social Security issued the National Occupational Standards for Domestic Service Providers, which, for the first time, recognized domestic work as a formal occupation (Liu 2017). Following the 2008 global financial crisis, the state started to push for the marketization of domestic services as part of its efforts to expand the service sector (interview with Zhang Xianmin, 15 February 2021). An inter-departmental joint meeting scheme was established to support the development of a domestic service sector. In 2009, the joint meeting implemented a domestic service project that would provide training and job placements to domestic workers, mainly through domestic service companies. In 2010, the State Council issued Guidelines for the Development of the Domestic Service Industry (No. 43 of the

State Council), which explicitly promoted the marketization, industrialization and socialization of household services, with domestic service companies playing a central role.

In 2012, the state promulgated the Interim Measures for the Administration of the Household Service Sector (State Council of the PRC 2012). As the only legislation regulating the domestic service sector, the Interim Measures, consistent with China's labour contract law, defines families or individuals contracting domestic workers as 'consumers' of domestic services rather than 'employers' of domestic workers. The current legal framework excludes domestic workers who do not have signed contracts with any domestic service company – and are, therefore, deemed informal – from the protection of China's labour law while shielding family employers from their legal responsibilities towards such workers (Liu 2017).

Starting in 2017, the state incorporated the domestic service industry into its national development strategies. At this stage, the focus of state policy was to expedite the professionalization, standardization and formalization of the sector. In 2019, the state issued Guidelines for Improving the Quality and Capacity of the Domestic Service Industry (State Council of the PRC 2019). As part of this endeavour, the state offered subsidies and tax rebates to domestic service companies and channelled large amounts of funding for them to train workers. The state also used these companies to promote the formalization of the domestic service sector. For example, some local governments subsidized the enrolment of domestic workers in employee's insurance by domestic service companies.

However, the process of formalization of the domestic service sector was fragmented and its overall impact limited, as less than 2 per cent of domestic workers in Beijing, Jinan and Changsha were formally employed through written and signed labour contracts and had access to employee's insurance (Sa and Liu 2022). Furthermore, many provisions of the Interim Measures remained unimplemented (Liu 2017).

2.3 Social protection for internal labour migrants

Prior to the 1980s, China had strictly restricted rural-to-urban migration for more than two decades as a part of its state-led industrialization. As established in previous sections, the *hukou* system enforced rural-urban segregation affecting resource distribution and access to services (Cheng and Selden 1994). Post the 1980s, the restrictions on rural-to-urban labour mobility were gradually relaxed but the *hukou* system and its rural-urban division of welfare provisions persisted. As a result, migrant workers faced significant difficulties in accessing secure jobs, social security and social services in destination cities, and many of them left children behind in rural areas.

In response, the state, over the past two decades, introduced a series of policy measures that expanded the coverage of rural social safety nets and integrated rural populations into urban social security systems (Li, S. et al. 2013). In 2010, the State Council announced that the *hukou* system would be replaced by a system of residence permits to enable rural migrants to enjoy the same social security benefits as urban residents. In some developed areas, the *hukou* reforms gave rural farmers access to integrated systems for social security and social services, but the level of benefits they enjoyed was relatively low given their lower incomes. Despite the new measures, therefore, rural-to-urban migrant workers' access to social security and social services remained limited in most receiving urban areas (Li, Y. et al. 2021).

The era of market reform in China thus witnessed the privatization of care responsibilities, and the marketization and commodification of care provisions. The main focus of state policies on paid care was to promote employment, reduce poverty and stimulate economic development. As part of their task of supporting state policies, the women's federations were actively involved in the marketization and commodification of care provisions. However, little or no attention was paid to the rights and interests of domestic workers. As a result, there is currently no labour and social protection for informal domestic workers or regulations for family employers.

2.4 Precarity of domestic workers in the pre-pandemic period

Domestic workers who were employed informally had to rely on rural or urban resident's social insurance schemes rather than employee's insurance.[3] Their working conditions were poor, as they worked longer hours, received lower wages and had unstable jobs compared with other workers (Wang and Wu 2016). It was hard for them to negotiate working hours and workloads, as there was no clear boundary between work and life, particularly for live-in domestic workers (Ma 2015). On an average, live-in workers in Beijing and Jinan worked more than thirteen hours per day and eighty-three hours each week (Sa and Liu 2022). Domestic workers' incomes remained relatively low. According to Dong et al. (2016), they earned 20 per cent less than other types of service workers with the same human capital characteristics. Sa and Liu (2022) show that the hourly pay of domestic workers in Beijing was lower than the local minimum hourly wage of other informal workers. The labour devaluation was particularly salient among elder care workers who are considered to perform 'dirty work'. Their hourly pay was about two-thirds of other service and informal workers (Dong et al. 2016, Sa and Liu 2022).

The 'hidden' nature of paid care labour in private households alongside informal employment relations rendered domestic workers vulnerable to multiple labour rights violations (Sa and Liu 2022), of which the most prominent was the lack of rest time. More than 28 per cent of domestic workers in Beijing did not have weekly breaks and 20 per cent did not take days off on public holidays. Their right to compensation was also violated. Of the domestic workers interviewed in Beijing for this study, more than 40 per cent said they worked overtime on weekends or public holidays without receiving the level of compensation mandated by China's labour law. Working in private households also endangered their personal safety and health. Nearly 12 per cent of domestic workers interviewed in Beijing reported being insulted or intimidated themselves, and more than 30 per cent reported that their co-workers experienced sexual harassment by family employers. These poor labour conditions were exacerbated by the pandemic.

3. Impact of Covid-19 on China's domestic workers

3.1 China's pandemic policy response

Following the outbreak of the pandemic in early 2020, China took speedy measures to expand access to health care benefits. It ensured free testing, extended a medical benefits package to include drugs and medical services necessary for Covid-19 treatment and made medical treatment accessible to those who were not insured, irrespective of their ability to settle co-payments. In addition, the government ensured that medical facilities received the funds needed for treatment in advance to prevent any exclusions from care due to financial constraints (Stern-Plaza et al. 2021).

The state's economic relief measures prioritized financial support to enterprises to enable them to resume production. In February 2020, the state extended the tax payment window for enterprises affected by the pandemic (Ministry of Finance and the State Administration of Taxation 2020, No. 8). In May 2020, it reduced rents for the hardest hit small and micro enterprises

(National Development and Reform Commission 2020, No. 734). In June 2020, it took multiple measures to enable domestic service companies to resume operations, reducing their financial burden and enabling them to expand and improve the quality of their services. Besides offering tax relief and deductions and other forms of financial support to domestic service companies, the state also exempted them from paying the social insurance premiums for their formal employees (National Development and Reform Commission 2020). In contrast, the state did not provide any cash transfers or reductions in and exemptions from insurance premiums to workers, all of whom were badly affected by the pandemic.

3.2 Economic burdens on domestic workers during the pandemic

To avoid a large-scale spread of the Covid-19 epidemic, the government implemented a nationwide lockdown in January 2020. Among other impacts, the initial lockdown prevented migrant domestic workers who spent the Spring Festival break in their hometowns from returning to work. A survey by the Beijing Hongyan Social Work Service Center (2020) shows that 70–80 per cent of migrant domestic workers stopped working or lost jobs at the time due to restricted mobility, perceived health risks and a drastic reduction in the demand for their services (Xing 2021, Yu et al. 2021). The chapters on Jamaica and Malaysia (Constable; Shreedaran and Ne Foo, this volume) similarly demonstrate how mobility restrictions, among other measures, to combat the Covid-19 outbreak had immediate negative impacts on domestic workers' employment and economic livelihoods. States' pandemic policy responses often left migrants, including internal migrants, at the margins of social protection schemes (Dewan; Burnett, this volume).

In China, the pandemic had sustained negative effects on domestic workers' economic livelihoods. The Zero-Covid-19 policy made it difficult for migrant domestic workers to travel between home and work. Two research participants for this study who worked as managers of small domestic service companies in Jinan said that only 70 per cent of domestic workers signed with their agencies resumed work after the initial lockdown and some quit their jobs because of the fear of contracting the virus while at work.

In large cities like Beijing and Nanjing, most domestic workers resumed work after the initial lockdown was lifted, but the work of live-out workers was interrupted every time there was a small-scale outbreak. Li, the branch manager of a domestic service company in Nanjing, told us:

About 50 per cent of live-out *A'yi* [nanny in Chinese] in our branch stopped working due to this new wave of outbreak [in Nanjing in July 2021]. If one [person] is found infected, the entire neighbourhood is closed. Now I have an order here but I can't arrange it because it's risky [. . .] A customer asked if I can guarantee that the *A'yi* is not infected. This *A'yi* has tested negative twice but I still can't guarantee. So *A'yi* stopped her work at his home [. . .] Many part-time *A'yi* are scared of not being able to work.

Live-in domestic workers, particularly maternal care workers, experienced job instability as well (Xing 2021). As manager Li explained:

Maternal care workers experience difficulties going to work now. Many of them are migrants from other provinces. Some have to go back to their hometowns after they finish one monthly order. It is difficult for them to travel between cities.

The decreased demand for their services also made live-in workers' jobs unstable. Liu, the manager of domestic service company in Jinan pointed out, 'Because customers [family employers] are also affected by the economic downturn, they now tend to hire part-time workers instead of live-in ones. They think live-in workers cost too much.' Chen, a live-in child care worker in Nanjing, changed three employers after resuming work in May 2020. 'They [her first employer after the outbreak] are migrants who worked hard to buy their own house here. When the closure was relaxed and their children grew older, they hired a part-time domestic worker and fired me,' she told us. The pandemic thus exacerbated the uncertainties of work and life. 'It's much harder to find a good employer now than before. Those who do this work all have economic hardships just like us. At this age, we need to support children and ageing parents,' Chen added.

While the emergency economic relief measures allowed domestic service companies to cope, informally employed domestic workers barely benefitted from them. Manager Liu said:

Even for a small enterprise like us, with eight or nine employees, it's a heavy burden to pay social insurance premiums. So the reduction in premiums is very helpful [. . .] but this policy only benefits formal employees, not frontline domestic workers.

In fact, all domestic workers interviewed for this study said they neither received any cash transfers nor benefitted from any reduction in or exemption from social insurance premiums during the pandemic. In the absence of state relief, workers' benefits depended on the 'kindness' of employers and domestic service companies. In order to retain workers, some companies reduced their service fees and negotiated financial compensations with the employing families, on workers' behalf.

3.3　Health impact of Covid-19 on domestic workers

The immediate problems faced by domestic workers stemmed from the lack of access to personal protective equipment (PPE) for several months following the outbreak of the health crisis. The face-to-face work performed by domestic workers made it crucial for them to be protected. But while public health agencies introduced guidelines for the prevention of Covid-19 among domestic workers, they did not mandate that employer families and domestic service companies provide PPEs to their workers. Hongyan Social Work Service Center's (2020) survey of migrant domestic workers in Beijing shows that 50 per cent needed help in obtaining masks and other PPEs. Companies provided PPEs to their management staff, but frontline domestic workers had to fend for themselves. Manager Li reported:

> Because of last year's serious shortage of protective materials, *A'yi* had to prepare [masks] themselves. We told them, since you work at customers' homes, you must take protective measures. [. . .] There are so many workers, you couldn't count on the company to provide protective materials. [. . .] Some nice customers would give *A'yi* some masks.

Another common health problem that emerged from the interviews is the psychological stress that domestic workers underwent due to anxieties over loss of jobs and incomes, and the consequent strain on family livelihoods. The Hongyan Social Work Service Center survey (2020) indicated that about 90 per cent of migrant domestic workers had such concerns. Chen, the child care worker from Nanjing, stayed in her hometown in Hubei province during the initial lockdown and spoke of the anxieties she experienced at the time: 'We are migrant workers. All of a sudden, the family has no income and the epidemic is so serious. We were really worried that we couldn't get out and we were trapped there.'

The outbreak of Covid-19 had particularly grave health consequences for live-in domestic workers whose working conditions worsened during the lockdowns. Most live-in workers interviewed reported heavier workloads either because their employers developed higher standards of cleanliness and disinfection or due to the lack of help from family caregivers. Su, a live-in elder care worker in Beijing, said, 'The elder's children sometimes came and helped a bit before [the pandemic], but now they can't come. I have to take care of her myself. I'm so tired.' It was common for live-in elder care workers to report high levels of psychological stress due to the rigid mobility restrictions and lack of breaks during the lockdowns. Su added:

> They [employing family] don't let me go out because I take care of the elderly. Although there isn't so much change in my work, I feel stressed and tired. If I could take four days off each month like before and go out to relax, my mood would be different.

Most interviewees could no longer take regular work breaks even after the peak restriction period. As manager Li explained:

> After things went back to normal last fall, many employing families were afraid of the infection and asked *A'yi* to not go home during the weekends. Instead, they were ready to pay *A'yi* for overtime work on the weekends or asked *A'yi* to save her break time for later.

The lack of weekly breaks had a negative impact on live-in workers' mental health. Chen reported:

> I planned to save two days from last month to take a rest this month. But now I am trapped in Nanjing and can't go back home again. I feel depressed. [. . .] A colleague of mine used to take two days off each month. Now she can't take breaks either, which makes her feel stressed out.

Elder care workers who stayed in the hospital during the pandemic were saddled with extended working hours and heightened psychological stress. With hospitals taking extremely restrictive measures to prevent transmission during the pandemic, Shi, an elder care worker in Beijing, had to stay on in the hospital for a couple of weeks with the elder woman under her care. She reported:

> In the hospital, it is not the same as at home. I feel more tired here .[. . .] Each patient's family can only leave one person here and other family members are not allowed to come. [. . .] At home, when I've done the work, I can take a short rest. Now, I get up at 5:30 in the morning and work until 9 o'clock in the evening.

Even short-term work in the hospital was stressful for Shi. 'I feel like I'm jailed here. I can step out of the ward only when I need to get hot water. We're not allowed to leave this room otherwise,' she said.

4. China's Covid-19 domestic work policies: A case of path dependency

The testimonies offered above reflect the fragmented nature of China's policies on care and domestic workers' social protection, which cushioned domestic service companies more than the workers themselves. The state's domestic work-related pandemic response policies are closely related to its development strategy in the reform era and, in that sense, can be described as stagnant and path dependent.

As explained in Section 2, since the beginning of the reforms of the late 1970s, the Chinese state prioritized economic growth and efficiency while lowering labour standards and relegating the provision of welfare and care to households in order to keep expenditure on social protection and social reproduction low (Connelly et al. 2018, Huang 2020). The labour rights and interests of domestic workers, who constitute a large section of China's informal workers, have not been a focal policy concern for a long time. The national labour standards stipulated in China's labour law, covering labour contracts, remuneration, working and rest hours, paid leave, wage arrears, maternity leave and allowances, are stricter than the international labour standards set forth in the ILO Convention on Domestic Workers (No. 189) (Liu 2017). However, the vast majority of the country's domestic workers are informally employed and not protected by labour laws as a result of pro-market bias in the reform era. The economic reforms, while bringing about rapid economic growth and poverty alleviation, dramatically increased social inequalities, particularly between rural and urban residents, and formal and informal workers (Cook and Dong 2011; Li, S. et al. 2013).

Domestic workers' vulnerabilities during the pandemic can also be attributed to gender biases in state policies. Care work is a public good because the time and effort involved in the daily work of caring for others ensure the well being and proper functioning of society and the economy (Folbre and Nelson 2000). Globally, most care work is done by women. Even when it is paid work, there is often a low value assigned to it. Women's over-representation in the poorly paid care labour force undervalues their work and leads to few or no employment-related social protections (McCrum 2021).

In China, the neglect of gender in care policies in general and pandemic-related policies in particular also reflects a deep-rooted gender bias in the policy making process (Bahn et al. 2020). The state's retreat from the provision of care and social protection in the reform era went hand-in-hand with its shift from a Marxist gender-egalitarian ideology to a rejuvenated Confucian patriarchal tradition aligned with neoliberalism (Ji et al. 2017). Under these circumstances, the issue of care receded from public policy and was perceived as women's duty and a private matter for families. In addition, the domestic service sector was transformed into a utilitarian tool to realize the state's goal of rapid economic growth at the cost of domestic workers' rights and interests.

The lack of appropriate policy responses was also the result of weak social dialogue regarding domestic workers in China. Due to the state's control over trade unions and the fact that private households are the site of domestic work, such workers in China have historically not been unionized and have a weak class consciousness (Liu 2017, Tong 2018). There is thus a dearth of voices of domestic workers in the public sphere. Women's federations, which formally represent the rights and interests of women, support the state's policy for the domestic service industry. As such, their main focus is the promotion of employment and poverty alleviation among poor rural women and laid-off women workers through the provision of domestic services for urban families. The federations, therefore, perceive female domestic workers as women fulfilling traditional gender roles rather than as workers, neglecting their labour rights and interests in the process. As a result, discussions about female domestic workers' labour issues are largely absent from the public discourse.

5. Conclusion and recommendations for policy transformation

This chapter demonstrates that the Covid-19 pandemic had negative impacts on domestic workers' employment, working conditions and mental health. While some informal domestic workers experienced job and income losses without compensation, all of them had no access to employment-based social protection, including the provision of PPEs and economic relief measures. While the working conditions of live-in workers were badly affected, all domestic workers experienced heightened psychological stress during the course of the pandemic as a result of job and income insecurity, risk of exposure to infections, excessive workloads and the lack of work breaks. These empirical findings, coupled with the contextual background, suggest that while domestic workers' pre-pandemic conditions were shaped by the intertwining effects of the state's care and labour policies, the market and gender, the pandemic intensified their precarities with regards to working conditions, livelihoods and psychological well being.

These findings also suggest that there is space for transformative policies in China. However, whether or not such policies will be enacted and implemented remains a matter of debate. While the two interviewees from NGOs providing social services to domestic workers were optimistic about the scope for such policies, others held different views. The optimists anticipated that recent labour and demographic changes would lead to policy changes in China. There are currently 220 million informal workers in urban China, of whom over 11 per cent work in the service sector, including domestic services (Huang 2020). The number of informal workers has been increasing faster than ever with the rise of the platform economy, particularly in the aftermath of the Covid-19 pandemic. In response to the large number of labour rights disputes involving informal workers, the government has begun to develop policies to improve labour and social protections for them. In July 2021, the state issued Guidelines for Protecting the Labour Rights and Interests of Workers Employed in New Forms of Economy (Ministry of Human Resources and Social Security of the PRC 2021, No. 56), which mandate the formalization of employment relations of platform workers; set standards for informal workers' working hours and remuneration; provide access to social insurance, occupational safety and health; and integrate rural migrants into the urban social security system. While cities like Shenzhen and Hangzhou have proposed work-related injury insurance cover for informal workers and the removal of barriers for rural migrants' enrolment in social insurance, most of these measures have not been institutionalized at the time of writing (July 2023).

A rapidly ageing population, declining fertility and small family size have led to population and social policy reforms that allow married couples to have three children and subsidize elder care provisions. However, China's care deficit remains one of the biggest barriers to achieving these policy goals. The two interviewees from NGOs saw the current situation as an opportunity to recognize the value of care work and improve domestic workers' labour and social protections.

Academic research, however, suggests that China's care policies are unlikely to change. For instance, Xu's (2022) policy analysis indicates that the state has issued numerous documents in the past few years to address its ageing population and elder care crisis. Yet, care workers who provide care labour for the elderly remain invisibilized and their labour is devalued (Dong et al. 2016, Sa and Liu 2022). Xu (2020) argues that the commodification and privatization of elder care provision in China, in line with the global trend, is a deliberate policy aimed at creating positive conditions for the domestic service market to flourish at the expense of social reproduction and care.

That said, based on the findings of this study, we still see space for policy advocacy for domestic workers' labour rights in China, and make the following recommendations:

i)	It is imperative that the government change its development approach and pay more attention to social equity and distribution. Greater commitments are needed to promote the social protection of domestic workers as part of broader policy initiatives to integrate rural and urban social security and social service systems.

ii)	It is crucial to formulate special laws and regulations to protect the labour rights and interests of domestic workers and regulate the behaviour of family employers to make them conform to international labour standards.

iii)	The government should place gender at the centre of its policy making process aimed at solving the problem of care deficit. In this regard, women's federations need to actively advocate for domestic workers' labour rights and interests, focus on changing social norms that devalue care work, which is mainly performed by women, and ensure that workers' voices are heard. The development of class consciousness among domestic workers and the creation of spaces for their organizing will be crucial steps in this direction.

Notes

1	The author would like to thank Professor Claire Slatter and DAWN's project team for their helpful suggestions for revision, and Yiping Cai and Junyue Qian for their insights during the entire writing process. The views expressed in the chapter are the sole responsibility of the author.

2	NGOs and interviewees are unnamed or have been given pseudonyms to protect their anonymity.

3	The urban employee's insurance scheme provides better protection than rural or urban resident's insurance schemes. It covers five types of insurance, including medical insurance, pension insurance, unemployment insurance, work-related injury insurance and maternity insurance. The resident's insurance scheme only covers medical and pension insurance, which have lower premiums than the employee's insurance.

References

Bahn, K., Cohen, J. and Meulen Rodgers, Y. van der (2020), 'Feminist Perspective on COVID-19 and the Value of Care Work Globally', *Gender Work and Organization*, 27(5): 695–99. Available at: https://doi.org/10.1111/gwao.12459 (accessed 16 November 2023).

Beijing Hongyan Social Work Service Center (2020), 'Post-Coronavirus, China Must Come to the Aid of Its Domestic Workers', *Sixth Tone*, 23 March. Available at: https://www.sixthtone.com/news/1005327 (accessed 8 December 2023).

Cheng, T. and Selden, M. (1994), 'The Origins and Social Consequences of China's Hukou System', *The China Quarterly*, 139: 644–68. Available at: https://www.jstor.org/stable/655134 (accessed 16 November 2023).

Connelly, R., Dong, X., Jacobsen, J. and Zhao, Y. (2018), 'The Care Economy in Post-reform China: Feminist Research on Unpaid and Paid Work and Well-being', *Feminist Economics*, 24(2): 1–30. Available at: https://doi.org/10.1080/13545701.2018.1441534 (accessed 16 November 2023).

Cook, S. and Dong, X. (2011), 'Harsh Choices: Chinese Women's Paid Work and Unpaid Care Responsibilities Under Economic Reform', *Development and Change*, 42(4): 947–65. Available at: https://doi.org/10.1111/j.1467-7660.2011.01721.x (accessed 16 November 2023).

Dong, X., Feng, J. and Yu, Y. (2016), 'Relative Pay of Domestic Eldercare Workers in Shanghai, China', *Feminist Economics*, 23(1): 1–24. Available at: https://doi.org/10.1080/13545701.2016.1143108 (accessed 16 November 2023).

Folbre, N. and Nelson, J.A. (2000), 'For Love or Money – or Both?', *Journal of Economic Perspectives*, 14(4): 123–40. DOI: 10.1257/jep.14.4.123 (accessed 16 November 2023).

Huang, Z. (2020), *China's New Informal Economy: Practice and Theory*, Nanning, Guangxi: Guangxi Normal University Press (in Chinese).

Ji, Y, Wu, X., Sun, S. and He, G. (2017), 'Unequal Care, Unequal Work: Toward a More Comprehensive Understanding of Gender Inequality in Post-reform Urban China', *Sex Roles: A Journal of Research*, 77 (11–12): 765–778. Available at: https://doi.org/10.1007/s11199-017-0751-1 (accessed 16 November 2023).

Llavaneras Blanco, M. and Cuervo, M.G. (2021), 'The Pandemic as a Portal: Policy Transformations Disputing the New Normal', DAWN Discussion Paper No. 32. Available at: https://dawnnet.org/wp-content/uploads/2021/04/DAWN-Discussion-Paper-32_The-Pandemic-as-a-Portal.pdf (accessed 16 November 2023).

ILO (2021), 'Making Decent Work A Reality for Domestic Workers: Progress and Prospects Ten Years After the Adoption of the Domestic Workers Convention, 2011 (No. 189)', Geneva: ILO.

Stern-Plaza, M., Tessier, L., Frota, F. and Lönnroth, K. (2021), 'Health Protection and Sickness Benefits to Face the COVID-19 Pandemic in Asia', in A. Peres, R. Brito, C. Bilo and M. Balboni (eds), *What's Next for Social Protection in Light of COVID-19: Challenges Ahead, Policy in Focus*, 22–24, International Policy Center for Inclusive

Growth, Brazil. Available at: https://ipcig.org/sites/default/files/pub/en/PIF48_ What_s_next_for_social_protection_in_light_of_COVID_19_challenges_ahead.pdf (accessed 16 November 2023).

Li, Y., Wang, X., Tan, S., Jia, Y and Lian, W. (2021), 'Leave No One Behind: Preliminary Development Assessment of Vulnerable Groups of Women', *Journal of Shandong Women's University*, 1: 30–46 (in Chinese).

Li, S., Sicular, T. and Zhao, Z. (2013), 'Long-term Trends for Income and Wage Inequality in China', Unpublished manuscript. Retrieved from: https://hceconomics.uchicago. edu/sites/default/files/file_uploads/ChaoFu-Slides.pdf (accessed 9 January 2024).

Liu, M. (2017), 'Migrants and Cities: Research Report on Recruitment, Employment, and Working Conditions of Domestic Workers in China', Working Paper, Conditions of Work and Employment Series No. 92, ILO, Geneva. Available at: https://www.ilo.org/ wcmsp5/groups/public/---ed_protect/---protrav/---travail/documents/publication/ wcms_559247.pdf (accessed 16 November 2023).

McCrum, C. (2021), 'Gender-responsive Social Protection in Times of COVID-19', in A. Peres, R. Brito, C. Bilo and M. Balboni (eds), *What's Next for Social Protection in Light of COVID-19: Challenges Ahead, Policy in Focus*, 10–13, International Policy Center for Inclusive Growth, Brazil. Available at: https://ipcig.org/sites/default/files/pub/en/ PIF48_What_s_next_for_social_protection_in_light_of_COVID_19_challenges_ ahead.pdf (accessed 16 November 2023).

Ministry of Finance and the State Administration of Taxation (2020), 'Announcement of Tax Policies to Support the Prevention and Control of the COVID-19 Infection (No. 8)' (in Chinese). Available at: https://www.ndrc.gov.cn/xwdt/ztzl/jdstjjqycb/ zccs/202012/t20201228_1260552_ext.html (accessed 16 November 2023).

Ministry of Human Resources and Social Security of the PRC (2021), 'Guidelines for Protecting the Labor Rights and Interests of Workers Employed in the New Forms of Economy (No. 56)' (in Chinese). Available at: http://www.gov.cn/xinwen/2021-07/23/ content_5626787.htm (accessed 16 November 2023).

Ma, Dan (2015), 'A Study of the Labor Process of Live-in Domestic Workers in Beijing', *Chinese Workers*, 2: 18–22 (in Chinese).

National Development and Reform Commission (2020), 'Guidelines to Further Support Small and Micro Enterprises and Private Businesses in the Service Industry to Alleviate Stress of Housing Rent During the COVID-19 Pandemic (No. 734)' (in Chinese). Available at: https://www.ndrc.gov.cn/xxgk/zcfb/ghxwj/202005/ t20200509_1227769_ext.html (accessed 16 November 2023).

National Development and Reform Commission (2020), 'The National Development and Reform Commission and Other Ministries and Commissions Have Taken Multiple Measures to Support Domestic Enterprises to Prevent the Epidemic and Resume Production' (in Chinese). Available at: https://www.ndrc.gov.cn/xwdt/ztzl/ jzfwytzkr/bjlxhyzd/202006/t20200601_1229706.html (accessed 16 November 2023).

Qianzhan Industry Research Institute (2021), 'An Analysis of the Market Size and Development Prospects of China's Domestic Service Industry in 2021' (in Chinese).

Available at: https://xw.qianzhan.com/trends/detail/506/211108-e7ec6 867.html (accessed 16 November 2023).

Sa, Z. and Liu, J. (2022), 'Making an Invisible Care Workforce Visible: A Survey of Domestic Workers in Three Cities in China', *China Population and Development Studies*, 6: 95–113. Available at: https://doi.org/10.1007/s42379-022-00104-1 (accessed 16 November 2023).

State Council of the PRC (2012), 'Interim Measures for the Administration of Family Services Sector (No. 11, Ministry of Commerce)'. Available at: http://en.pkulaw.cn/display.aspx?cgid=191714&lib=law (accessed 16 November 2023).

State Council of the PRC (2019), 'Guidelines for the Increase of Quality and Capacity of the Domestic Service Industry (No. 30)' (in Chinese). Available at: http://www.gov.cn/zhengce/content/ 2019-06/26/content_5403340.htm (accessed 16 November 2023).

Tong, X. (2018), 'Gender Labour Regimes: On the Organizing of Domestic Workers in Urban China', *Asian Journal of German and European Studies*, 3, 14. Available at: https://doi.org/10.1186/s40856-018-0036-7 (accessed 16 November 2023).

Wang, J. and Wu, B. (2016), 'Domestic Helpers as Frontline Workers in China's Home-based Elder Care: A Systematic Review', *Journal of Women & Aging*, 29(4): 294–305. Available at: https://doi.org/10.1080/08952841.2016.1187536 (accessed 16 November 2023).

Xing, C. (2021), 'The 'Hyper Precarity' of Informal Employment under the COVID-19 Pandemic and Workers' Coping Strategies: Taking Postpartum Doulas in Beijing as an Example', *Journal of Chinese Women's Studies*, 3: 37–52 (in Chinese). Available at: https://www.fnyjlc.com/EN/abstract/abstract1003.shtml (accessed 8 December 2023).

Xu, F. (2022), 'Building China's Eldercare Market: The Imperatives of Capital Accumulation and Social Stability', *Social Sciences*, 11(5): 212. Available at: https://doi.org/10.3390/socsci11050212 (accessed 8 December 2023).

Yu, H., Zhang, Y. and Yang, T. (2021), Building New Ecology for China's Domestic Service Industry. Beijing: China's Labor and Social Security Press (in Chinese).

Section II

Attempting to Depart from Path Dependence

5

Who Really Wins? Kiribati Labour Mobility Schemes in the Post-Covid Era

Roi Burnett

1. Introduction

Migration and mobility are no new concepts to those living in the Republic of Kiribati, an atoll nation in the central Pacific. Atoll life has long required I-Kiribati to be expert navigators of the ocean, as they traversed the region for resources, adventures and opportunities. In colonial times, I-Kiribati displayed resilience in the face of forced migration and resettlement, which established I-Kiribati communities in the Solomon Islands and in Rabi, Fiji. In contemporary times, contending with the impacts of climate change and other pressing development challenges, I-Kiribati are once again moving across the region as seafarers on international ships and, more recently, on temporary labour mobility schemes in search of better employment opportunities.

Over the last fifteen years, hundreds of I-Kiribati men and women have sought seasonal employment as fruit pickers and on farms under the Seasonal Worker Programme (SWP) and the Pacific Labour Scheme (PLS) in Australia, now amalgamated under the Pacific Australia Labour Mobility (PALM) Scheme,[1] as well as the Recognised Seasonal Employer (RSE) Scheme in New Zealand. In recent years, I-Kiribati have also found work in Australia's tourism, hospitality, meat processing, forestry and aged care industries. These 'guestworker' schemes are often lauded for representing the best practices of international labour mobility policies (ILO 2019, Gibson and McKenzie 2014) due to the 'triple wins' (and, in certain cases, quadruple wins) they ostensibly bestow on all involved stakeholders. The schemes allow the labour-receiving countries Australia and New Zealand to address critical domestic labour shortages; enable the labour-sending Pacific countries, particularly Kiribati, to address rising unemployment and contribute to sustainable development; and benefit workers by giving them access to employment and higher income. They also benefit ancillary or wraparound services, such as transport and accommodation providers, in the host countries (Underhill-Sem and Marsters 2017).

In early 2020, the Covid-19 pandemic brought labour mobility in the Pacific to a standstill. Border closures and lockdowns left I-Kiribati seasonal workers stranded throughout Australia and New Zealand. At the same time, the pandemic made visible the longstanding inequities embedded within these schemes, including the precarity of temporary migrant labour, gender biases and asymmetrical relationships between key players. This, coupled with the economic benefits accrued by the Australian and New Zealand economies from the Pacific Labour Mobility (PLM) schemes and the relatively fewer benefits for the sending Pacific countries and workers, raised a crucial question: who is really winning by participating in labour mobility?

This chapter outlines the changes that have taken place for I-Kiribati seasonal workers in particular and PLM policies in general as new and reinvigorated forms of solidarity and social organizing emerged in the midst of pandemic-related struggles. Relationships between employers, employees and community organizations have strengthened, giving rise to innovative worker welfare initiatives. Wider political shifts have led to a renewed focus on workers' welfare and improved schemes that ensure fair working and living conditions. However, this chapter also argues that further work is needed to ensure that the objectives of the PLM schemes, particularly sustainable development for Kiribati and other Pacific Island countries (PICs), are met. Until there are adequate reintegration policies, skill development pathways, and gender-responsive and transformative approaches to achieve this aim, the promised triple win of labour mobility will remain elusive.

2. Kiribati and Pacific Labour Mobility

Over the last fifteen years, the New Zealand and Australian governments have progressively introduced temporary labour migration schemes with participating PICs. In 2007, New Zealand introduced the RSE scheme to respond to labour shortages in its domestic horticulture sector. Australia established the SWP in 2008 and the PLS in 2018, both modelled on the RSE. All three schemes, the RSE, the SWP and the PLS, have the dual objective of meeting the labour needs of the receiving countries and contributing to the economic development of the participating countries through workers' earnings and remittances. Indeed,

PICs have played a key role in the development of these schemes since their inception.

Considered a least developed country[2] by the United Nations, labour mobility is one of the few viable ways for Kiribati to address its growing unemployment rate[3] and usher in sustainable development through remittances sent home by workers.[4] Indeed, the Kiribati government has actively lobbied for the expansion of these schemes (RNZ 2019a) and recognized the importance of migration and labour mobility in several key policy documents.[5] Employment under the PLM schemes is also an attractive opportunity for I-Kiribati nationals. As of 2015, unemployment in Kiribati stood at 41.3 per cent (NSO 2019), prompting several public and regional institutions to attempt to improve these figures. For instance, the Marine Training Centre (MTC) trains qualified seafarers and fishing vessel personnel while the Kiribati Institute of Technology (KIT), accredited to Australian universities (and institutes), trains trade workers and aged care workers; the University of the South Pacific also has a campus in South Tarawa. However, applications for seasonal work far outweighs the opportunities available, with the SWP and RSE schemes only employing about 2.5 per cent of Kiribati's total workforce (ibid.). Though most seasonal workers are from the main island of South Tarawa, the Kiribati government has put in place an island quota system to equitably spread employment opportunities across the thirty-three islands. The problem, however, is that only a small number of workers are recruited from Kiribati each season, meaning that very few are selected from individual islands. In fact, Kiribati constitutes one of the smallest workforces under the PLM schemes compared with other participating PICs.

While there is no disputing the positive impacts that seasonal work has for I-Kiribati nationals, including the ability to remit money back home to their families and developing valuable skills and networks (Cornish et al. 2022), what is less discussed are the disproportionate gains and asymmetrical relationships embedded within labour mobility schemes. The triple win rhetoric and the dual objective of contributing to sustainable development in the sending countries and addressing critical labour shortages in the receiving countries give these schemes the guise of a mutually beneficial arrangement. However, a key criticism of the PLM schemes, aside from allegations of worker exploitation, has been that they are 'a road with no end' (MacWilliam 2022). It has been argued that without proper reintegration pathways and skill development for workers to achieve the promised objective of sustainable development, these schemes contribute to and produce non-development (ibid.). In other words, the schemes reproduce the socioeconomic conditions that form the basis of a never-ending supply of migrant labour from the Pacific. For I-Kiribati working on these schemes, there is a 'permanent' aspect to the 'temporary' nature of their labour, with many workers opting to return on these schemes year after year.

3. Covid-19 and the predicament of I-Kiribati workers

In March 2020, international border closures and the cessation of mobility left hundreds of I-Kiribati seasonal workers stuck in Australia and New Zealand. Around 159 workers were stranded in Australia under the SWP and 286 remained in New Zealand under the RSE (IOM 2020, Bedford et al. 2021). Those who had found pre-assigned employment on these schemes were unable to leave Kiribati. Workers who were stranded experienced reduced working hours and wages, with no repatriation pathways home. Although both Australia and New Zealand addressed, quite early on, concerns related to the legality of their stay through visa extensions and redeployment options, workers continued to be stuck in limbo throughout the pandemic. The extended stay proved particularly difficult for six I-Kiribati women who were pregnant and preparing to give birth at the time.

3.1 **Restrictive visa conditions**

The RSE and SWP policies dictate that workers be issued an employer-specific limited purpose visa that ties their legal status in the country to employment with their government-approved employer. Workers are not allowed to find alternative employment and are only eligible to stay in the country for the duration of their visas, which is typically nine to eleven months (Bedford 2020, Bedford and Bailey 2022). With international borders closed during the pandemic, all I-Kiribati workers faced the possibility of breaching their visa conditions and illegally residing in Australia and New Zealand. Furthermore, workers who found themselves without work could not legally find employment elsewhere. In response to these challenges, Australia and New Zealand implemented a series of temporary changes to visa conditions for seasonal workers, including granting continuous visa extensions to those unable to return home (Askola 2021), as elaborated in Table 5.1. Employers and workers welcomed these changes, but many were unhappy with the level of bureaucracy involved in arranging visa extensions and variations for workers. Long processing and approval times left workers in limbo, and many had to rely on their savings to get

Table 5.1 Australian and New Zealand Covid-19 Labour Mobility Policy Responses

Policy area	Australia	New Zealand
Visa conditions	Visa extensions: the government made temporary changes to visa arrangements, allowing Pacific workers to continue working until the pandemic has passed. Temporary visa changes: seasonal workers were allowed to move between sponsors/approved employers during the Covid-19 period.	Visa extensions: the government announced a series of visa extensions for RSE workers who could not return home. Variations in visa conditions: workers were allowed to shift between different regions and crops. Time-limited visa changes: stranded RSE workers were allowed to do up to 15 hours of part-time work in any industry.
Financial assistance	There was no federal government support, but state-based measures were put in place, often with assistance from the Red Cross. Workers were able to access up to AU$10,000 (or approximately US$7,000) of their superannuation.	Between July and December 2020, the temporary Visitor Care Manaaki Manuhiri programme, implemented by the Department of Internal Affairs (DIA), made in-kind support available to cover essential costs such as rent, utility bills and food. RSE workers without work or with insufficient hours of work to meet their expenses were eligible to apply, and the assistance was paid directly to RSE employers based on the living costs they deducted from workers. Between December 2020 and August 2021, temporary visa holders in hardship due to Covid-19 could get an Emergency Benefit from the Work and Income service at the Ministry of Social Development (MSD).
Repatriation	The Palladium Group advised the repatriation of seasonal workers. Repatriation pathways for I-Kiribati workers remained unclear, as there were no direct flights to the country from Australia.	New Zealand's Ministry of Foreign Affairs and Trade (MFAT) led repatriation efforts in late 2020 for some Pacific workers, but there were no pathways home for I-Kiribati seasonal workers as there were no direct flights to the country from New Zealand.

Table 5.1 (*Continued*)

Policy area	Australia	New Zealand
Health	Covid-19-related medical and quarantine costs were covered by health insurance and/or employer.	Covid-19-related medical and quarantine costs were covered by health insurance and/or employer.
Other support measures	In October 2020, the government introduced the Safeguarding the Welfare of Workers package, which set aside AU$9 million to support Pacific and Timorese workers.	For workers who faced reduced working hours, the MFAT provided opportunities for further training through the Vakameasina programme.

Source: Compiled by author based on data from Ministry of Foreign Affairs and Trade, New Zealand and Department of Foreign Affairs and Trade, Australia.

through these periods of no or reduced work, in turn impacting their ability to remit money back home (Bedford 2020, Petrou et al. 2021). A key issue tied to the strict visa conditions was the inability of workers to voice grievances or report issues to their employers. I-Kiribati workers were reluctant to speak up for fear of being sent home or not being hired in subsequent seasons by their employers (R Namoori-Sinclair, personal communication, 2 February 2023).[6]

3.2 Limited financial support

When compared with other Pacific Island workers, I-Kiribati workers experienced significant reductions in working hours during the pandemic-related lockdowns and many spent long periods without work (IOM 2020). Data suggests that around 77 per cent of all I-Kiribati seasonal workers experienced lower earnings while the corresponding figure for workers from Fiji and Tonga stood at 62 per cent and 57 per cent, respectively (Doan et al. 2020). I-Kiribati workers saw a 54.9 per cent reduction in total earnings compared with 35.1 per cent for workers from Fiji and 51.7 per cent for workers from Tonga (ibid.). Consequently, I-Kiribati workers were not able to save as much as they would during a normal season and had to cut down on their own living expenses. Remittances sent home dropped 54.8 per cent for SWP/PLS/PALM workers and 41.4 per cent for workers employed under the RSE (ibid.).

As with other temporary migrants in New Zealand and Australia, seasonal workers typically do not have access to public income and welfare support, something that was also observed in other cases such as that of migrant domestic workers in Malaysia (Shreedharan and Ne Foo, this volume). During the Covid-19 crisis, New Zealand's Department of Internal Affairs (DIA) in association with the New Zealand Red Cross responded to this policy gap by launching an assistance programme for migrants experiencing hardship. It offered in-kind support to cover essential costs such as rent, utility bills and food. RSE workers without work or with insufficient work to meet their expenses were eligible to apply and assistance was paid directly to the RSE employers based on workers' living costs. The initiative enabled workers to retain their savings and remit to families back home.

Australia did not provide any federal support packages to seasonal workers but put in place limited state-based measures in the form of one-off emergency payments, among other things, delivered with assistance from the Red Cross (Bedford and Bailey 2022). I-Kiribati SWP workers and diaspora communities in Australia pointed out that government financial support would have been invaluable at the time (Petrou et al. 2021). Instead, financial support for SWP workers came from employers, local communities and diaspora groups. In some cases, family members at home sent money to support workers. In addition, workers were able to access up to AU$10,000 (approximately US$7,000) of their superannuation fund, which, under normal circumstances, they could not until the end of their contract.

3.3 Gaps in workers' welfare

Temporary labour schemes operate in and rely on a context in which the mobility of workers from destination to host countries (and vice versa) remains unrestricted. One of the most significant and complex aspects of PLM during the pandemic was the repatriation of seasonal workers, which was easier for countries where commercial flights were available. For I-Kiribati seasonal workers, however, no clear repatriation pathways were available till the country reopened its borders in August 2022. The 286 I-Kiribati workers who entered New Zealand before the onset of the pandemic spent nearly three years away from home. As such, they went through three consecutive seasons of picking and packing fruit without the usual breaks back in Kiribati to recover from the strenuous eight to ten hour days/nights in the fields and the packhouses.

An extended stay allowed workers to earn more but also led to issues and tensions. Especially the early months of the pandemic were filled with uncertainties. When seasonal workers, categorized as 'essential workers', returned to work, they did so under restricted conditions with little personal space, thus increasing the threat of contagion. Workers felt isolated not only from their families but also from the usual support structures they regularly accessed in their host communities. Employers, liaison officers and RSE and PALM team leaders spoke of declining worker productivity, mental health issues, increased alcohol consumption and the inability to access health care services (Bedford and Bailey 2022; R Namoori-Sinclair, personal communication, 2 February 2023).

3.4 Challenges in accessing sexual and reproductive health rights

For I-Kiribati women employed under the RSE scheme, access to maternity protection and sexual and reproductive health rights (SRHR) and services was a key issue arising from the pandemic-induced extended stay. Some experienced an increase in sexually transmitted infections (Bedford and Tekenene 2021). Of the forty-seven women stranded, six reported being pregnant and, of them, five had to give birth in New Zealand. In previous years, an RSE woman who became pregnant received support from employers to return home to give birth (Bailey 2021, Bedford et al. 2021). This became impossible during Covid-19. As in pre-pandemic times, RSE workers were unable to access New Zealand's public health system free of charge and were instead covered under the mandatory medical insurance, which was deducted weekly or fortnightly from their pay. The RSE medical insurance did not cover pregnancy and childbirth costs, which could exceed NZ$9,000 (approximately US$6,000) and fell directly on women workers themselves.

While the RSE scheme attempted to promote education and sexual health (Bailey 2020), discussions about the latter were often avoided for reasons that were cultural, religious or perceived to be too personal. Yet, such conversations are essential as sexual relationships do occur during seasonal workers' contracts and, in many cases, directly affect women's livelihoods. Also paramount is culturally appropriate access to sexual and reproductive health services. A survey conducted by Australia's Anti-Slavery Taskforce revealed that Pacific female seasonal workers were more likely to experience sexual harassment and abuse but were unable to speak out for fear of losing their jobs (RNZ 2022a). This raises serious questions around the design of these schemes and the inequities they produce in terms of women's ability to fully participate in them.

In recent years, governments have prioritized increasing the number of women hired under these schemes. It is important, however, that such efforts do not become a matter of simply improving the gender balance in seasonal worker statistics. If the shared experiences of I-Kiribati women RSE workers are anything to go by, the design of temporary labour mobility arrangements with regards to

SRHR do not account for gender inequalities. This has already prompted calls for greater focus on how such policies shape the experiences of temporary women migrants from Kiribati (Kagan 2016). Against this backdrop, the pandemic once again emphasized the urgent need for more gender-responsive and transformative approaches to PLM schemes, including appropriate SRHR services and education, and access to and greater recognition of women's and labour rights.

4. Strengthened relationships and moments of solidarity

Based on the above-mentioned responses of the Australian and New Zealand governments to the Covid-19 pandemic, specifically in the context of the PLM schemes, I had initially concluded that these policies had remained largely unchanged. However, since then, significant shifts have occurred in the PLM landscape in the form of renewed commitments from concerned stakeholders to ensure workers' welfare and fairer living and working conditions. New and strengthened relationships have emerged between workers, employees, civil society groups and diaspora Kiribati communities, leading to innovative initiatives and care practices.

4.1 Media reporting, national inquiries and investigations

Prior to the pandemic, the labour of temporary migrants (including backpackers, working holiday makers and Pacific seasonal workers) in the horticulture and agriculture industries remained largely hidden. But the pandemic and its consequent labour shortages shone a spotlight on the essential role played by Pacific migrant workers in New Zealand and Australian food supply chains. As temporary migrants in these industries returned home by mid-2020 (Barry 2022), Australian employers' demand for Pacific seasonal workers increased to fill critical labour gaps (Stead and Petrou 2022).

The renewed attention on the labour of Pacific migrants coincided with widespread media scrutiny of the PLM schemes. Several media outlets reported stories of worker exploitation, wage theft and abuse, which offered insights into the experiences of seasonal migrant workers (Howes 2020, Baker 2021, Kelly 2021, Johnston 2022). Mass media attention, coupled with pressure exerted by labour unions, led the PLM schemes to be subjected to parliamentary scrutiny and national inquiries both in Australia and New Zealand. The Australian Senate Select Committee on Job Security held two hearings on the former SWP as part of a wider review of the 'impact of insecure or precarious employment on the economy, wages, social cohesion and workplace rights and conditions' (Sharman and Howes 2022). Following the inquiry, Australia announced significant changes such as greater monitoring of employers by government agencies and greater involvement of labour unions in collective bargaining for workers (ibid.).

In New Zealand, wages and employment conditions under the RSE scheme were reviewed as part of a parliamentary select committee inquiry into the Fair Pay Agreements Bill, which was passed into law in December 2022. The law aims to improve working conditions and outcomes for employees across sectors through a union-led compulsory bargaining process. More recently, an investigation led by the Equal Employment Opportunities Commissioner found major gaps in the RSE scheme, which enabled a systematic pattern of human rights abuses of seasonal workers (RNZ 2022b). This included unreasonable pay deductions, denial of personal and cultural freedoms, poor access to health care and grossly inadequate housing. The Commissioner's report went so far as to liken the treatment of RSE workers to slavery. The observations of the report will likely shape the New Zealand government's own review of the scheme (which commenced in 2019 but remained largely stalled during the pandemic) and lead to better working conditions and accommodations for RSE workers.

4.2 Glimpses of solidarity

The pandemic witnessed new forms of solidarity and social organizing and led to the emergence of new stakeholders concerned with workers' welfare. Stead (2022) highlights the campaigns run by the United Workers Union (UWU) in Australia that brought together migrant workers, international students and casual hospitality workers under a common political cause. As discussed in Section 3, seasonal workers, like other temporary migrants in Australia, do not have access to welfare support and social security (Clibborn and Wright 2018). During the Covid-19 lockdown, temporary migrants were excluded from the federal government's narrowly focused pandemic job subsidy scheme, JobKeeper, which only covered citizens and permanent resident workers in full-time or part-time roles. Much like the organizing seen among migrant domestic workers in Malaysia (Sreedharan and Ne Foo, this volume), seasonal workers, alongside other temporary migrant workers, united at 'digital picket' lines held over Zoom and social media, and at meetings organized on Facebook livestream.

While this moment of solidarity united those experiencing precarity, it should be noted that the uptake of unions and social organizing has historically been low among seasonal workers. The structural issues associated with these schemes make it difficult for them to collectively organize and rally against exploitative conditions for fear of being sent home or blacklisted from the programme. Another complexity that influences workers' ability to collectively organize is that sending PIC governments and communities often discourage seasonal workers from joining unions because these outcomes reflect badly on the sending countries (GCU Press 2022, Solomon Times 2021, Lesa 2019).

4.3 Support from civil society and diaspora community groups

The exceptional circumstances of the pandemic spurred support for workers among non-governmental organizations (NGOs), diaspora Pacific communities and employers. A product of these strengthened relationships was the SWP Community Connections initiative. Administered by the Salvation Army in Australia, the initiative provides additional welfare support to workers, including counselling and helpline access, and assists them to better integrate and connect with their host communities by advancing cultural understandings between seasonal workers and local communities (Cash 2021). Alongside the Salvation Army, the initiative brought together employers, the Australian government and the Queensland, New South Wales and South Australia Pacific Island Councils as well as the Uniting Church in Victoria and Tasmania. In Tasmania, the initiative employed an I-Kiribati in the role of a community connections worker to help seasonal workers ease into life in Australia and facilitate connections between local churches and I-Kiribati workers (Humphries 2022).

Members of Kiribati diaspora groups also played a significant role in supporting Pacific seasonal workers during the pandemic. This was particularly evident among Kiribati communities in Australia and New Zealand who rallied around stranded workers who could not return home. In New Zealand, members of the diaspora housed six pregnant I-Kiribati women and their newborns (Bedford and Tekenene 2021). In Victoria, Australia, the local Kiribati community ran a fundraising campaign to support a pregnant worker unable to return home to Kiribati.[7]

5. New political possibilities in the pandemic conjuncture

While the renewed focus on workers' well being was certainly influenced by the solidarity movements forged during the pandemic, a key shift in the PLM landscape occurred with the May 2022 election of the new Australian Labour government. The administration led by Prime Minister Anthony Albanese announced a suite of positive and transformative reforms to the PALM scheme in Australia. Notable among them was the initiative to allow seasonal workers on long-term visas to bring their immediate family members to the host country. While the rollout of the reform was originally intended to take place in the last quarter of 2023, the Australian government confirmed at the Pacific Labour Mobility Annual Meeting (PLMAM) held in November that year that a trial phase open only to long-term workers from Timor-Leste and Kiribati would begin in January 2024. The government explained the delay by citing the need to put in place certain legislative and administrative arrangements before families begin to arrive in Australia. To be eligible for the accompaniment visa, workers would have to spend twelve months in Australia with eighteen months remaining on their visas. Once implemented, the reform would allow partners of workers to work and study in Australia, their children to attend public schools while paying domestic fees and their families to access assistance benefits as well as Medicare, Australia's universal health insurance scheme (Pacific Australia Labour Mobility 2023). With the pandemic highlighting the impact of family separation on the well being of workers and their families, the announcement was especially welcomed by those on extended four-year contracts. Other proposed reforms included the coverage of travel costs of Pacific migrant workers by the federal government instead of employers and the discontinuation of the Australian agriculture visa, which is now redirected through the PALM scheme (Albanese 2022).

The PLM changes announced by the Labour government are part of a new phase of diplomacy in the region. In the years preceding the election, Australia's coalition government shared a contentious relationship with its Pacific neighbours because of the country's failure to adhere to domestic and international standards on reduction in greenhouse gas emissions in the face of grave threats posed by global warming. Kiribati and other PICs have expressed frustration at Australia's lack of action and have sought other international platforms and donors to voice their concerns (RNZ 2019b).[8] Australia's renewed engagement and commitments have also emerged in the wake of China's growing influence in the Pacific. In 2019, Kiribati made international headlines when it announced that it would cut ties with Taiwan to establish relations with Beijing. While there were numerous rumours and media speculation around this decision, Kiribati President Taneti Maamau has often claimed that China is the better development partner to tackle both domestic and global issues, including climate change (Westerman 2019, Pala 2020). Against this backdrop, the new Australian Labour government has committed to 'listen' more to its 'Pacific family' by promising an increase in foreign aid, a restoration of its climate leadership and reforms in the PALM scheme (Hurst and Murphy 2022). However, geopolitical tensions persist in terms of broader mobility issues within the Pacific. Samoan Prime Minister Fiame Naomi Mata'afa has recently called for an European Union-style movement of labour, among other things, between PICs and Australia and New Zealand (Neilson 2023).[9]

The PLM reforms have been welcomed by workers and PIC governments, but outstanding issues remain unaddressed. At the PLMAM held in November 2022, sending and receiving governments, employers and other stakeholders met to discuss PLM and raised a number of issues, including cooperation and coordination between the sending countries and improving the recognition of Pacific qualifications (Bedford and Sharman 2022). The key theme of the 2022 PLMAM, Reinvigorating Labour Mobility Cooperation for Development, guided conversations throughout the four-day event[10] and was particularly evident during the third day of the conference in discussions on the reintegration of workers back into their home communities. Delegates acknowledged that returning workers are currently not supported to contribute to local development, with many lacking the capacity to apply the benefits of their earnings and the skills they gained overseas. As a result, many workers opt to return on the PLM schemes year after year.

Reintegration policies for returning workers is one of the ways in which labour mobility schemes are believed to contribute to economic development. Such policies can serve as channels for harnessing the skills and financial capital of returning workers by providing them with avenues to invest their earnings into private enterprises and undertake further skills training. Without these pathways, the potential development benefits of labour mobility in the PICs are unlikely to be fully realized. PIC delegates at the PLMAM accepted the proposal for a Framework for Pacific Labour Mobility Economic Reintegration that aims to build decent employment pathways for returning migrants, facilitates transfer of financial returns and fosters entrepreneurship, supports higher education opportunities for returning migrant youth workers and supports polices that cover the three former aims (PLMAM 2022). However, the effectiveness of regional platforms like the PLMAM in advancing issues pertaining to PLM, including reintegration, has previously been questioned (Curtain 2018, Bedford and Sharman 2022) since these have long been recurring items on the agenda.

Moreover, in the smaller sending countries, the matter of reintegrating returning workers to foster national economic development has little relevance. Kiribati has one of the smallest numbers of participating workers, constituting less than 5 per cent of all seasonal workers hired under the PLM schemes (Underhill-Sem and Marsters 2017). As such, there are simply not enough workers on these schemes to create a significant development impact. One of the reasons for such low participation by countries like Kiribati is the demand-driven nature of temporary labour mobility schemes, with employers deciding to recruit from a subset of countries in the region, mainly Vanuatu, Samoa and Tonga (Howes et al. 2022).

Notably, the PLM schemes cause the local economies of these larger participating countries more harm than good. Samoa, Fiji, Vanuatu and Tonga have admitted that the 'brain drain' resulting from these schemes is a growing concern (Curtain 2022). During a visit to New Zealand in 2022, Samoa's prime minister emphasized the need for seasonal work schemes to ensure that human resource constraints in Samoa are dealt with in a balanced manner (Ah Tong 2022). In Samoa, labour mobility schemes have negatively impacted both public and private sectors, particularly the manufacturing and tourism industries that have been losing workers to these schemes. There have been instances of teachers and other highly qualified workers applying for jobs on these schemes because of better renumeration.

A review of the SWP in 2016 concluded that no verified empirical data was available showing specific linkages between remittances under the scheme and economic development in Pacific countries. Similar limitations have also been recognized in relation to New Zealand's longer-running RSE scheme (Craven 2015, Underhill-Sem and Marsters 2017). What is clear, however, are the economic gains accruing to Australia and New Zealand from the labour of Pacific seasonal workers. Between 2018 and 2022, Australian employers earned roughly AU$289 million (US$202 million) in profits while AU$184 million (US$128 million) reached Pacific home communities (Petrou and Connell 2023). The value of crops harvested during the pandemic was also considerably greater than the wages (and remittances) of Pacific workers (ibid). The larger RSE participating countries see the 'triple wins' tipping in favour of New Zealand employers and the larger horticulture and agriculture sectors, with many Pacific nations claiming that the scheme is undermining community and local development (Movono et al. 2023). This goes to show the uneven 'wins' and asymmetrical relationships embedded within the PLM schemes (MacWilliam 2022, Perkiss et al. 2022).

6. Conclusion

This chapter sought to provide an overview of the changes that have occurred in Kiribati in the context of the temporary labour mobility schemes in the pandemic conjuncture. In the months following periods of extended lockdowns in 2020 and 2021, the situation for I-Kiribati seasonal workers and the wider Pacific labour mobility landscape has changed significantly. The unique circumstances of the pandemic exposed the inequitable experiences of I-Kiribati seasonal workers and simultaneously led to the flourishing of new and strengthened relationships and moments of solidarity. This resulted in a renewed focus on workers' welfare and led to much-needed change in the PLM schemes. The relationships formed during the pandemic between workers and their host communities will also continue to benefit new and returning workers as they settle into Australia and New Zealand. We have already begun to see the effects of the reforms announced by the new Australian Labour government. The family accompaniment visas, particularly for workers on four-year contracts, will go far in addressing the negative impacts caused by family separation.

However, this chapter has also shown that the very design of the PLM schemes and the wider labour mobility policy landscape in which I-Kiribati workers are embedded are characterized by unequal power relations between the sending and receiving governments. The positive development impacts promised to PICs, especially smaller island nations such as Kiribati, are yet to fructify. The limited opportunities available to I-Kiribati to partake in these schemes mean that the economic development impacts are negligible even as the social costs are high, especially in the context of immobilities that marked the first year of the pandemic. With national aspirations in Kiribati to expand these schemes, there is also a need to focus on the reintegration of returning workers. However, as long as the schemes are not meeting their development objectives in the sending countries, the labour mobility policy will remain skewed.

Notes

1 On 4 April 2022, the SWP and the PLS were consolidated to form the Pacific Australia Labour Mobility (PALM) Scheme. However, workers continue to work under the SWP and PLS until the expiry of their contracts. See: https://www.ato.gov. au/Business/PAYG-withholding/In-detail/Seasonal-Worker-Program/.

2 In 2018, Kiribati was recommended for graduation from least developed country status by the Committee for Development Policy. However, this decision has been deferred to 2024. See: https://www.un.org/development/desa/dpad/least-developed-country-category-kiribati.html.

3 Kiribati has long engaged in seafaring. Many I-Kiribati nationals are employed on foreign fishing vessels and send home remittances that are cumulatively larger compared with those from the PLM schemes, as pointed out by Maria Borovnik in her extensive research. However, for the purposes of this chapter, I am solely focusing on the PLM schemes in the Covid-19 context.

4 In 2020, personal remittances received in Kiribati made up 8.4 per cent of GDP, down from 11.5 per cent in the previous year (World Bank 2020).

5 For example, see <u>Kiribati Joint Implementation Plan (KJIP) 2019-2028</u>, <u>Kiribati Development Plan 2020-2023</u>, <u>Kiribati National Labour Migration Policy</u> and <u>Kiribati 20-Year Vision 2016-2036 (KV20)</u>.

6 Personal communication with Kiribati Welfare Officer at the Pacific Labour Mobility Annual Meeting.

7 See: https://www.facebook.com/MauriVKA/photos/-urgent-help-for-our-kiribati-seasonal-worker-who-is-about-to-give-birth-here-in/3000183303564990/?paipv=0&eav=AfbH7hTQIVEiiq-9SGxQfQ4S3tHMkIAf0Od2RMJD-H5wK_UU465_FYqRoCCa68TivJQ&_rdr.

8 Vanuatu successfully campaigned for the adoption of a United Nations General Assembly resolution on a non-binding advisory opinion by the International Court of Justice on how existing international laws can be used to strengthen action on climate change. See: https://www.vanuatuicj.com/.

9 See also: https://www.abc.net.au/pacific/programs/pacificbeat/prasad-calls-for-free-travel-between-australia-and-nz/102476574.

10 Key issues raised by PIC delegates included standards of worker accommodation, worker disengagement from the programme, enhancement and protection of worker well being, and operational issues such as better pre-departure briefings, easier access to superannuation and meeting deployment timelines. Pacific delegates also put forward the need for a cultural competency framework to be developed for use in Australia and New Zealand. They requested that employers have access to cultural competency training (Bedford and Sharman 2022).

References

Ah Tong, Matai'a Lanuola Tusani T. (2022), 'Seasonal Workers Scheme Needs Balance: P.M. Fiame', *Samoa Observor*, 14 June. Available at: https://www.samoaobserver.ws/category/samoa/98657 (accessed 20 February 2023).

Albanese, H.A. (2022), 'Labor's Plan for a Stronger Pacific Family', Media Release, *anthonyalbanese.com*, 26 April, Available at: https://anthonyalbanese.com.au/media-centre/labors-plan-for-a-stronger-pacific-family (accessed 20 January 2023).

Askola, H., Forbes-Mewett, H. and Shmihelska, O. (2021), 'Migrant Precariousness in the Time of COVID-19: Migrant Workers, Risks and Rights', Castan Centre for Human Rights Law, Monash University. Available at: https://research.monash.edu/en/publications/migrant-precariousness-in-the-time-of-covid-19-migrant-workers-ri (accessed 20 January 2023).

Bailey, R. (2021), 'Border Closures: Experiences of Ni-Vanuatu Recognized Seasonal Employer Scheme Workers', *Oceania*, 90(S1): 68–74. Available at: https://doi.org/10.1002/ocea.5268 (accessed 2 February 2023).

Baker, R. (2021), 'Pacific Island Meat Workers on $9 Per Hour After Wage Deductions', *The Sydney Morning Herald*, 12 September. Available at: https://www.smh.com.au/business/workplace/pacific-island-meat-workers-on-9-per-hour-after-wage-deductions-20210912-p58qyg.html (accessed 2 February 2023).

Barry, K. (2022), 'Australia's Borders are Open, So Where Are all the Backpackers?', *The Conversation*, 3 November. Available: https://theconversation.com/australias-borders-are-open-so-where-are-all-the-backpackers-192614 (accessed 20 July 2023).

Bedford, C. and Bailey, R. (2022), 'Managing Worker Wellbeing during COVID-19: Pacific Seasonal Workers in Australia and New Zealand', Australian National University. Available at: https://openresearch-repository.anu.edu.au/handle/1885/269938 (accessed 23 January 2023).

Bedford, C., Bedford, R. and Tekenene, R. (2021), 'I-Kiribati Female Seasonal Workers in New Zealand: Lived Experiences', *Dev Policy Blog*, Australian National University, 1 September. Available at: https://devpolicy.org/i-kiribati-female-seasonal-workers-in-new-zealand-lived-experiences-20210901/ (accessed 10 January 2023).

Bedford, C. (2020), 'RSE COVID-19 Responses, Supporting Seasonal Workers in New Zealand', *Dev Policy Blog*, Australian National University, 9 July. Available at: https://devpolicy.org/rse-covid-19-responses-supporting-seasonal-workers-in-new-zealand-20200709-2/#:~:text=Under%20Alert%20Level%204%2C%20the,work%2C%20and%20in%20their%20accommodation (accessed 23 January 2023).

Bedford, C. and Sharman, E. (2022), 'The Pacific Labour Mobility Annual Meeting: Finding its Feet', *Dev Policy Blog*, Australian National University, 7 December. Available at: https://devpolicy.org/pacific-labour-mobility-annual-meeting-finding-its-feet-20221207/ (accessed 20 January 2023).

Cash, H.M. (2021), 'Strengthening Community Connections for Seasonal Workers', *Ministers' Media Centre*, 29 March. Available at: https://ministers.dese.gov.au/cash/strengthening-community-connections-seasonal-workers (accessed 23 January 2023).

Clibborn, S. and Wright, C.F. (2018), 'Employer Theft of Temporary Migrant Workers' Wages in Australia: Why has the State Failed to Act?', *The Economic and Labour Relations Review*, 29(2), 207–227. Available at: https://doi.org/10.1177/1035304618765906 (accessed 23 January 2023).

Cornish, G.E., Pearson, J., McNamara, K.E., Alofa, P. and McMichael, C. (2022), 'Experiences of I-Kiribati with Labor Mobility Schemes', *Asian and Pacific Migration Journal*, 31(2): 162–175. Available at: https://doi.org/10.1177/01171968221107 (accessed 2 January 2023).

Craven, L.K. (2015), 'Migration-Affected Change and Vulnerability in Rural Vanuatu', *Asia Pacific Viewpoint*, 56(2): 223–236. Available at: https://doi.org/10.1111/apv.12066 (accessed 2 January 2023).

Curtain, R. (2022), 'Brain Drain 1: A Growing Concern', *Dev Policy Blog*, Australian National University, 13 October. Available at: https://devpolicy.org/brain-drain-1-a-growing-concern-20221013/ (accessed 1 January 2023).

Curtain, R. (2018), 'What Can Papua New Guinea Do to Lift Its Numbers in the Seasonal Worker Programs of Australia and New Zealand?', Development Policy Centre Discussion Paper No. 70, Australian National University. Available: https://papers.ssrn.com/sol3/papers.cfm?abstract_id=3255353 (accessed 23 January 2023).

Doan, D., Dornan, M., Parsons, K., Petrou, K. and Yi, S. (2020), 'Pacific Labor Mobility, Migration and Remittances in Times of COVID-19: Interim Report', World Bank Group. Available at: https://documents1.worldbank.org/curated/en/430961606712129708/pdf/Pacific-Labor-Mobility-Migration-and-Remittances-in-Times-of-COVID-19-Interim-Report.pdf (accessed 23 January 2023).

GCU Press (2022), 'Seasonal Workers Reminded to Be Good Ambassadors', 22 September. Available at: https://solomons.gov.sb/seasonal-workers-reminded-to-be-good-ambassadors/ (accessed 16 January 2023).

Gibson, J. and McKenzie, D. (2014), 'The Development Impact of a Best Practice Seasonal Worker Policy', *The Review of Economics and Statistics*, 96(2): 229–243. Available at: https://doi.org/10.1162/REST_a_00383 (accessed 16 January 2023).

Howes, S. (2020), 'Pacific Labour Mobility in the Media Spotlight', *Dev Policy Blog*, Australian National University, 19 June. Available at: https://devpolicy.org/pacific-labour-mobility-in-the-media-spotlight/ (accessed 2 January 2023).

Howes, S., Curtain, R. and Sharman, E. (2022), 'Labour Mobility in the Pacific: Transformational and/or Negligible?', *Dev Policy Blog*, Australian National University, 10 October. Available at: https://devpolicy.org/labour-mobility-in-the-pacific-transformational-and-or-negligible-20221010/ (accessed 1 January 2023).

Humphries, A. (2022), 'Man for all Seasons', Uniting Church in Australia. Available at: https://victas.uca.org.au/man-for-all-seasons/?utm_source=rss&utm_medium=rss&utm_campaign=man-for-all-seasons (accessed 25 February 2023).

Hurst, M. and Murphy, K. (2022), 'China's Pacific Plan is 'Clear' but so Is Australia's Intention to be Regional Partner of Choice, Penny Wong Says', *The Guardian*, 25 May. Available at: https://www.theguardian.com/australia-news/2022/may/25/penny-wong-set-to-travel-to-fiji-on-thursday-coinciding-with-chinese-ministers-pacific-tour (accessed 22 November 2023).

ILO (2019), 'Labour Mobility in Pacific Island Countries', Suva, Fiji. Available at: https://www.ilo.org/wcmsp5/groups/public/---asia/---ro-bangkok/---ilo-suva/documents/publication/wcms_712549.pdf (accessed 25 February 2023).

IOM (2020), 'Rapid Assessment of the Socioeconomic Impacts of COVID-19 on Labour Mobility in the Pacific Region', Suva, Fiji. Available at: https://publications.iom.int/system/files/pdf/iom-rapid-assessment-report.pdf (accessed 25 February 2023).

Johnston, K. (2022), 'Blatant Exploitation': Migrant Workers Packed in Freezing, Damp Rooms for $150 a Week', *Stuff*, 8 August. Available at: https://www.stuff.co.nz/business/129496019/blatant-exploitation-migrant-workers-packed-in-freezing-damp-rooms-for-150-a-week#:~:text—igrant%20horticulture%20workers%20are%20being,then%20refused%20paid%20sick%20leave (accessed 16 January 2023).

Kagan, S. (2016), 'On the Ship, You Can Do Anything; The Impact of International Cruiseship Employment for I-Kiribati Women', *The Journal of the Pacific Studies*, 35(3): 34–51. Available at: https://doi.org/10.33318/jpacs.2016.36(1)-3 (accessed 5 January 2023).

Kelly, C. (2021), 'Sixteen Deaths in Australia's Troubled Seasonal Workers Program since Pandemic', *The Guardian*, 11 November. Available: https://www.theguardian.com/australia-news/2021/nov/12/sixteen-deaths-in-australias-troubled-seasonal-workers-program-since-pandemic (accessed 5 January 2023).

Lesa, M.K. (2019), 'P.M. Tells "Proud Ambassadors" No Alcohol And Extra Marital Affairs', *Samoa Observor*, 15 November. Available at: https://www.samoaobserver.ws/category/samoa/53304 (accessed 5 January 2023).

MacWilliam, S. (2022), 'A Road With No End: Making the South Pacific a Permanent Labour Reserve', *Journal of Contemporary Asia*, 52(5): 830–854. Available at: https://doi.org/10.1080/00472336.2021.1975306 (accessed 26 June 2023).

Movono, A., Scheyvens, R. and Auckram, S. (2023), 'NZ Wants More Seasonal Workers – But Pacific Nations No Longer Want to Be the 'Outposts' that 'Grow' Them', *The Conversation*, 16 November. Available at: https://theconversation.com/nz-wants-more-seasonal-workers-but-pacific-nations-no-longer-want-to-be-the-outposts-that-grow-them-217790 (accessed 27 November 2023).

Neilson, M. (2023), 'Samoa PM Calls Out NZ and Australia over 'Pacific Family', Urges EU-Style Free Movement of Labour and Travel', *NZ Herald*, 22 March. Available at: https://www.nzherald.co.nz/nz/politics/samoa-pm-calls-out-nz-and-australia-over-pacific-family-urges-eu-style-free-movement-of-labour-and-travel/E2JBKV5OU5CEXJBCIRJL3GFPSM/ (accessed 26 June 2023).

New Zealand Red Cross (2021), 'Migration Scoping Report Identifying Current and Emerging Issues in Key Migrant Population Groups in New Zealand', New Zealand Red Cross, Wellington, Available at: https://media.redcross.org.nz/media/documents/RC_Migration_Scoping_Report_2021.pdf (accessed 20 November 2021).

NSO (2019), 'Unemployment Rate 1990-2015'. Available at: nso.gov.ki/statistics/social/ (accessed December 2021).

Pacific Australia Labour Mobility (2023), 'Family Accompaniment – Frequently Asked Questions for Workers'. Available: https://www.palmscheme.gov.au/resources/family-accompaniment-faqs (accessed 20 July 2023).

Pala, C. (2020), 'Kiribati's President's Plans to Raise Islands in Fight against Sea-Level Rise', *The Guardian*, 10 August. Available at: https://www.theguardian.com/world/2020/aug/10/kiribatis-presidents-plans-to-raise-islands-in-fight-against-sea-level-rise (accessed 23 January 2023).

Perkiss, S., Taule'alo, T., Dun, O., Klocker, N., Liki, A. and Tanima, F. (2022), 'Exploring Accountability of Australia and New Zealand's Temporary Labour Mobility Programmes in Samoa using a Talanoa Approach', *Accounting, Auditing & Accountability Journal*, 35(4): 1061–1092. Available at: https://www.proquest.com/docview/2645735873 (accessed 23 January 2023).

Petrou, K., Dun, O., Farbotko, C. and Kitara, T. (2021), 'Pacific Labour Mobility on Pause: Consequences of Temporary Immobility During the Pandemic', in Yonique Campbell and John Connell (eds), *COVID in the Islands: A Comparative Perspective on the Caribbean and the Pacific*, 299–319, Singapore: Springer Nature: Singapore.

Petrou, K. and Connell, J. (2023), 'Our 'Pacific Family'. Heroes, Guests, Workers or a Precariat?', *Australian Geographer*, 54(2): 125–135. Available at: https://doi.org/10.1080/00049182.2023.2203348 (accessed 23 January 2023).

PLMAM (2022), 'Concept Note – A Framework for Pacific Labour Mobility Economic Integration'. Available at: https://pacerplus.org/assets/PLMAM-2022/Discussion-Paper-3.1_-Concept-Note-A-Framework-for-Pacific-Labour-Mobility-Economic-Reintegration.pdf (accessed 22 November 2023).

RNZ (2019a), 'Kiribati Wants More Seasonal Workers to Aust, NZ'. 12 April. Available at: https://www.rnz.co.nz/international/pacific-news/386844/kiribati-wants-more-seasonal-workers-to-aust-nz (accessed 20 January 2023).

RNZ (2019b), 'Kiribati Frustrated by Australian Indifference to Climate Change', 29 August. Available at: https://www.rnz.co.nz/international/pacific-news/397753/kiribati-frustrated-by-australian-indifference-to-climate-change (accessed 23 January 2023).

RNZ (2022a), 'Abused RSE Workers in Australia too Afraid to Speak Out', 16 May. Available at: https://www.rnz.co.nz/international/pacific-news/467200/abused-rse-workers-in-australia-too-afraid-to-speak-out (accessed 20 January 2023).

RNZ (2022b), 'RSE Worker Treatment like 'Slavery', Says Equal Employment Opportunities Commissioner', 12 December. Available: https://www.rnz.co.nz/news/national/480556/rse-worker-treatment-like-slavery-says-equal-employment-opportunities-commissioner (accessed 23 January 2023).

Sharman, E. and Howes, S. (2022), 'Seasonal Work at the Job Security Inquiry: What Did We Learn?', *Dev Policy Blog*, Australian National University, 1 April. Available:

https://devpolicy.org/seasonal-work-at-the-job-security-inquiry-20220401/ (accessed 23 January 2023).

Solomon Times (2021), 'Beck Reminds Seasonal Workers: "Be Good Ambassadors for the Country"', 10 September. Available at: https://www.solomontimes.com/news/beck-reminds-seasonal-workers-be-good-ambassadors-for-the-country/11088 (accessed 23 January 2023).

Stead, V. (2022), 'Temporariness made Interminable: Pacific Islander Farmworkers in Australia and the Enduring Crises of Global Agricultural Production', *Journal of Agrarian Change*, 23(3): 579–589. Available at: https://doi.org/10.1111/joac.12524 (accessed 23 January 2023).

Stead, V. and Petrou, K. (2022), 'Beyond the 'Triple Win': Pacific Islander Farmworkers' Use of Social Media to Navigate Labour Mobility Costs and Possibilities through the COVID-19 Pandemic', *Journal of Ethnic and Migration Studies*, 49(9): 2194–2212, Available at: https://www.tandfonline.com/doi/full/10.1080/1369183X.2022.2138288 (accessed 23 January 2023).

Underhill-Sem, Y. and Marsters, E. (2017), 'Labour Mobility in the Pacific: A Systematic Literature Review of Development Impacts', New Zealand Institute of Pacific Research. Available at: https://www.palmscheme.gov.au/sites/default/files/2022-05/UNDERHILL%20SEM%202017%20LM%20in%20Pacific%20-%20Literature%20review.pdf (accessed 23 January 2023).

Westerman, A. (2019), 'Some Pacific Island Nations Are Turning To China. Climate Change Is A Factor', *NPR*, 23 November. Available at: https://www.npr.org/2019/11/23/775986892/some-pacific-island-nations-are-turning-to-china-climate-change-is-a-factor (accessed 5 January 2024).

World Bank (2020), 'Personal Remittances, Received ($ of GDP) – Kiribati'. Available at: https://data.worldbank.org/indicator/BX.TRF.PWKR.DT.GD.ZS?locations=KI (accessed 23 January 2023).

6

Social Protection versus Orthodoxy in the Covid-19 Pandemic: Lessons from South Africa

Busi Sibeko

1. Introduction

The Covid-19 pandemic worsened the manifold crises that South Africa has been dealing with for decades. Coming on the heels of multiple cycles of austerity, the pandemic further diluted the weak and poorly implemented social protections offered by the government. Amid the state's failure to create decent work opportunities and sustainable livelihoods for a majority of the marginalized population, the Covid-19 crisis raised questions about how society is organized around productive and reproductive work. At the same time, the pandemic provided an opportunity to rethink how macroeconomic policy could be used to fulfil the state's responsibility of providing social protection for those left vulnerable by the socioeconomic system.

Even before the pandemic, South Africa had a well-established social assistance programme driven by the Constitutional mandate that 'everyone has the right to have access to social security, including, if they are unable to support themselves and their dependants' (SA Department of Justice, 1996, Chapter 2). This mandate ensures the minimum social protections below which no one should fall over their entire lifecycle. As such, a significant proportion of the government's social spending has taken the form of grants aimed at addressing historical and ongoing intersectional racialized and gendered inequalities. Cumulatively, the number of recipients of all such grants increased from nearly 4 million (9 per cent of the population) in April 2001 to over 18 million (30 per cent of the population) in 2021 (Zulu 2021). The staggering increase can be attributed to changes in the eligibility criteria, such as raising the age limit for the Child

Support Grant (CSG),[1] and the failure to address the socioeconomic dispossession of the Black majority. The grants are subject to income-based means testing and include the Old Age Pension (OAP), Social Relief of Distress (SRD) Grant, Disability Grant (DG), Foster Care Grant (FCG), Care Dependency Grant (CDG) and the CSG. All grants fall below the national minimum wage of 3,904 South African rand (R) (US$266) per month and their beneficiaries include permanent residents, refugees and South African citizens. As provided by the Constitution, during the Covid-19 crisis, these grants continued to be made available through state provisioning (SA Department of Justice, 1996, Chapter 2).

This chapter focuses on the Covid-19 SRD Grant that was introduced by the South African government a month after the commencement of the first lockdown, targeting unemployed individuals between the ages of eighteen and fifty-nine. It also briefly discusses the Caregiver Allowance provided to caregivers who received the CSG on behalf of children in their care. Based on these policy innovations, the chapter reflects on the prospects of a Universal Basic Income Grant (UBIG) in South Africa.

Despite the temporary expansion of these grants during Covid-19, social security in South Africa currently stands threatened as the National Treasury accelerates its International Monetary Fund (IMF)-endorsed austerity programme that began in 2014 (IMF 2020a). Understood as a fiscal policy implemented by a state to solve debt and growth problems during a period of economic stagnation, austerity typically takes the form of budget cuts and/or higher taxes (Wren-Lewis 2015). In the South African context, austerity, in part, explains why social protection has been implemented in a stop-start manner, with civil society having to continuously advocate for such measures. This chapter demonstrates how, despite some progressive policies, the global health emergency also witnessed the perpetuation of pre-pandemic orthodoxies, which will likely cement the status quo of austerity moving forward. Based on DAWN's Policy Transformations analytical framework, the chapter argues that during Covid-19, the country's policy regime was marked by a business-as-usual approach (Llavaneras Blanco and Cuervo 2021).

2. Context

2.1 The foundations of a social crisis

To understand the need for social assistance in South Africa, we must first examine how production and social reproduction were shaped by settler colonization and Apartheid (1948–94). The systemic oppression of Black labour shaped asymmetrical power relations in industrialization and wealth accumulation processes, and, more generally, in capitalist accumulation. This system exploited the cheap labour of Black men and the unpaid and underpaid work of Black and coloured women.[2]

A feminist approach to understanding social reproduction requires that we take into account i) diversity in household configurations, ii) inequalities within households, iii) inter-household relations and iv) longitudinal processes (Stevano 2020). Such an approach should also account for the racialized and gendered sociospatial legacies of the apartheid state, which enforced spatial and socioeconomic separations between production and social reproduction (Cousins et al. 2018).

The system of internal labour migration, which was established to supply cheap labour to the mining industry, marginalized the land-based livelihoods of the rural population, with few offsetting employment opportunities. Those left behind in the former *Bantustans* (Black homelands geographically determined by the colonial regime and formalized under Apartheid) had to undertake additional unpaid labour, such as subsistence agriculture and child rearing, to compensate for the labour force sent to the cities and the mines. These structures separated Black men from their families, and contributed to the long-term fragmentation of families and men's detachment from child care (Budlender and Lund 2011). Black women faced a disproportionate burden of social reproduction as white women hired them as domestic workers to take care of their homes and children (Sibeko 2021). Care was thus deliberately feminized and racialized as well as deeply shaped by economic disparities. Furthermore, the absence of wages and state support for Black women made social reproduction extremely difficult. These processes systematically undermined women's bargaining power, which is determined by quantifiable (i.e., economic assets) and non-quantifiable (i.e., community-based support) factors (Agarwal 1997). Cousins et al. (2018) argue that policies for land reform, accumulation and social reproduction should take into account land and property rights, fragmented classes of labour, communal areas, customary norms and values, and customary and social institutions. Against this backdrop, social protection in the form of grants has been critical to the social reproduction of the Black population, particularly women, children and those excluded from the waged economy.

2.2 The current context: Multiple crises

After almost three decades of democracy, South Africa faces multiple crises. It has one of the highest levels of inequality globally, with the average per capita income in large cities twice that of rural provinces (Stats SA 2020, IMF 2020b). Women earn 30 per cent less than men on average, with Black women earning 40 per cent less, and with larger disparities amongst low-skilled workers. Wealth distribution is even more unequal, with the wealthiest 1 per cent of the population owning half the country's wealth and the top 10 per cent owning at least 90–95 per cent (Stent 2020). Wealth is concentrated along race and gender lines, with a larger proportion held by white men. This perpetuates a cyclical crisis of social reproduction and other broader crises, especially among the Black working class. In 2015, 55 per cent of the population, or 30 million people, lived below the official poverty line of R992 (US$67) per person per month. Poverty was higher among female-headed households (49 per cent) than male-headed households (33 per cent). A quarter of the population lived in extreme poverty, unable to afford enough food to meet their basic physical needs (Stats SA 2017).

South Africa's National Development Plan suggests employment as the best way to provide incomes and secure livelihoods (South African Government 2012). Yet in 2015, 54 per cent of full-time workers earned below the poverty line of R4,125 (US$281) per person per month used by Finn (2018).[3] In the fourth quarter of 2019, the unemployment rate stood at 29 per cent.[4] The corresponding figure for young Black women was 59 per cent, twice as high as the national average and seven times greater than that of the white population (Stats SA 2019).

The pandemic exacerbated this already dire situation. By the second quarter of 2021, unemployment had increased to 34 per cent, the highest since 2008 (Stats SA 2021). By the expanded definition of unemployment,[5] the figure stood at 44 per cent. When segregated by gender and race, Black women's unemployment rate stood at 41 per cent; it was 53 per cent as per the expanded definition. Youth in the age categories of fifteen to twenty-four and twenty-five to thirty-four recorded the highest unemployment rates of 64 per cent and 43 per cent, respectively.

Historically, Black and coloured women were either excluded from waged work or 'over-represented in the lowest-paying occupations (domestic work) and under-represented in the highest-paying occupations (legislators, senior officials, managers)' (Mosomi 2019: 8). South Africa also has a persistent gender wage gap. The Employment Equity Act [No. 55 of 1998] to eliminate gender and race wage disparity has not been adequately implemented.

In addition, the integration of women into the workforce generally assumes 'workers' full-time and lifelong participation in the workforce' and does not consider 'how those workers are sustained or how their households are structured' (Sibeko 2021). Black women in particular perform at least five times more social reproductive activities than men (Oxfam South Africa 2019). Unpaid and underpaid labour is thus extracted from working-class women on two fronts: waged work and unpaid housework.

The country's economic position was precarious even before the pandemic. Growth has been trending downwards since 2010–11, averaging just below 2 per cent between 2011 and 2018 (Sibeko and Isaacs 2020). In 2019, South Africa experienced its third recession since 1994. Despite the downturn, the government, since 2014, has been implementing several austerity measures in the form of cuts to health and education budgets, which are integral to social reproduction. To be sure, South Africa is not a recipient of conditional loans from the Bretton Woods institutions. Rather, its pursuit of austerity reflects a self-enforced neoliberal agenda. The National Treasury (2021) justifies this by arguing that government borrowing 'crowds out' private investment – a tenet of neoclassical economics – and budgetary cuts are, therefore, necessary to appease credit rating agencies and the markets. Globally, the crowding out argument has been central to the implementation of austerity and the enforcement of a financial architecture that prioritizes profits over the rights and survival of citizens.

2.3　Social assistance policies: Crucial but insufficient

Historically, civil society organizations (CSOs) in South Africa have advocated for increased social security. In the 1980s, trade unions called for social pensions to be expanded to include Black workers. The CSG was introduced in 1998 (Westphal 2016). In the late 1990s and early 2000s, CSOs and sections of the government also pushed for a Basic Income Grant (BIG). In 2002, the Taylor Committee, established by the government to inquire into a Comprehensive System of Social Protection, recommended a grant for those excluded from social assistance (Taylor et al. 2002), but this was never acted upon.

Over time, the value of grants declined vis-à-vis the different poverty lines used in South Africa (Budget Justice Coalition 2020).[6] The CSG, which in 2011–12 covered 79 per cent of the cost of basic foodstuff necessary to avoid hunger, covered 71 per cent of the same cost by 2018–19 (ibid.). In the 2021 Budget, the CSG was R445 (US$30) but the food poverty line stood at R585 (US$40). In 2022, the grant was revised to R480 (US$33), or R720 (US$49) for orphans under the care of relatives, versus an updated food poverty line of R624 (US$43) (South

Table 6.1 South Africa's Social Grants, 2021

Grant	Amount (per month)
Old Age Pension	R1,860 (US$126)
Disability Grant	R1,780 (US$121)
Foster Care Grant	R1,000 (US$68)
Care Dependency Grant	R1,860 (US$126)
Child Support Grant	R425 (US$29)
Social Relief of Distress Grant	R350 (US$23.8)

Source: Compiled by author based on data from South African Social Security Agency (2021).

African Government 2022). The OAP declined between 2014 and 2019 relative to the upper-bound poverty line.

At the onset of the pandemic, all grants (as outlined in Table 6.1) were insufficient to meet the full basic needs of households relative to the monthly food basket price of over R4,000 (US$250) per month (Pietermaritzburg Economic Justice & Dignity Group 2021). Thereafter, the government intervened to introduce new grants and protect households against anticipated large-scale job losses, increased hunger and a negative economic outlook.

3. The Covid-19 social security response

The revised grant amounts notwithstanding, South Africa's pandemic response was biased towards rescuing businesses rather than offering social protection, thus highlighting the state's contradictory role under neoliberalism – limiting 'interference' in the market but supporting businesses during crises (Clarke and Newman 2012). This also demonstrates a bias towards so-called 'productive' expenditure versus 'consumption'.

In April 2020, South African President Cyril Ramaphosa announced a R500-billion (US$34 billion) Covid-19 response package, the largest on the African continent. However, its weak implementation reinforced an ongoing conservative fiscal policy trajectory. The financial year 2020–21 saw only a R36-billion (US$2.5 billion) net increase in non-interest spending (spending on everything but debt). The Budget was reconfigured to move funds from other departments to the department of health (or within the department) to reflect the Covid-19 allocation. For example, R2.1 billion (US$140 million) was cut from the education budget and redirected towards health (Budget Justice Coalition 2020).

In other words, there was no new money going into the fiscus at the scale announced, meaning that the package announced by the president never quite materialized.

Of the stated R500-billion emergency response, R50 billion (US$3.4 billion) was allocated towards social security, which included i) an SRD Grant of R350 (US$23.8) per month between May and October 2020, and later extended to April 2021; ii) a Caregiver Allowance of R300 (US$20.4) in May 2020 and, thereafter, R500 (US$34) per month until October 2020; and iii) an R250 (US$17) increase per month in all grants between May and October 2020. The SRD Grant was available to unemployed people between the ages of eighteen and fifty-nine with limited income. The Caregiver Allowance was provided to caregivers who received the CSG on behalf of children in their care.

The Covid-19 SRD Grant was withdrawn in April 2021, prompting many CSOs to demand its reinstatement. During its implementation, CSOs had also called for an increase in the quantum of the grant and an expansion in its eligibility criteria, which excluded many vulnerable groups. But the government did not heed these calls despite the fact that 10 million people, including 3 million children, were affected by hunger between April and May 2021 (#PayTheGrants 2020), and a looming third wave of the pandemic portended additional lockdowns and further livelihood constraints for the vulnerable population. The grants were presumably stopped because of the government's perceived fiscal pressures and the false assumption that the country had passed the rescue phase and was now in recovery. Visagie and Turok (2020) warn that temporary grants may 'create vulnerabilities in poor communities if they are withdrawn prematurely'. This was likely the case when the SRD Grant was temporarily withdrawn. It was reinstated four months later.

3.1 Geographic distribution

The spatial inequalities produced by Apartheid placed socioeconomically marginalized people in remote areas, thus necessitating a targeted implementation of social security grants during the pandemic. The government's approach worked for rural applicants, who were the highest recipients of the SRD Grant, as shown in Table 6.2.

However, the grant's reach was not as successful among the more heterogenous urban population, of whom shack dwellers were the most vulnerable. About 23 per cent of this group went hungry between April and May 2021 compared with 14 per cent of the urban population on average (Githahu 2021). Yet, only a small proportion of shack dwellers received any form of social security grants, in part due to their inability to produce a home address to claim such benefits (Visagie and Turok 2020).[7]

Table 6.2 Access to South African Covid-19 SRD Grants by Geographic Location in June 2020

Geographic location	Access (%)
Rural	33
Cities and towns	24
Metropolitans	21
Peri-urban areas	29
Townships	27
Shack dwellers (those in informal settlements and backyards)	18
Suburbs	16

Source: Compiled by the author using data from Visagie and Turok (2020).

3.2 Exclusion of women and vulnerable groups

The Covid-19 SRD Grant provided a lifeline to about 6 million unemployed people. Despite the fact that it was lower than the food poverty line of R585 (US$40), 10 per cent of households solely depended on this grant for an income. Based on this data, Spaul et al. (2021) argue that the grant was well targeted and alleviated the hardships experienced, especially by poor households, during the pandemic. However, they overlook its lack of gender sensitivity and exclusion of vulnerable groups.

Initially, women, refugees and asylum seekers were heavily excluded from the SRD Grant. Receiving the Caregiver Allowance made them ineligible for the SRD Grant, which remained the case even after the former grant ended on 31 October 2020. Thereafter, from 1 November 2020, a mother and child were expected to survive on a CSG of R500 (US$34) per month, which was insufficient to meet their basic needs. It is, therefore, unsurprising that of the 6.4 million people who had received the SRD Grant between May and November 2020, only 32.1 per cent were women (Department of Social Development 2021). Most women were excluded because they received the Caregiver Allowance, despite the fact that they experienced disproportionately higher unemployment than men.

Asylum seekers and special permit holders became eligible for the SRD Grant only after litigation by the Scalabrini Center (Scalabrini Institute 2020). Even after the court order, the process of putting a payment system in place was delayed, and no payments were made to asylum seekers in 2020. The bulk of the work to ensure access to the Covid-19 SRD Grant was done by CSOs and community-based advice offices (Mncube et al. 2020).

Additional challenges included unfair rejections of grant applications caused by outdated government databases and delays in grant rollouts. This meant it took longer for the money to reach recipients. During the first phase of the rollout, 571,724 approved grants remained uncollected due to systematic failures such as poor communication with beneficiaries, costs associated with collecting grants, online application systems being only available in English, geographic challenges and a lack of capacity (Sonjica 2021).[8] In August 2021, when the SRD Grant was reinstated, the Department of Social Development allowed only twenty-seven days for applicants to make their claims. Many whose grant applications were initially declined were still struggling with the appeals process, which had a short application window.

The #PayTheGrants movement[9] and other CSOs have flagged the use of means testing as a leading cause for rejection of grant applications, arguing that it fails to consider the diverse strategies employed by households for survival. SRD Grants were declined when applicants received funds into their accounts during the previous month (South African Government 2020). As such, the system failed to consider complex intra- and inter-household income distribution. It did not, for instance, account for inter-household transfers from Black workers to other members of their extended family and family networks, which has historically subsidized the state's failures.[10] This meant that money flowing into bank accounts could be remittances from family members rather than income earned by the grant applicant. The system also didn't account for an estimated 11 million South Africans who are unbanked or underbanked and may be sharing accounts (BusinessTech 2019).

3.3 Reinstatement and extension of the SRD Grant

After its temporary withdrawal in April 2021, the SRD Grant was revised and reinstated the same year in August amid a wave of violent protests and looting following the arrest of former South African President Jacob Zuma. The R38-billion (US$2.6 billion) package continued till March 2022, with applicants having to reapply for the new iteration of the programme, which now included caregivers. The means testing criterion was relaxed and the income required for eligibility was raised to the food poverty line (R585 or US$40 at the time).

Following the reinstatement of the grant, over 12 million people applied, but as of September 2021, only 7 million applications were approved and 4.7 million applicants were paid (Zeeman 2021). Such a slow rollout during a crisis was a critical concern. On the positive side, the inclusion of caregivers ensured that a majority of applicants were women (52 per cent) and young people between the ages of eighteen and thirty-five (62 per cent).

In the earlier rounds, the government spent a significant portion of the pandemic response funds on social relief (and more resources were made available in the first year). However, in the 2022 Budget, only R44 billion (US$2.6 million) was allocated to serve 10.5 million people until the end of March 2023. The allocation was not enough to cover the 10.9 million people originally identified as potential beneficiaries of the SRD Grant, prompting the Department of Social Development to once again amend eligibility criteria and decrease the number of applicants to remain within the grant allocation. This amendment meant that 400,000 people earlier deemed eligible for the grant no longer qualified.

There is broad acknowledgement that a crisis of social reproduction persists in South Africa and, with recent global shocks, households face a heightened cost of living crisis. In 2022, the National Treasury noted that '[a]lthough BIG or permanent SRD-350 is preferred option for DSD [the Department of Social Development], option 3 in Presidency Paper: SRD-Job-seeker grant and SRD-caregiver grant might be an acceptable compromise'. Beyond costs to the fiscus, the Treasury did not specify why the caregiver and job-seeker grants were deemed better alternatives than the UBIG and other grants, and whether substantive research had been conducted on the success or failure of the initially proposed grants. The Treasury maintained that a longer-term commitment to social protection requires higher taxes and leads to more debt, thus unwittingly acknowledging that fiscal surplus is the desired outcome in the medium term.

3.4 The Caregiver Allowance

The Caregiver Allowance is essentially a top-up to the CSG but given directly to caregivers as opposed to the child. The grant was an outcome of the government's desire to support households while reducing total costs. While President Ramaphosa promised a R500 (US$34) top-up to the CSG per month per child in April 2020 (Holmes and Hunt 2021), the minister of finance and social development diluted this commitment to R300 (US$20.4) per child in May. The top-up was raised to R500 per caregiver between June and October that year.

According to the government, the implementation of the Caregiver Allowance offset the exclusion of caregivers from the SRD Grant. Caregivers were better off, the government argued, because the top-up provided them R500 instead of the R350 SRD Grant. At the same time, the government claimed that the R500 was meant to provide additional support to children, thus unwittingly indicating that caregivers themselves were not receiving any benefit and were unfairly excluded from the SRD Grant.

Caregivers were likely left out because of exaggerated fears of double-dipping into grants. Their exclusion effectively saved the state R13 billion (US$0.9 billion) (Broughton 2020) but resulted in at least 6.6 million children continuing to live below the food poverty line (Hall 2023). This policy move was driven by the prevailing austerity logic, which disproportionately affected women. As the primary caregivers of their households, women bore an increased financial burden at a time when food prices were increasing, school feeding schemes were closed and jobs were being lost. The impacts of disruptions in the school feeding schemes were similar to those seen in Ghana (Torvikey and Marfo, this volume), where such programmes were halted at the height of the pandemic.[11]

The state's pandemic response also failed to consider the structural inequalities that caregivers already faced. During the first lockdown, two-thirds of those who lost their jobs were women, poor folks, black Africans and informal workers (Casale and Posel 2020). Women predominate in the non-essential retail and service occupations, which were not allowed to operate during lockdowns. Informal workers, who are disproportionately women, were also barred from operating.

Similar to Roopnarine and Brizan's findings in Trinidad and Tobago (this volume), the implementation of lockdowns disproportionately increased women's unpaid work, which was already high relative to that of men before the pandemic. Casale and Posel (2020) show that 'nearly 80% of women who were spending more time than usual on child care were spending more than 4 extra hours a day on it, compared to 65% of men'. Even in households that paid for domestic care work, the absence of workers due to lockdowns meant that social reproductive labour had to be internalized (Sibeko et al. 2021).

Despite being one of the first countries in the world to consider gender-responsive budgeting, policies in South Africa have not considered the care work undertaken by women. During the pandemic, many CSOs denounced the 'anti women' and 'anti poor' stance of the government's policy response (see #PayTheGrants 2020).[12] Eventually, the efforts of CSOs and progressive research institutions proved instrumental in getting caregivers included in the SRD Grant.

In the long term, grants like the SRD and the Caregiver Allowance could be a way to value and compensate women's work in the economy. Feminists have argued that an unconditional income independent of paid work would enhance women's agency in families, households, workplaces and the community, with particular benefits for those facing multiple and intersecting forms of discrimination (Williams 2021). Granlund and Hochfeld point out that 'South Africa's cash transfers have largely had positive social transformative effects on individuals, in relation to a sense of dignity, autonomy and increased decision-making powers for primary caregivers, usually mothers or grandmothers. Positive effects were also perceived in relation to these households and communities, although some contested effects and limitations were also found' (2019: 1230). They further argue 'that gaining access to an independent income, in this case, the CSG, offers the potential to challenge a subordinate role with less economic and social power within the family and community, and therefore potentially rebalance unequal power relations' (ibid.: 1233). A caregiver grant, or a wage-independent grant like a BIG, would help diversify the sources of income households need to sustain themselves.

4. Transformative potential? Calls for (U)BIG amid continued orthodoxy

The Covid-19 crisis demonstrated the need for a comprehensive social protection programme and led to renewed calls for a BIG in South Africa (Institute for Economic Justice 2021a, #PayTheGrants 2020). The Department of Social Development echoed calls from CSOs, such as the Institute for Economic Justice (IEJ), Studies in Poverty and Inequality Institute (SPII), #PayTheGrants and Black Sash,[13] to use the Covid-19 SRD Grant as a stepping stone towards a BIG (Omarjee 2021).[14] The National Treasury, however, clung to its austerity agenda, claiming that a BIG would be unaffordable. Despite evidence to the contrary, the Treasury pushed the notion that grants create dependency and social welfare systems weaken incentives to join the labour force (Hanna 2021).

Feminist economists have long called for a non-commodified means of existence that is also non-conditional (Williams 2021). Schulz argues that a UBIG, 'if unconditional and at a level covering basic needs, would help tackle the structural inequalities inherited from the past, due to the sexual divide between the public and private sphere', and would be critical in delinking social protection from waged labour, which would eliminate women's structural exclusion (2017: 1).

There is a relevant debate to be had around the risk of expanding financial capitalism via cash transfers (see, for example, the discussion proposed by Fernández Cervantes in this volume). Lavinas argues that the expansion of the social protection system has happened in tandem with the 'expansion of the financial system to every end, across all levels of society', and cautions against the intertwining of financialized capitalism and social protection (2017: 7). Mies et al. (1988) argue that women's bodies and labour are the 'last colony' of accumulation, as they are introduced as new subjects of capitalism in exploitative and violent ways. In South Africa, the government appointed private financial services provider Cash Paymaster Services (CPS) to assist with the distribution of grants through biometric-enabled smart cards. The integration of CPS led to increased financialization of those previously seen as 'unbankable', but the impact on racialized and poor women and other marginalized groups remains to be analysed.

Prior to the 2021 Medium-Term Budget Policy Statement, the Treasury was reportedly considering a family grant to be given to one member of a household instead of individual grants (Human 2021). However, such a measure assumes unitary households and ignores internal fragmentations, which reproduce inequalities and power differentials within families. A report by the Southern African Labour and Development Research Unit (SALDRU) demonstrated that a family grant would be unfeasible given that South Africa does not have a household registry, and would lead to high levels of exclusion (Goldman et al. 2021). CSOs also critiqued the government's 'secretive and closed-door' approach to the proposal (#PayTheGrants 2021).

Although the BIG has gained traction among various constituencies, my concern remains that delivered in the context of austerity, it could lead to further public disinvestment such as the rollback of basic services. This concern is shared by Lavinas (2020) in the context of Brazil. I also share Gronbach's (2019) caution against policies that shift from the 'provision of free or affordable public services to facilitating access to consumer loans', thus paving the way for privatization. In this approach, poverty is seen as a symptom of financial exclusion rather than an outcome of systemic issues that reproduce adverse outcomes.

The extreme austerity adopted by the South African government in the 2020 Budget (prior to the pandemic) should have been abandoned, but it wasn't. In October 2020, then Finance Minister Tito Mboweni said that 'the Cabinet remain[s] resolute and will walk through the narrow gate towards fiscal sustainability' (National Treasury 2021). In line with traditional neoliberal orthodoxy, the Treasury plans to achieve a fiscal surplus by 2024–25, which will be followed by debt stabilization. This is despite a recent warning by the IMF that 'countries should not run larger budget surpluses to bring down the debt, but should instead allow growth to bring down debt-to-GDP ratios organically' (Chamon and Ostry 2021).

The premature withdrawal of Covid-19 relief measures is consistent with the orthodox assumption that cutting government spending has relatively little adverse effect on aggregate demand. However, studies have shown that, during recessionary times, the effect of government spending cuts on output is larger than anticipated (UNCTAD 2019). Furthering the view that social spending on grants creates dependency and that jobs and social protection are competing interests, current Finance Minister Enoch Godongwana (2021) has argued that, instead of a UBIG, the government should spend on upskilling people. This goes against the Constitutional mandate that the government must provide adequate social protection even when there are jobs.

5. Conclusion

The Covid-19 crisis laid bare the flaws of the current social protection system, including the lack of gender sensitivity in policy design. Without adequate social protection, including social assistance, that considers gender, race, geography and other intersectionalities, the crisis of social reproduction is likely to continue. It will be further exacerbated by austerity, which reduces the availability of, access to and quality of basic services essential for social reproduction.

South Africa's experience is also a cautionary tale against the provisioning of social protection in a context of orthodoxy. Even as sections of the government, notably the Department of Social Development, proposed innovative methods to provide social security, other powerful factions remained committed to the orthodox or business-as-usual approach. Despite internal tensions among different government bodies, the Treasury's commitment to austerity prevailed, thus confirming that governments 'may carry on with the same old policies even though there may be an uneasy awareness that more is needed' (Llavaneras Blanco and Cuervo 2021: 12).

A transformative approach in South Africa requires a systemic review of the current social protection system. It necessitates reconceptualizing what a comprehensive system of social protection should look like amid high levels of unemployment, poverty and structural inequality. Such a system needs to consider historical and ongoing intersectional racialized and gendered inequalities in the economy. Policy needs to ensure a minimum social floor for all, which includes a minimum income and access to quality basic services. However, a social floor cannot be achieved in a context of austerity. Instead, fiscal policy should be used as an essential tool in South Africa's repertoire to move it onto a new, inclusive, more stable and sustainable development path. For social protection to be realized in the country, neoliberalism must be abandoned. Instead, what is needed is the adoption of a socioeconomic framework that enables a regenerative interaction between public investment, labour productivity, socioeconomic development, rights and equity. Without such a fundamental rethink of economics in South Africa, everyday life will remain unviable for the majority.

Notes

1   Initially, the CSG only covered children up to seven years. Over time, the eligibility criteria was amended to eighteen years through incremental changes.
2   The communities designated as coloured have primarily descended from the Khoisan people who originally inhabited the western parts of South Africa, enslaved Asians and Africans brought to the Cape from the earliest years of the colony, European settlers and other Africans.
3   This poverty line accounts for the cost of basic needs of South Africans, linking individual wages to household poverty (Finn 2018).
4   Unemployed persons include those who i) were not employed in the reference week and ii) were available to work but did not look for work because they were discouraged or for other reasons (Stats SA 2021).
5   The expanded unemployment figure includes anyone who is out of a job and wants a job, but is not looking for work at any given time (Stats SA 2021).
6   Different poverty lines are applied in different contexts in South Africa. These include the food poverty line and one for the working poor (Finn 2018).
7   Visagie and Turok (2020) also found that migration status amongst shack dwellers was another relevant factor for their limited access to grants.
8   It is important to note that applications were available through SMS, WhatsApp, online and physical means. These multiple channels were needed since internet penetration in the country is not yet widespread.
9   #PayTheGrants emerged from the Covid-19 People's Coalition, an emerging civil society collective seeking to ensure that South Africa's response to the crisis is rooted in social justice and democratic principles.
10 This is often referred to as the 'black tax'.

11 It is important to highlight the role of CSOs in galvanizing resources to support households at the local level by distributing basic goods, particularly food, and raising awareness around the virus throughout the pandemic (Hamann 2020).

12 The statements were made by the C19-People's Coalition Cash Transfers Working Group, Institute for Economic Justice and Black Sash.

13 A human rights organization advocating for social justice.

14 On 8 August 2021, the Department of Social Development published a green paper on a Comprehensive Social Security and Retirement Reform, in which it proposed the introduction of a BIG. Between 2017 and 2021, South Africa declared three national states of disaster for drought. In addition, major droughts have been experienced in 2020 and 2022. These disasters have prompted several government responses, including social relief from emergency reserves.

References

Agarwal, B. (1997), 'Bargaining" and Gender Relations: Within and Beyond the Household', *Feminist Economics*, 3(1): 1–51. Available at: https://doi.org/10.1080/135457097338799 (accessed 9 October 2021).

Broughton, T. (2020), 'Covid-19: Increase in Social Grants Not Good Enough, Say Critics', *GroundUp*, 29 April. Available at: https://www.groundup.org.za/article/covid-19-increase-social-grants-announced-last-week-are-not-pro-poor-first-appeared-says-civil-society/ (accessed 18 November 2023).

Budget Justice Coalition (2020), 'Submission by the Budget Justice Coalition to the Select and Standing Committees on Finance on the 2020 Medium-Term Budget Policy Statement'. Available at: https://static.pmg.org.za/201104MTBPS_Submission_to_Finance_Committees_by_the_BJC.PDF (accessed 23 December 2023).

Budlender, D. and Lund, F. (2011), 'South Africa: A Legacy of Family Disruption', *Development and Change*, 42(4): 925–946. Available at: https://doi.org/10.1111/j.1467-7660.2011.01715.x (accessed 9 October 2021).

BusinessTech (2019), 'Discovery Has the Big Banks Nervous', 13 February. Available at: https://businesstech.co.za/news/banking/298810/discovery-has-the-big-banks-nervous/ (accessed 29 November 2021).

Casale, D. and Posel, D. (2021), 'The Gendered Effects of the Covid-19 Crisis and Ongoing Lockdown in South Africa: Evidence from NIDS-CRAM Waves 1 – 3'. Available at: https://cramsurvey.org/wp-content/uploads/2021/02/4.-Casale-D.-Shepherd-D.-2021-The-gendered-effects-of-the-Covid-19-crisis-and-ongoing-lockdown-in-South-Africa-Evidence-from-NIDS-CRAM-Waves-1-3.pdf (accessed 29 November 2021).

Chamon, M. and Ostry, J. (2021), 'A Future with High Public Debt: Low-for-Long Is Not Low Forever', *IMF Blog*, 20 April. Available at: https://www.imf.org/en/Blogs/

Articles/2021/04/20/a-future-with-high-public-debt-low-for-long-is-not-low-forever (accessed 25 May 2023).

Clarke, J. and Newman, J. (2012), 'The Alchemy of Austerity', *Critical Social Policy*, 32(3): 299–319. Available at: https://doi.org/10.1177/0261018312444405 (accessed 9 October 2021).

Cousins, B., Genis, A. and Clarke, J. (2018), 'The Potential of Agriculture and Land Reform to Generate Jobs', PLAAS Policy Brief No. 51, Cape Town: Institute for Poverty, Land and Agrarian Studies, University of the Western Cape. Available at: https://repository.uwc.ac.za/xmlui/bitstream/handle/10566/4305/pb_51_potential_agriculture_land_reform_generate_job_2018.pdf?sequence=1&isAllowed=y (accessed 9 October 2021).

Department of Social Development (2021), 'The Rapid Assessment of the Implementation and Utilisation of the Special Covid SRD Grant', Government of South Africa. Available at: https://www.dsd.gov.za/index.php/component/jdownloads/?task=download.send&id=316:the-rapid-assessment-of-the-implementation-and-utilisation-of-the-special-covid-19-srd-grant&catid=7&m=0&Itemid=101 (accessed 16 November 2023).

Finn, A. (2018), 'A National Minimum Wage in the Context of the South African Labour Market', National Minimum Wage Research Initiative, Working Paper Series No. 1, University of the Witwatersrand. Available at: http://nationalminimumwage.co.za/wp-content/uploads/2015/09/NMW-RI-Descriptive-Statistics-Final.pdf (accessed 9 October 2021).

Githahu, M. (2021), 'Child Hunger Remains Extremely High, Shack Dwellers Worst Off, Survey Finds,' *IOL*, 9 July. Available at: https://www.iol.co.za/capeargus/news/child-hunger-remains-extremely-high-shack-dwellers-worst-off-survey-finds-5671dc07-8e5d-4e44-8a32-4ad451b1c3b6 (accessed 9 October 2021).

Godongwana, E. (2021), 'We Must Balance Growth Interventions, Job Creation, Social Grants', *BusinessDay*, 29 July. Available at: https://www.businesslive.co.za/bd/opinion/2021-07-29-enoch-godongwana-we-must-balance-growth-interventions-job-creation-social-grants/ (accessed 29 November 2021).

Goldman, M., Bassier, I., Budlender, J., Mzankomo, L., Woolard, I., Leibbrandt, M. and UNU-WIDER (2021), 'Simulation of Options to Replace the Special COVID-19 Social Relief of Distress Grant and Close the Poverty Gap at the Food Poverty Line', WIDER Working Paper No. 2021/165, The United Nations University World Institute for Development Economics Research (UNU-WIDER), Helsinki. Available at: https://www.econstor.eu/bitstream/10419/248379/1/wp2021-165.pdf (accessed 9 October 2021).

Granlund, S. and Hochfeld, T. (2019), ''That Child Support Grant Gives Me Powers' – Exploring Social and Relational Aspects of Cash Transfers in South Africa in Times of Livelihood Change', *The Journal of Development Studies*, 56(6): 1230–1244. Available at: https://doi.org/10.1080/00220388.2019.1650170 (accessed 29 November 2021).

Gronbach, L. (2019), 'Financialising Poverty: Social Grants and Financial Inclusion in South Africa, *socialprotection.org*, 2 January. Available at: https://socialprotection.org/discover/blog/financialising-poverty-social-grants-and-financial-inclusion-south-africa (accessed 15 January 2023).

Hall, K. (2023), 'Child Poverty', Children Count: Statistics on Children in South Africa, Children's Institute, University of Cape Town. Available at: http://childrencount.uct.ac.za/indicator.php?domain=2&indicator=98 (accessed 18 November 2023).

Hamann, R. (2020), 'Civil Society Groups that Mobilised around COVID-19 Face Important Choices', *The Conversation*, 3 July. Available at: https://theconversation.com/civil-society-groups-that-mobilised-around-covid-19-face-important-choices-140989 (accessed 15 January 2023).

Hanna, B.R. (2019), 'Dispelling the Myth of Welfare Dependency', *Harvard Kennedy School Evidence for Policy Design*, 9 August. Available at: https://epod.cid.harvard.edu/article/dispelling-myth-welfare-dependency (accessed 29 November 2021).

Holmes, R. and Hunt, A. (2021), 'Have Social Protection Responses to Covid-19 Undermined or Supported Gender Equality? Emerging Lessons from a Gender Perspective', Working Paper, *ODI*, 9 June. Available at: https://odi.org/en/publications/have-social-protection-responses-to-covid-19-undermined-or-supported-gender-equality-emerging-lessons-from-a-gender-perspective/ (accessed 9 December 2023).

Human, L. (2021), 'Showdown over Proposed Family Grant', *GroundUp*, 29 October. Available at: https://www.groundup.org.za/article/showdown-over-family-grant/ (accessed 29 November 2021).

Institute for Economic Justice (2020), 'COVID-19 – An Emergency Rescue Package for South Africa', Covid-19 Response Policy Brief No. 1. Available at: https://www.iej.org.za/covid-19-an-emergency-rescue-package-for-south-africa/ (accessed 25 January 2023).

Institute for Economic Justice (2021a), 'Economic Relief in the Face of the Third Wave', Covid-19 Response, Policy Brief No. 4. Available at: https://www.iej.org.za/wp-content/uploads/2021/07/IEJ-COVID-19-policy-brief-series-4-Emergency-relief-package.pdf (accessed 9 October 2021).

Institute for Economic Justice (2021b), 'Introducing a Universal Basic Income Guarantee for South Africa: Towards Income for All', Social Policy Brief Series No. 1. Available at: https://www.iej.org.za/introducing-a-universal-basic-income-guarantee-for-south-africa/ (accessed 9 October 2021).

IMF (2020a), 'IMF Executive Board Concludes 2019 Article IV Consultation with South Africa', Press Release. Available at: https://www.imf.org/en/News/Articles/2020/01/29/pr2023-south-africa-imf-executive-board-concludes-2019-article-iv-consultation (accessed 9 October 2021).

IMF (2020b), 'Six Charts Explain South Africa's Inequality', IMF News: IMF Country Focus. Available at: https://www.imf.org/en/News/Articles/2020/01/29/na012820six-charts-on-south-africas-persistent-and-multi-faceted-inequality (accessed 9 October 2021).

Lavinas, L. (2017), *The Takeover of Social Policy by Financialization: The Brazilian Paradox*, New York: Palgrave Macmillan.

Lindiwe, Z. (2021), 'Budget Vote 19 Speech by the Minister of Social Development, Ms Lindiwe Zulu, MP to the National Council of Provinces (NCOP)', National Council of Provinces. Available at: https://www.dsd.gov.za/index.php/21-latest-news/367-budget-vote-19-speech-by-the-minister-of-social-development-ms-lindiwe-zulu-mp-to-the-national-council-of-provinces-ncop (accessed 9 October 2021).

Llavaneras Blanco, M. and Cuervo, M.G. (2021), 'The Pandemic as a Portal: Policy Transformations Disputing the New Normal', Discussion Paper No. 32, DAWN. Available at: https://dawnnet.org/wp-content/uploads/2021/04/DAWN-Discussion-Paper-32_The-Pandemic-as-a-Portal.pdf (accessed 9 October 2021).

Mies, M., Bennholdt-Thomsen, V. and Werlhof, C. (1988), *Women: The Last Colony*, London: Zed Books.

Mncube, Z., Zduńczyk, K., Brown, K., Gasela, B., Tyrrell, R.J. and Kimmie, Z. (2020), 'Human Rights Diagnosis: Community Advice Offices and COVID-19', *Foundation for Human Rights*. Available at: https://www.fhr.org.za/2020/09/20/human-rights-diagnosis-community-advice-offices-and-covid-19-snapshot/ (accessed 9 October 2021).

Mosomi, J. (2019), 'Distributional Changes in the Gender Wage Gap in the Post-Apartheid South African Labour Market', WIDER Working Paper 2019/17, United Nations University. Available at: https://www.wider.unu.edu/sites/default/files/Publications/Working-paper/PDF/wp-2019-17.pdf (accessed 9 October 2021).

National Treasury (2021), Minister Tito Mboweni: 2021 Budget Speech. Available at: https://www.gov.za/speeches/minister-tito-mboweni-2021-budget-speech-24-feb-2021-0000 (accessed 9 October 2021).

National Treasury (2022), 'Consideration When Deciding on the Future of the R350 Grant', *GroundUp*. Available at: https://www.groundup.org.za/media/uploads/documents/consideration_when_deciding_on_the_future_of_the_r350_grant_2.pdf (accessed 15 January 2023).

Omarjee, L. (2021), 'Basic Income Grant: Social Development Department Vows to Continue 'Fight' for It', *News24*, 21 October. Available at: https://www.news24.com/fin24/economy/basic-income-grant-social-development-department-vows-to-continue-fight-for-it-20211021 (accessed 10 January 2022).

Ostry, J. and Chamon, M. (2021), 'A Future with High Public Debt: Low-for-Long Is Not Low Forever', *IMF Blog*, 3 January. Available at: https://blogs.imf.org/2021/04/20/a-future-with-high-public-debt-low-for-long-is-not-low-forever/ (accessed 29 November 2021).

Oxfam South Africa (2019), Annual Inequality Reports. Available at: https://www.oxfam.org.za/resources/annual-inequality-reports/ (accessed 29 November 2021).

Patel, L., Knijn, T. and Van Wel, F. (2015), 'Child Support Grants in South Africa: A Pathway to Women's Empowerment and Child Well-being?', *Journal of Social Policy*, 44(2): 377–397. Available at: https://doi.org/10.1017/S0047279414000919 (accessed 9 October 2021).

#PayTheGrants (2020), 'Coalition Statement: President's Inadequate Grant Announcement Is Deeply Anti-Women and Anti-Poor'. Available at: https://c19peoplescoalition.org.za/coalition-statement-presidents-inadequate-grant-announcement-is-deeply-anti-women-and-anti-poor/ (accessed 9 October 2021).

#PayTheGrants (2021), '#PaytheGrants Joint Statement: On SONA and Extension of the SRD R350 Grant'. Available at: https://c19peoplescoalition.org.za/paythegrants-joint-statement-on-sona-extension-of-the-srd-r350-grant/ (accessed 22 January 2024).

Pietermaritzburg Economic Justice & Dignity Group (2021), Household Affordability Index. Available at: https://pmbejd.org.za/wp-content/uploads/2021/10/October-2021-Household-Affordability-Index-PMBEJD_27102021.pdf (accessed 9 October 2021).

SA Department of Justice (1996), The Constitution of the Republic of South Africa. Available at: https://www.justice.gov.za/legislation/constitution/saconstitution-web-eng.pdf (accessed 9 October 2021).

Scalabrini Institute (2020), 'Victory in Covid-19 Social Relief Grant Court Case', Press Release, 19 June. Available at: https://www.scalabrini.org.za/victory-in-covid19-social-relief-grant-court-case/ (accessed 29 November 2021).

Schulz, P. (2017), 'Universal Basic Income in a Feminist Perspective and Gender Analysis', *Global Social Policy*, 17(1): 89–92. Available at: https://doi.org/10.1177/1468018116686503 (accessed 29 November 2021).

Sibeko, B. (2019), 'The Cost of Austerity: Lessons For South Africa', Institute for Economic Justice Working Paper Series, No. 2. Available at: https://iej.org.za/wp-content/uploads/2020/02/The-cost-austerity-lessons-for-South-Africa-IEJ-30-10-2019.pdf (accessed 9 October 2021).

Sibeko, B. (2021), 'South Africa Needs Feminist Economics, Now', *New Frame*, 29 June. Available at: https://allafrica.com/stories/202107020873.html (accessed 9 October 2021).

Sibeko, B. and Isaacs, G. (2020), 'A Fiscal Stimulus for South Africa', Institute for Economic Justice Working Paper Series, No. 3. Available at: https://iej.org.za/wp-content/uploads/2020/08/A-fiscal-stimulus-for-South-Africa-Final-IEJ.pdf (accessed 9 October 2021).

Sibeko, B., Phalatse, S. and Ossome, L. (2021), 'Feminist Proposals on Macroeconomic Policies needed for a COVID-19 Economic Recovery', Nawi-Femnet. Available at: https://www.iej.org.za/wp-content/uploads/2021/07/FeministMacroeconomicPolicies-Briefing.pdf (accessed 29 November 2021).

Sonjica, N. (2021), 'R350 Social Relief Grant Mired in Challenges Despite its Benefits, Says Black Sash', *Sowetan Live*, 27 July. Available at: https://www.sowetanlive.co.za/

news/south-africa/2021-07-27-r350-social-relief-grant-mired-in-challenges-despite-its-benefits-says-black-sash/ (accessed 29 November 2021).

South African Government (2012), National Development Plan 2030. Available at: https://www.gov.za/issues/national-development-plan-2030 (accessed 9 October 2021).

South African Government (2020), 'SASSA on Coronavirus Covid-19 Social Relief of Distress Grant Rejection Rates'. Available at: https://www.gov.za/news/media-statements/sassa-coronavirus-covid-19-social-relief-distress-grant-rejection-rates-30 (accessed 5 January 2024).

South African Government (2022), 'Social Development Updates Portfolio Committee on the New CSG Top Grant'. Available at: https://www.gov.za/news/media-statements/social-development-updates-portfolio-committee-new-csg-top-grant-24-aug-2022 (accessed 9 January 2024).

Spaul, N. et al. (2021), 'Synthesis Report, NIDS-CRAM Wave 5'. Available at: https://cramsurvey.org/wp-content/uploads/2021/07/1.-Spaull-N.-Daniels-R.-C-et-al.-2021-NIDS-CRAM-Wave-5-Synthesis-Report.pdf (accessed 9 October 2021).

Stats SA (2017), 'Poverty Trends in South Africa: An Examination of Absolute Poverty between 2006 and 2015', No. 03–10–06. Available at: https://www.statssa.gov.za/publications/Report-03-10-06/Report-03-10-062015.pdf (accessed 9 October 2021).

Stats SA (2019), 'Quarterly Labour Force Survey, Quarter 4'. Available at: https://www.statssa.gov.za/publications/P0211/P02114thQuarter2019.pdf (accessed 5 January 2024).

Stats SA (2020), 'How Unequal is South Africa?'. Available at: http://www.statssa.gov.za/?p=12930 (accessed 9 October 2021).

Stats SA (2021), 'Quarterly Labour Force Survey, Quarter 3'. Available at: https://www.statssa.gov.za/publications/P0211/P02113rdQuarter2021.pdf (accessed 5 January 2024).

Stent, J. (2020), 'Shocking Study Reveals 15% of SA's Wealth is in Hands of Only 3,500 people', *IOL*, 12 March. Available at: https://www.iol.co.za/news/south-africa/shocking-study-reveals-15-of-sas-wealth-is-in-hands-of-only-3-500-people-44622062 (accessed 9 October 2021).

Sulla, V. (2020), 'Poverty & Equity Brief: South Afirica', World Bank. Available at: https://databank.worldbank.org/data/download/poverty/33EF03BB-9722-4AE2-ABC7-AA2972D68AFE/Global_POVEQ_ZAF.pdf (accessed 9 October 2021).

Taylor, V., Makiwane, F. and Masilela, E. (2020), *Transforming the Present – Protecting the Future: Consolidated Report*, Northwestern University. Available at: http://books.google.com/books?id=jPg5AQAAMAAJ (accessed 9 October 2021).

UNCTAD (2019), 'Trade and Development Report: Financing a Global Green New Deal'. Available at: https://unctad.org/en/PublicationChapters/tdr2019ch3_en.pdf (accessed 9 October 2021).

Visagie, J. and Turok, I. (2020), 'The Uneven Geography of the COVID-19 Crisis (Wave 2). National Income Dynamics Study (NIDS) – Coronavirus Rapid Mobile Survey

(CRAM)'. Available at: https://cramsurvey.org/wp-content/uploads/2020/09/14.-Visagie-J.-_-Turok-I.-2020-The-uneven-geography-of-the-COVID-19-crisis.pdf (accessed 9 October 2021).

Westphal, T. (2016), 'South Africa: Extending Social Protection to Children', ILO Social Protection Department. Available at: https://www.social-protection.org/gimi/ShowRessource.action;jsessionid=rDv64jMWrf_OkfRcXH8YtxewqNe_UMF1VYbzxcSLKQgR5F6PGWWn!-491661851?id=53472 (accessed 9 October 2021).

Williams L. (2021), 'Universal Basic Income: Potential and Limitations from a Gender Perspective', Policy Brief No. 22, UN Women. Available at: https://www.unwomen.org/en/digital-library/publications/2021/04/policy-brief-universal-basic-income (accessed 9 October 2021).

Wren-Lewis, S. (2015), 'Defining Austerity. Mainly Macro'. Retrieved from: https://mainlymacro.blogspot.com/2015/12/defining-austerity.html (accessed 9 October 2021).

Zeeman, K. (2021), 'More than 5-Million New People Applied for the R350 Grant this Time Around', *TimesLive*, 10 September. Available at: https://www.timeslive.co.za/news/south-africa/2021-09-10-more-than-5-million-new-people-applied-for-the-r350-grant-this-time-around/ (accessed 9 October 2021).

7

Barbados: Pandemic, Economic Restructuring and the Social Organization of Care

Daniele Bobb and Leigh-Ann Worrell

1. Introduction

Worldwide, care work, whether paid or unpaid, was pivotal to the survival of economies during the Covid-19 pandemic. In Barbados, too, social reproduction played a crucial role in the country's policy response as it grappled with the socioeconomic fallouts of the global health crisis while attempting to sustain the livelihoods of those affected. What complicated matters was that the island nation, at the time, was also navigating an economic restructuring programme led by the International Monetary Fund (IMF).

Known as the Barbados Economic and Transformation (BERT) Plan, the programme was introduced in 2018 under the auspices of the IMF's Extended Fund Facility (EFF). It was aimed at addressing the country's external debt problem, characterized by a precarious balance of payments, while protecting the social sector. In its design, the BERT Plan sought to align the government's anti-poverty and sectoral strategies with the United Nations' Sustainable Development Goals (SDGs). As such, it focused on strengthening social safety nets by increasing the minimum wage rate and expanding its coverage, among other things, while simultaneously bringing down external debt (CDB 2018).

What is remarkable in this context is how Barbados prioritized care and social spending in the face of austerity. This chapter examines this prioritization from a Caribbean feminist lens by analysing two policies, namely the Adopt Our Families Programme (earlier called the Adopt A Family Programme or AAFP) and the increase in and expansion of the minimum wage, implemented during the first two years of Covid-19. At first glance, these policy responses appear to be, and indeed were, bold and crucial. However, an exhaustive scrutiny of their fine print also lead us to conclude that they reproduced existing issues with the social organization of care and missed opportunities in the path of transforming the way care labour is distributed among households, communities, the market and the Barbadian state.

Fraga and Rodríguez Enríquez (this volume) define the social organization of care as the way care needs are met by interactions between households, the state, the market and community organizations. They argue that for care to be just, it should be of good quality and offer universal coverage (ibid.). In other words, how care is organized becomes important in mapping inequalities across various contexts. For care to evolve as a socioeconomic process that involves diverse actors and unfolds in a transformative and feminist manner, two factors are critical: care labour must be redistributed in ways that reduce the burden of unpaid labour on women, especially those living in poverty, and care services must be made easily accessible. Specifically in the case of Barbados, the question then arises: how does a government usher in a transformative social organization of care while navigating fiscal austerity and a pandemic?

In this context, it is worth noting that Barbados Prime Minister Mia Mottley has increasingly become an international representative of small island developing states (SIDS) in global negotiations linked to development finance. Her first speech at the 2018 United Nations General Assembly (UNGA) meeting addressed the inequities in an international financial order designed to serve the interests of the industrialized countries of the global North. It was an outspoken challenge to member states on behalf of the SIDS. Mottley has since articulated these themes at the Climate Conferences (COP26, '27 and '28) and the UN Conference on Trade and Development (UNCTAD). Specifically, she has called for reform of the Bretton Woods institutions and a new international economic order, echoing similar calls from the G-77 countries in the 1970s. She has leveraged the climate crisis to argue for special clauses in debt finance that account for climate uncertainties and has asserted that countries like Barbados that are at risk of climate catastrophes should be granted access to concessionary finance.

We argue that while Mottley's approach to the country's macroeconomic issues has been path breaking, with the potential for transformative change, it has not necessarily been feminist. On the one hand, care was a central component of her government's pandemic response policies, which advocated for inclusive social security and accounted for the needs of vulnerable groups. On the other hand, her government's approach to care lacked sustained institutional support; it was restricted to providing monetary assistance to households confronting pandemic-related job losses and an increased burden of unpaid domestic care work primarily done by women. There was no child care policy during the Covid-19 lockdown period, and the institutional support offered by the Child Care Board was limited. Elder care was also limited during this period. In addition, state agencies prohibited children from being at workplaces in an effort to protect them from the virus. These policy responses illustrate how a siloed understanding of care could potentially reproduce gendered and class-based inequalities.

Using Barbados as a case study, this chapter analyses the interlinkages between macroeconomic and care policies as well as the power relations that inform and implement such policies through the lens of Caribbean feminist theory (Wilson et al. 2019). It uses an intersectional lens to examine the impacts of such policies on livelihoods and the social organization of care. In particular, the chapter interrogates the gendered impacts of two key policies, namely the AAFP and the increase in and expansion of the minimum wage, implemented at a time when the island nation was battling the socioeconomic impacts of Covid-19. Additionally, it undertakes a multivariate analysis to account for how intersectionality plays out in lives at the margins, allowing us to evaluate the impact and future potential of these policies.

This case study is based on primary and secondary data such as government press releases, IMF documents, statements delivered by ministers of state and newspaper reports. An interview with a social protection/poverty alleviation specialist working with the AAFP provides further insights. The chapter utilizes feminist discourse analysis, which allows us to assess the language of the policies being studied as well as the underlying assumptions and ideologies that guide policy development in Barbados.

2. The Barbados economy: A brief backdrop

The Caribbean region shares a colonial history of enslavement and resource extraction by imperial countries that left it with limited policy autonomy, a heavy reliance on international loans and high levels of external debt. This structural dependency was further exacerbated by natural disasters, global economic recessions and infrastructural needs.

Barbados is the most easterly of the Caribbean islands in the Lesser Antilles of the West Indies and is home to 287,724 people. It is a high-income service economy that depends primarily on tourism, which contributes 17 per cent of its gross domestic product (GDP) (World Bank 2021). Like most SIDS, the country has significant exposure to and remains vulnerable to climate change, specifically changes in weather patterns, a rise in sea levels and an increase in atmospheric pressure (CDB 2018).[1]

2.1 Why Barbados needed the BERT Plan

Barbados' main economic sectors, which include financial services and construction in addition to tourism, were negatively affected by the 2008–09 global financial crisis, culminating in an economic recession in 2018. Public debt ballooned from over 55 per cent of GDP in 2008 to 158 per cent in 2017, leading to a slowdown in economic growth and prompting downgrades in credit ratings (World Bank 2021).

In 2018, Barbados' debt-to-GDP ratio stood at 175 per cent (Deutsche Welle 2018), the fourth highest in the world, resulting in higher taxes and layoffs. By the end of that year, real output declined by 0.6 per cent due to a confluence of local and external shocks (Ministry of Economic Affairs and Investment 2018). In October of the same year, the country embarked on the BERT Plan. This IMF-led debt restructuring programme aimed to align the government's anti-poverty and sectoral strategies with the SDGs, particularly in the areas of fiscal policy; increased social protection access and higher social spending floors; improved financial innovation, regulation and inclusion; and climate-resilient, carbon-neutral and marine-conscious public and private investment for growth (CDB 2018).

These adjustments were intended to be transformative. The BERT Plan incorporated several initiatives meant to strengthen social safety nets in the face of impending austerity. These included a 5 per cent wage increase for public servants, an increase in the minimum non-contributory pension from 155 Barbados dollars (BBD$) (US$77.50) to BBD$225 (US$112.50) per week (Nation News 2018), and a temporary increase in the funding for welfare and poverty alleviation programmes to the tune of BBD$5 million (US$2.5 million). However, as the onset of the pandemic in early 2020 led to salary cuts and job losses, citizens felt the pressure of higher taxes on utilities such as water and fuel, which were meant to increase fiscal revenue.

2.2 End of the BERT Plan and the rebuilding stage

While the first iteration of the BERT Plan ended in September 2022, the Barbados government extended its loan for another thirty-six months, borrowing an additional BBD\$227 million (US\$113 million) under the IMF's EFF programme. Prime Minister Mottley's administration also received access to the IMF's new Resilience and Sustainability Fund (RSF) to the tune of BBD\$380 million (US\$189 million). Another US\$100-million loan (approximately BBD\$201 million) was secured from the World Bank to support Barbados' climate resilience efforts (World Bank 2023). The prime minister stated that these measures would protect Barbadians from the effects of climate change and create opportunities for green and blue jobs and investments (ibid.).

However, the government did not incorporate a gender lens into its plans to 'build back better'. In fact, the language of its build back policies can be described as masculinist, as the focus was on integrating men into the workforce through the creation and expansion of jobs in male-dominated fields, such as construction and capital projects,[2] with no mention of the social organization of care and women's care work.

2.3 The social care policy landscape

This is not to say that attention to social care and protection is absent from Barbados' policy landscape in general. On the contrary, given the colonial legacies and constrained macroeconomic context, it is significant that Barbados is one of the few Caribbean countries to invest heavily in social policy, offering free tertiary education, public health care services, low-cost public day care services and a National Insurance Scheme (NIS). Like other newly independent countries in the Caribbean, Barbados experimented with a blend of social welfare policies in the 1960s and 1970s as it sought to develop a sense of what it would take to create a new and free nation. These policies included state investments in health care, national insurance and education. The NIS was created in 1967 as a way for Barbadians to receive pensions, sickness benefits and maternity cover.[3] These policies, some of which continue to this day, proved instrumental in expanding the social welfare functions of the postcolonial state and creating a new Black middle class (Barriteau 1996).

According to the UN Research Institute for Social Development (UNRISD), transformative policies should 'fundamentally change social institutions and relations to make them more inclusive and equitable, and [. . .] redistribute power and economic resources' (2017: 1). Overall, the Barbados government's demonstrated commitment to social care and protection points to a willingness to move towards progressive, even if not feminist, policies as opposed to simply maintaining the status quo.

3. Covid-19 social care and protection policies: Transformative or status quo?

During the lockdown period of the Covid-19 pandemic, several social responses were rolled out by the state. Such policies include the distribution of food hampers among targeted communities, a 40 per cent increase in welfare payments and cash transfer programmes such as the AAFP, which saw approximately 5,000 households receive assistance (Barbados Today 2021).

3.1 Adopt Our Families Programme: Benefitting women but leaving care burdens unchanged

The AAFP in particular was funded through a combination of public funds and donations from families earning over BBD$100,000 (US$50,000) annually who were encouraged to 'adopt a vulnerable family' (ECLAC n.d.). It was introduced by the Barbados government in April 2020 to provide a monthly monetary transfer of BBD$600 (US$300) to families with members who had lost jobs during the pandemic (Joseph 2020).

At its onset, the AAFP was meant to serve 1,500 families made vulnerable by Covid-19, but that number ballooned to 5,000 by April 2021 (Austin 2021) following an application and subsequent assessment process. In order to be eligible for assistance under the AAFP, households had to meet at least one of the following two criteria: i) they had to be ineligible for other forms of financial assistance such as national insurance, and/or ii) they had to be registered with the Household Mitigation Unit (HMU). The HMU was created by the government to support people who had lost their public sector jobs in the 2018 and 2019 retrenchments associated with the IMF restructuring. Of the 1,500 workers who lost their jobs under the retrenchment component of the BERT Plan, around 1,100 were women, mostly in administrative support roles. Sixty-two per cent of these women were their families' breadwinners.

More women, especially those who were household heads, received assistance under the AAFP than men.[4] This makes sense in light of a 2020 survey that found that women were three times as likely as men (8.2 per cent women versus 2.7 per cent men) to indicate that they were unemployed and not seeking work because they were 'keeping the house'[5] (Statistical Service Labour Force Survey 2020).

While the AAFP was scaled down in June 2021 and halted thereafter, it lasted well past its initial cut-off date of 31 March 2021 (Joseph 2020, Jones 2021).[6] It is promising that a care policy like the AAFP was prominent in Barbados' pandemic response and that it was implemented at a time when the country was experiencing financial shocks as a result of the global health crisis and a structural adjustment programme. It was a progressive initiative in that it prioritized social spending and attended to those who had become jobless as a result of the pandemic. Through the programme, the government injected resources into the social organization of care by way of cash transfers funded by the state and private donations.

However, a serious shortcoming of the policy was that its design and implementation did not alter the distribution of care responsibilities in ways that would reduce the burden borne by households. As such, the AAFP was a missed opportunity to increase public service provisions and foster a more fair and equitable social organization of care. Even as most beneficiaries of the AAFP were women, their centrality reaffirmed the existing sexual division of labour in which women are deemed the main providers of care. This gendered and familialist social organization of care remained unchanged under the policy.

3.2 The minimum wage policy: Increase and expansion in a time of crisis

Minimum wage is the lowest legally permissible wage in a country. Often, an increase in the minimum wage is seen as a means to reduce poverty. According to the Barbados Survey of Living Conditions, the poverty line in Barbados in 2016 was BBD$636.17 (US$318) per person per month, which is approximately BBD$160 (US$80) per person per week (Beuermann et al. 2018). In the same year, the minimum wage stood at BBD$6.26 (US$3.13) per hour, or BBD$250.40 (US$125.20) for a forty-hour week. This rate remained unchanged in the subsequent years, despite an almost 55 per cent increase in prices in the country.

It changed only in March 2020, a year after Minister of Labour Colin Jordan announced plans to implement a nationwide increase in the minimum wage[7] and bring more categories of workers, including gas station attendants and clerks, under its fold (Barbados Today 2019). This was a positive shift given that historically only certain categories of workers, such as shop assistants, domestic workers and agricultural workers, were covered by the minimum wage legislation in Barbados (Downes 2008). After a series of discussions with the social partnership – a tripartite group comprising the government, labour unions and the private sector – Barbados' new minimum wage of BBD$8.50 (US$4.25) per hour took effect on 1 April 2021 (The Barbados Advocate 2021). However, the minimum wage remained below the inflated living wage of BBD$12 (US$6) per hour (Barbados Underground 2021).

Care work is essential to sustaining our societies, even though it continues to be invisibilized, done primarily by women and devalued. While paid care work continues to be grossly underpaid, the pandemic showed that this work is both hazardous and requires unique skills. The increase in and expanded coverage of the minimum wage recognized precisely these gaps in existing care policies and sought to usher in transformative change by acknowledging and accounting for care workers among the lowest-paid workers in the country.

The private sector in Barbados, however, did not perceive the timing of the new minimum wage policy to be financially 'right'. This even as companies benefitted from a reduction in corporate tax rates in 2019–20 following the recession. Private actors voiced concerns about the policy being implemented at a time when the tourism industry faced the onslaught of the Covid-19 pandemic and asked for a delay until 2022.

Amid such pressure from the private sector, the government's decision to increase the minimum wage was a bold one and also crucial given the increase in the number of people living in poverty. It especially benefitted workers in the retail sector, those working in gas stations and domestic workers, some of whom were included under the fold of the minimum wage for the first time. This initiative was transformative not only due to its timing (during the pandemic), but also because, as Prime Minister Mottley noted, 'the last minimum payment for shop assistants was introduced almost a decade or more ago, in a world that has seen price increases of more than 40 per cent' (Caribbean National Weekly 2021). Her statement marked an official recognition that wages are not commensurate with living costs and reflected the government's interest in improving the quality of life of those in the lower-wage categories. At the same time, Mottley noted that 'history has shown that those benefitting [from the increase in minimum wage] contributed more to the economic activity in the country' (ibid.), suggesting that the initiative was driven by economic reasons.

Most people who earn the minimum wage in Barbados are women between the ages of twenty and forty-nine. The types of jobs that are associated with the minimum wage, such as shop assistants and domestic workers, are also primarily done by women. Raising the general minimum wage, therefore, especially benefitted low-wage women workers, who are also the primary supporters of their families. Conversely, it made women workers vulnerable to layoffs and reduced working hours as workplaces navigated the cost of the higher minimum wage for their businesses. That said, given that women head most single-parent households, a higher minimum wage can, in the long run, have a welfare-positive and economically stimulative ripple effect on families and communities, despite the associated risk of layoffs (UNDP, UNICEF and UN Women 2020).[8]

A feminist challenge in this regard was that even as wages increased, the gender gaps between highly feminized and highly masculinized jobs stayed intact. While the Barbados government increased the minimum wage and expanded its coverage, it did not address the gender wage gap. A comparison between the national minimum wage rate and wages in a male-dominated job, such as security services, exemplifies this point. Table 7.1 details the minimum hourly, weekly, monthly and overtime rates (on ordinary days and public holidays) for contract workers in general, while Table 7.2 details the hourly, weekly, monthly and overtime rates of minimum pay (on ordinary days and public holidays) for security guards in particular. A comparison between the figures in the two tables shows that as the overall minimum wage was raised, the wages of security guards increased proportionately. The gender wage gap was reproduced as men working in security services in Barbados already earned 7 per cent more than women.[9] The government's lack of attention to the gender wage gap is especially concerning given that closing this gap was a stated goal of the ruling party.[10] We believe that the Barbados social security system can cushion the potential socioeconomic fallout of reducing this gender gap through the Reverse Tax Credit (RTC). This initiative provides a tax credit to employed persons who earn less than BBD$25,000 (US$12,400) per annum (Government of Barbados 2019) and would particularly benefit women who are disproportionally represented in lower-wage jobs.

Table 7.1 General Minimum Wage Rates in Barbados, 2021

Minimum wage rates	National minimum pay rate
The minimum rate of wages payable weekly for forty hours of work	US$170 (BBD$340) per week
The minimum rate of wages payable daily for an eight-hour workday, where an employee is not employed on a weekly basis	US$34 (BBD$68) per day
The minimum rate of wages payable hourly where an employee is not employed on a weekly or daily basis	US$4.35 (BBD$8.50) per hour
Minimum overtime rates	
The minimum overtime rate of wages payable for ordinary working days	US$6.37 (BBD$12.75) per hour or part thereof
The minimum overtime rate of wages for public holidays	US$8.50 (BBD$17) per hour or part thereof

Source: Compiled by authors using information from the Government of Barbados Ministry of Labour, 2021. See https://gisbarbados.gov.bb/download/minimum-wage-national-and-sectoral-minimum-wage-order-2021/.

Table 7.2 Sectoral Minimum Rate of Pay for Barbadian Security Guards, 2021

Minimum wage rates	National minimum pay rate
The minimum rate of wages payable weekly for forty hours of work	US$185 (BBD$370) per week
The minimum rate of wages payable daily for an eight-hour workday where a security guard is not employed on a weekly basis	US$37 (BBD$74) per day
The minimum rate of wages payable hourly where a security guard is not employed on a weekly or daily basis	US$4.63 (BBD$9.25) per hour
Minimum overtime rates	
The minimum overtime rate of wages payable for ordinary working days	US$6.94 (BBD$13.88) per hour or part thereof
The minimum overtime rate of wages for public holidays	US$9.25 (BBD$18.50) per hour or part thereof

Source: Compiled by authors using information from the Government of Barbados Ministry of Labour, 2021. See: https://gisbarbados.gov.bb/download/minimum-wage-national-and-sectoral-minimum-wage-order-2021/.

Another shortcoming of the increase in the minimum wage was that it did not address the rising unemployment rate. This, too, had a disproportionate impact on women, with 47.2 per cent of Barbadian women reporting losing their jobs versus 38.1 per cent men (Garavito et al. 2020).

Even though the higher minimum wage benefitted many women workers, it did not account for the complex ways in which gender shapes the distribution of paid and unpaid labour, and its monetary implications. The increase in the minimum wage during the pandemic recognized the socioeconomic vulnerability of some workers but did not ask pertinent questions around gender. It did not examine, for instance, why certain jobs are devalued and why women dominate those spaces, thereby reproducing these gendered inequalities. Such questions would have shed light on the fact that women have a higher unemployment rate, meaning that many do not benefit from an increase in the minimum wage and there is no 'feed through effect to the salaries of other workers' (Moore et al. 2009: 27). In fact, an increase in the minimum wage can reduce the hours and weeks worked and lead to unemployment and underemployment (ibid.).

4. Conclusion

This chapter assessed Barbados' policy changes during the pandemic and the impacts on care systems and livelihoods. Through an analysis of the AAFP and the policy to increase and expand the minimum wage, we proposed that gender was not positioned as pivotal in the formulation of pandemic policies and programmes, leading to limitations associated with reach, effectiveness, efficiency and access. Going forward, a gender analysis should inform and orient public policy development in order to strengthen public services such as day care centres for working-class mothers and a universal basic income.

While the AAFP and the policy to increase and expand the minimum wage were compatible with a 'universal and human rights-based approach', offered 'a new take on policy integration' and led to 'the empowered participation of all social actors in the decision-making processes', (UNRISD 2017:1), the social and environmental objectives of the policies were not put ahead of economic ones. The policies were driven primarily by economic imperatives as they sought to ensure the circulation of money within the economy via monetary transfers without fully addressing intersectional inequalities associated with care provision and labour valuation.

Furthermore, although the policies had some degree of transformational potential, they simultaneously reproduced inequalities among vulnerable groups, offering only micro-level and short-term gains for the benefit of the larger economy. While some programmes targeted vulnerable groups, they did so in a general sense (poor households, elderly, etc.) and did not specifically account for vulnerabilities associated with gender, sexual orientation and age (in the case of children). Thus, while they attempted to usher in social and economic gains to create transformation, these policies were insufficient to correct the imbalances in the social relations of gender. In fact, the AAFP and the minimum wage increase were one-off temporary measures rather than sustainable long-term initiatives. They were propelled by the ultimate goal of economic and fiscal growth. A transformative addition to these policies could be a basic universal care wage for unpaid care work and public investment in child care services. These could greatly improve the economic and social position of women, especially those who have been excluded from the labour force.

Following the UNRISD (2017), which calls for a focus on enhanced policy integration, we argue that the policy shortfalls identified in Barbados could be addressed, at least in part, by incorporating a gendered and intersectional analysis of all intended and ongoing programmes in order to arrive at policy responses that are truly transformative and feminist and that expand democracy and social justice (Llavaneras Blanco and Cuervo 2021).

Finally, we believe that a key indicator of the government's commitment to gender equality would be to inject human and financial resources into national gender institutions. The Bureau of Gender Affairs could play a central role in organizing inter-agency coordination on care leave policies, gender-equitable responses to socioeconomic crises and 'build back' initiatives. For decades, those in charge of mainstreaming gender in state policy making have not been given the human, technical and financial resources they need to carry out their work effectively. The need to close this critical gap is now more urgent and necessary than ever in order to avoid missing new opportunities to incorporate a feminist lens into Barbados' policy transformation.

Notes

1 The country faced significant damage due to La Soufrière's explosive volcanic eruption in April 2021 and Hurricane Elsa in July 2021.
2 There is a direct emphasis on training 'boys on the block' in order to address the increased crime rate.
3 See more at: https://www.nis.gov.bb/about-us/.
4 Based on an August 2021 interview with a social protection/poverty alleviation specialist working with the AAFP.
5 A Barbadian expression which means taking care of domestic duties required to maintain the household.
6 Following the end of the AAFP, the Ministry of People Empowerment and Elder Affairs, in June 2022, announced plans for the 1000 Families Programme, which would operate similarly to the AAFP. According to Minister Kirk Humphrey, the 1000 Families Programme seeks to specifically target the 'poorest of the poor' through both financial and non-financial support mechanisms such as educational support, counselling and cash transfers. Much like the AAFP, the government relied on donations from charities, ordinary citizens and corporations to co-fund the venture (Caribbean Broadcasting Company 2022).
7 See more at: https://www.minimum-wage.org/international/barbados.
8 There are simultaneous concerns about the growing inflation rate in the country. See: https://barbadostoday.bb/2022/12/03/soaring-prices/.
9 See here: https://www.salaryexplorer.com/average-salary-wage-comparison-barbados-c19.
10 See page 25 of the Barbados Labour Party Manifesto here: http://acuteinnovation.com/BLP/2018Manifesto/.

References

Austin, S. (2021), 'Adopt Our Families Extended But No New Beneficiaries', *Barbados Government Information Service*, 20 April. Available at: https://gisbarbados.gov.bb/blog/adopt-our-families-extended-but-no-new-beneficiaries/ (accessed 19 November 2023).

Barbados Today (2019), 'Minimum Wage Law 'on the Table', 2 May. Available at: https://barbadostoday.bb/2019/05/02/minimum-wage-law-on-the-table/ (accessed 6 December 2023).

Barbados Today (2021), 'Review and Re-Register of Adopt Our Families Programme', 26 June. Available at: https://barbadostoday.bb/2021/06/26/review-and-re-register-of-adopt-our-families-programme/ (accessed 6 December 2023).

Barbados Underground (2021), 'Increase in National Minimum Wage, after 9 Years', 1 April. Available at: https://barbadosunderground.net/2021/04/01/increase-in-national-minimum-wage-after-9-years/ (accessed 21 November 2021).

Barriteau, E. V., (1996), 'Structural Adjustment Policies in the Caribbean: A Feminist Perspective', *NWSA Journal*, 8(1): 142–156.. Available at: https://www.jstor.org/stable/4316428 (accessed 21 November 2023).

Beuermann, D., Flores Cruz, R. And Barbados Statistical Service (2018), 'Barbados Survey of Living Conditions: 2016', Inter-American Development Bank. Available at: https://publications.iadb.org/en/barbados-survey-living-conditions-2016 (accessed 6 December 2023).

Caribbean Broadcasting Company (2022), 'Minister Humphrey Clears the Air on Social Programme Targeting 1000 Families', 15 June [video]. Available at: https://www.youtube.com/watch?v=l0W1lRjdvGE (accessed 9 January 2024).

Caribbean National Weekly (2021), 'Barbados Minimum Wage Take Effect,' 2 April. Available at: https://www.caribbeannationalweekly.com/caribbean-breaking-news-featured/barbados-new-minimum-wage-takes-effect/ (accessed November 21, 2021).

CDB (2018), 'Country Economic Review Barbados'. Available at: https://www.caribank.org/publications-and-resources/resource-library/economic-reviews/country-economic-review-2018-barbados (accessed 21 November 2021).

Deutsche Welle (2018), 'Drowning in Debt – Barbados' Predicament Offers a Warning for Small Island Nations', 15 June. Available at: https://www.dw.com/en/drowning-in-debt-barbados-predicament-offers-a-warning-for-small-island-nations/a-44245771 (accessed 21 November 2023).

Downes, A. (2008), *The Impact of a Minimum Wage Policy on the Economy of Barbados*. Bridgetown: SALISES, The UWI.

ECLAC (n.d.), 'Initiatives Offered that Assisted Women During Covid 19 in Barbados', United Nations Economic Commission for Latin America and the Caribbean. Available at: https://www.cepal.org/sites/default/files/document/files/uneclac_observatory.pdf (accessed 19 November 2023).

Garavito, Maricruz A, Diether B, and Laura G. (2020), 'COVID-19: The Caribbean Crisis: Results from an Online Socioeconomic Survey', Inter-American Development Bank. Available at: https://publications.iadb.org/en/covid-19-the-caribbean-crisis-results-from-an-online-socioeconomic-survey (accessed 21 November 2021).

Government of Barbados (2019), Budgetary Proposals and Financial Statement 2019. Available at: https://www.barbadosparliament.com/uploads/document/9490e69647396a5d559bf968c298daab.pdf (accessed 9 January 2024).

Government of Barbados Ministry of Labour (2021), Minimum Wage (National and Sectoral Minimum Wage) Order, 2021. Available at: https://gisbarbados.gov.bb/download/minimum-wage-national-and-sectoral-minimum-wage-order-2021/ (accessed 6 December 2023).

Jones, L. (2021), 'Adopt-A-Family Programme Scaling Back', *Caribbean Broadcasting Corporation*, 27 June. Available at: https://www.cbc.bb/news/local-news/adopt-a-family-programme-scaling-back/ (accessed 6 December 2023).

Joseph, E. (2020), 'Government Adopt-A-Family Scheme to Continue until March', *Barbados Today*, 18 November. Available at: https://barbadostoday.bb/2020/11/18/government-adopt-a-family-scheme-to-continue-until-march/ (accessed 19 November 2023).

Llavaneras Blanco, M. and Cuervo, M.G. (2021), 'The Pandemic as a Portal: Policy Transformations Disputing the New Normal', DAWN Discussion Paper No. 32. Available at: https://dawnnet.org/wp-content/uploads/2021/04/DAWN-Discussion-Paper-32_The-Pandemic-as-a-Portal.pdf (accessed 24 August 2021).

Ministry of Economic Affairs and Investment (2018), 'Barbados Economic and Social Report 2018'. Available at: https://www.barbadosparliament.com/uploads/sittings/attachments/5b5ae68fb3456dec74db1d5ed1973d3d.pdf (accessed 8 January 2024).

Moore, W., Browne, R. and Thompson, S. (2009), 'The Potential Impact of a Minimum Wage on Poverty and Income Distribution in Barbados', *Journal of Eastern Caribbean Studies*, 34(1): 19–40. Available at: https://www.semanticscholar.org/paper/The-Potential-Impact-of-a-Minimum-Wage-on-Poverty-Moore-Browne/669373f04345ed8036fe4685ff1bf85fabea342c (accessed 21 November 2023).

Nation News (2018), 'BLP Clarifies Pension Promise', 6 May. Available at: https://www.nationnews.com/2018/05/06/blp-clarifies-pension-promise/ (accessed 6 December 2023).

Sevilla, A. and S. Smith, (2020), 'Baby Steps: The Gender Division of Childcare During the COVID-19 Pandemic', *Oxford Review of Economic Policy*, 36(1): 169–186. Available at: https://doi.org/10.1093/oxrep/graa027 (accessed 21 November 2023).

Statistical Service Labour Force Survey (2020), 'Statistical Bulletin: Continuous Household Labour Force Survey: 4th Quarter 2020'. Available at: https://stats.gov.bb/wp-content/uploads/2021/03/LFS_Bulletin_4Q2020.pdf (accessed 21 November 2023).

The Barbados Advocate (2021), 'Caddle: Right Time for Hike in Minimum Wage', 24 March. Available at: https://www.barbadosadvocate.com/news/caddle-right-time-hike-minimum-wage (accessed 28 August 2021).

UNDP, UNICEF and UN Women (2020), 'Barbados: Covid-19 Heat Report Human and Economic Assessment Of Impact'. Available at: https://www.undp.org/sites/g/files/zskgke326/files/migration/bb/3b9b3aaf77b8e1f3459c2636abf0eaaa53c1566181a3777cf2717b1ef1c137e1.pdf (accessed 23 November 2023).

UNRISD (2017), 'Transformative Policies for Sustainable Development: What Does It Take?', Research and Policy Brief 23: 1–2. Available at: https://cdn.unrisd.org/assets/library/briefs/pdf-files/rpb23-transformative-policies-flagship2016.pdf (accessed 20 November 2021).

Wilson, S., Nakhid, C., Fernandez-Santana, A. and Nakhid-Chatoor, M. (2019), 'An Interrogation of Research on Caribbean Social Issues: Establishing the Need for an Indigenous Caribbean Research Approach', *AlterNative: An International Journal of Indigenous Peoples*, 15(1): 3–12. Available at: https://doi.org/10.1177/1177180118803692 (accessed 23 November 2023).

World Bank (2021), 'Latin American and the Caribbean. Macro Poverty Outlook: Country-by-country Analysis and Projections for the Developing World. Annual Meetings, Report'. Available at: https://thedocs.worldbank.org/en/doc/77351105a334213c64122e44c2efe523-0500072021/related/mpo-am20-lac.pdf (accessed 21 November 2023).

World Bank (2023), 'World Bank Approves US$100 Million for Barbados' Green and Resilient Recovery', World Bank Press Release, 11 January. Available at: https://www.worldbank.org/en/news/press-release/2023/01/11/world-bank-approves-us-100-million-for-barbados-green-and-resilient-recovery (accessed 21 November 2023).

8

Conditional Cash Transfer Programmes in Bolivia during the Covid-19 Crisis: A Thwarted Redistributive Potential

Silvia Amparo Fernández Cervantes

1. Introduction

The Covid-19 pandemic arrived in Bolivia during a year of severe political crisis. In November 2019, the country faced a coup d'état that resulted in an authoritarian transitional government that lasted almost a year, followed by the eventual return to power of the Movement Towards Socialism (MAS) government, which has been in power for the last fourteen years. In the first year of the pandemic, these two successive governments implemented four emergency Conditional Cash Transfer Programmes (CCTPs), each provided on a one-off basis. CCTPs, by their very definition, involve a cash transfer from the state to recipients who meet certain conditions and maintain them over a period of time (McGuire 2013). The latest emergency programmes shared the characteristics and structures of past CCTPs in that they corrected the so-called distributive market failures by supporting consumption via monetary transfers but did not address income inequality or improve livelihoods. The one characteristic that set the pandemic CCTPs apart was their aspiration for universality, meaning that the cash transfers were distributed across all sections of the population regardless of differences in income.

This chapter uses a feminist economics framework and an intersectional lens to study the CCTPs implemented in Bolivia during the first year of the pandemic.[1] It argues that the two consecutive governments in charge of responding to the crisis implemented policies that were stagnant and an extension of pre-existing trajectories. These policies essentially reproduced the patriarchal, classist and racist economic and political structures that are legacies of Bolivia's colonial past and favour urban and non-indigenous elites. The chapter proposes that the principle of universality in the emergency CCTPs was a key reason for the reproduction of inequalities in Bolivian society against the backdrop of the pandemic. The framework of feminist economics allows us to analyse the functioning of the patriarchal order, the sexual division of labour in the economy and gendered intersectionalities. Following Picchio (2009), who argues that the conditions of capitalist production impact and determine the social reproduction of the population, this chapter analyses the differentiated impact of the unequal distribution of public resources during Covid-19 and reveals the tensions and inefficiencies in the economic system.

2. The backdrop

2.1 The Plurinational State of Bolivia

The Plurinational State of Bolivia is made up of thirty-six indigenous nations.[2] A large section of the population identifies itself as mestizo and a part of it identifies itself as white. In 2006, following the election of the country's first indigenous President, Evo Morales, emancipatory mobilizations led by indigenous peoples joined forces with movements led by peasants and other subordinate groups, leading to the setting up of a Constituent Assembly and the drafting of a new Constitution. In 2009, almost 200 years after the creation of the Bolivian Republic, plurinationality came to be recognized in the country with the adoption of the Constitution of the Plurinational State of Bolivia.[3]

Though Bolivian society is diverse in its origins, it remains underpinned by older colonial, capitalist and patriarchal structures of subordination, and deeply entrenched discrimination based on race, class and gender. This colonial heritage persists in the country's economic model, which is based on extractivism and dependent on international prices of hydrocarbons, minerals and other commodities.

The Covid-19 crisis brought to the fore the structural and irresolvable conflict between life and capital in Bolivia and prompted a rethink of the narrative of development, and the very nature of the capitalist system and its relation to culture and the patriarchal order. Capitalism, patriarchy and colonial invasions have underlined the establishment of capitalism as a global system since the sixteenth century (Federici 2015). For colonized peoples, the destruction of systems of redistribution and reciprocity, and communal land use; and the confiscation of territories and bodies, mainly of indigenous women, represented a deep and painful rupture of their social structures. Colonial domination mandated the adoption of modern rationality and the development of collaborative family structures underpinned by patriarchy (pre-existing among the original peoples as well), sexual division of labour and the sexual contract (Firestone 1976).

The racialization of class divisions in Bolivian society is a product of this colonial condition and is further strengthened by contemporary capitalism, which manifests in neo-extractivism, violent commodification of nature, and oppression and violence against women and indigenous peoples, resulting in a social life marked by inequality, scarcity, precarity and conflict. More than 500 years after the arrival of European colonizers in the Americas, the continued presence of this order of dominance could not have been possible without the forces of patriarchal colonialism and globalization that lay the foundations on which the whole world is built. It is in the bodies of indigenous peoples, *cholas*,[4] and peasant, middle-class and bourgeois women that patriarchy, capitalism and colonialism manifest their particularities.

Modern approaches to plurinationality pigeonhole the configuration and representation of society within a binary logic (Zavaleta 1979). In contrast, the Aymara approach to plurinationality, *Ch'ixi*, is far more expansive. According to Silvia Rivera's (2018) translation of the term, *Ch'ixi* refers to the coexistence of two contrasting and even antagonistic elements. As Rivera (ibid.) puts it, a *Ch'ixi* society not only refers to the human but encloses in itself 'antagonistic mandates' of a society, of a soul divided between white, indigenous and mestizo thought; it is a mixture that encloses its opposites. In the Bolivian context, plurinationality is part of the Constitution of the state and takes on an emancipatory connotation: it is an alternative to development and rooted in the concept of *vivir bien* or living well,[5] which centres the harmony between human beings and nature without exploitation and inequalities, in contrast to capitalist development. However, the modern approach to plurinationality is juxtaposed with the persistent condition of coloniality and manifests itself in the Bolivian government's right to development discourse,[6] which legitimizes the exploitation of nature. In this context, plurinationality becomes merely a symbol of political power and an illusion of equality.

2.2 The Bolivian Government's Productive Community Social Economic Model, 2006–2020

Between 2006 and 2020, Bolivia established the Productive Community Social Economic Model (Modelo Económico Social Comunitario Productivo or

MESCP). The model was a product of the emancipatory movements that led to the 2009 Bolivian Constitution and were later co-opted by the MAS government. As per its official rationale, the MESCP is aimed at strengthening the social community economy and moving towards achieving *vivir bien*. However, until 2019, the success of the model was measured in terms of the implementation of an expansive fiscal policy, growth of domestic consumption, macroeconomic stability and growth in the gross domestic product (GDP) (Ministry of Economy and Public Finance 2016, 2018 and 2019).

Under the MESCP, the state assumes the roles of producer, investor, entrepreneur and redistributor of wealth. The model combines pluralist principles with modernizing actions. Its emphasis is on dynamizing and steadily increasing domestic demand, and creating and/or enhancing markets (Ministry of Economy and Public Finance 2013a). The four pillars of the MESCP focus on i) growth and development based on extractivist policies; ii) the exploitation of natural resources and the redistribution of surpluses to sectors that generate income and employment; iii) income redistribution through CCTPs, public investments, wage increases, cross subsidies, etc.; and iv) the reduction of social inequality and poverty (Ministry of Economy and Public Finance 2013b).

Between 2008 and 2018, Bolivia's GDP grew at an annual average rate of 4.3 per cent, spurred by domestic demand invigorated by price subsidies and sustained growth in public investments (Ministry of Economy and Public Finance 2016, 2018 and 2019). By increasing consumption in the economy, CCTPs contributed to this growth as well. In 2011, Bolivia entered the category of middle-income countries, but the parameters that allowed for this classification obscured great inequalities between rural and urban areas, and indigenous and non-indigenous populations (see Annex 1, Table 8.2).

Using Household Survey data, Ugarte and Bolívar (2015) suggest that the implementation of CCTPs such as the Dignity Income, Juancito Pinto and Juana Azurduy vouchers reduced the incidence of moderate poverty in Bolivia by 8.2 per cent and extreme poverty by 9.6 per cent among groups that received the transfers in 2013. However, using 2009 data, Arauco et al. (2013) observe that CCTPs played a limited role in reducing income inequality. Coello and Fernández (2014) add to this discussion by arguing that the redistributive effects of CCTPs were even narrower when considering the impact of indirect taxes, which are uniformly applied across all income groups, thus affecting lower-income groups disproportionately.

Poverty disproportionally affects indigenous groups. As of 2020, more than 55 per cent of the rural population who declare themselves indigenous were living in moderate poverty and 31.3 per cent in extreme poverty. In urban areas, 36 per cent of the self-identified indigenous urban population was living in moderate poverty compared with 30 per cent of the non-indigenous population (see Annex 2, Table 8.3).

The year 2021 saw a restoration of democracy after the political crisis of the coup d'état and the subsequent return to power of the MAS government. This also meant a reinstatement of the MESCP. During that year, despite the difficulties wrought by the Covid-19 crisis, the Bolivian economy grew 6.1 per cent while the fiscal deficit declined to 9.3 per cent of GDP from 12.7 per cent in 2020 (Ministry of Economy and Public Finance 2022).

2.3 How Covid-19 exacerbated the 2019–20 political crisis

The Covid-19 pandemic found the country in a deep political crisis, with a rise in racism and religious fundamentalism. The mass protests that swept Bolivia between October and November 2019, encouraged by conservative forces, resulted in the national elections being declared null and void, and forced the resignation of Evo Morales and his MAS government. Conservative forces took advantage of the consequent power vacuum to install a transitional government in November 2019 with the support of the military and police.[7] This was followed by another twenty-one days of mobilizations that saw the country divided into two fronts: the indigenous peasant people and the subordinate classes against sectors of the capitalist oligarchy and the middle class. Finally, after eleven months of the transitional government, national elections were held in the country in October 2020, leading to the MAS government's return to power.

The initial cases of Covid-19 appeared amid the repressive regime of the transitional government, aggravating the country's already deficient public health and social protection systems. In turn, this government used the pandemic to justify further restrictions on democratic freedoms, banning meetings, allowing businesses to remain open only for designated days and hours, restricting the movement and gathering of people, suspending public and private services that support citizens and address violence against women, restricting health care to only address Covid-19, increasing the presence of armed forces on the streets and encouraging the rise of disinformation campaigns. This generated uncertainty that contributed to an environment of fear and defencelessness characteristic of the exercise of biopolitical control over the population. The social isolation measures prompted by the pandemic contributed further to the prevailing uncertainty.

Supreme Decree (DS) No. 4289 of 15 July 2020 and DS No. 4200 of 25 March 2020, both introduced by the authoritarian transitional government, legalized repression and authorized additional budgetary allocations to the police, thus strengthening the government's power (Ministry of the Presidency 2020a and 2020b). The violation of the human rights of the Aymara, Quechua, Guaraní, Guaraya and Chiquitana[8] internal migrant populations, among others, brought to the fore the racism and gender discrimination deeply rooted in Bolivia's social and political fabric. *Mujeres de pollera* or *cholas* faced different forms of violence and misogyny in urban centres. Forced by the need to generate income, these women set up natural medicine pharmacies on the streets, contributing to health care and tempering the devastating effects of the pandemic on the precarious public health system by making their ancestral knowledge and skills available to the population. Yet, they faced increased discrimination in the exercise of their economic, social and cultural rights.

3. Analysis of CCTPs during the pandemic

The main social policy response of the transitional government to Covid-19 was in line with the policies of other Latin American governments. It took the form of CCTPs, subsidies for basic consumption and tax relief for the private sector, among others.

CCTPs are an extension of the neoliberal logic that prevailed in the 1990s, which coincided with a decline in formal employment and a privatization of public goods and services, dramatically reducing the presence of the state in social services and increasing the influence of multilateral financial institutions. This neoliberal model also exacerbated the vulnerabilities of certain sections of the population, including women, whose unpaid care workloads increased. The prevalence of CCTPs confirms the continuity of this neoliberal model in the Plurinational State of Bolivia.

CCTPs in Latin America and the Caribbean share the following four characteristics: i) guaranteeing macroeconomic stability; ii) managing the social risk of groups vulnerable to economic, social, political and environmental impacts, and preventing chronic impoverishment; iii) strengthening human capital through education and health support programmes; and iv) focusing social spending on the poor in order to be more efficient. As per neoclassical economics, CCTPs are aimed at correcting market failures in the efficient redistribution of resources (World Bank 2009). According to UN Women, the

CCTPs that were issued in response to the Covid-19 crisis 'aimed to create new transfers to compensate for the situation of vulnerability of sectors that, due to social isolation, have lost their income or suffered significant reductions' (2020: 7). However, UN Women also pointed out that the formulation and implementation of these CCTPs did not take gender into consideration.

In order to analyse gender biases in the CCTPs introduced in Bolivia between March 2020 and January 2021, it is necessary to explore two central and interrelated elements that underpin these programmes, namely the process of capital valorization that governs all social structures and the sexual division of labour. According to Agenjo (2012), gender biases in the economy are classified into four main groups: i) mercantilist gender bias, which equates the economy with the market and conflates work with paid work; ii) androcentric gender bias, which excludes women's experiences and needs from the realm of the economy and invisibilizes reproductive work; iii) classist bias, which sets the bourgeois class as the model of women and family; and iv) ethnocentric bias, which imposes global and cultural hegemony and establishes the ways of doing and thinking of industrialized countries as the norm. According to Stotsky (2005), there are two main gender biases in fiscal policy: i) an explicit gender bias that dictates different characterizations and treatments for men and women in laws, policies, administrative procedures and informal practices; and ii) an implicit gender bias, in which normative and public policy provisions, due to social conventions and typical economic behaviour, have different consequences for men and women.

3.1 The Covid-19 emergency vouchers and their underlying biases

The Bolivian economy and labour market are characterized by high levels of informality and employment precarity. According to the Ministry of Economy and Public Finance (2020), 80 per cent of workers in the country are self-employed or self-generate their own employment in the informal sector, which is dominated by the lowest income quintiles. Of the total number of people employed in this sector, 77.8 per cent face highly precarious conditions. Seventy-three per cent of employed women are in the informal sector. These segments comprise poor and vulnerable households and a large part of the lower middle class (INE 2023a and 2023b).

The population employed in the informal sector was the worst affected by the social distancing measures and movement restrictions imposed by the pandemic. Many were forced to close their businesses and quit street vending, which is mostly carried out by women. The precarity faced by small businesses and street vendors stood in sharp contrast to measures such as tax relief, extensions of credit, specific subsidies and other benefits that were made available to the business sector. These emergency tax exemptions and benefits and the refinancing of credits with public resources in favour of private companies led to the loss of tax collection. The Ministry of Economy and Public Finance (2021a) estimated that the fiscal loss resulting from tax relief to the private sector stood at US$287 million, affecting the government's revenue and limiting redistributive policy. Against this backdrop, the Bolivian state introduced four CCTPs, collectively known as the Covid-19 emergency vouchers.

The first such voucher was introduced on 10 March 2020 under DS No. 4197 (Ministry of the Presidency 2020a). It was called *Bono Familia*, or the Family Voucher, and offered a one-off payment of US$71.73 for each child who attended public kindergarten, primary or secondary schools, or belonged to the corresponding age categories. In addition, it granted low-income households a 30 per cent reduction in electricity bills.

Thereafter, on 25 March 2020, DS No. 4200 introduced the *Bono Canasta Familiar* or the Family Basket Voucher (Ministry of the Presidency 2020b). Under this decree, the government implemented four policies, three of which are relevant to our analysis:

i)   The voucher was provided to low-income households;
ii)   These households could claim a subsidy on electricity bills worth less than US$20 and a 50 per cent subsidy on drinking water bills on a temporary basis;
iii) The armed forces and the police were authorized to apply coercive measures to ensure the maintenance of public order and social peace in response to the political situation in the country.

The Family Basket Voucher allocated US$57.38 per family, which was 8.47 per cent of the national minimum wage and 9.38 per cent of the national average real income. The voucher, which became effective after more than fifty days of complete quarantine, was distributed in a single delivery of cash and/or foodstuffs but did not meet a family's basic food and health requirements. This CCTP injected resources worth US$6.8 million into the market via households but managed to reach only 26.12 per cent of the total target population due to poor implementation.

Subsequently, DS No. 4215 of 14 April 2020 (Ministry of the Presidency 2020c) extended the coverage of the earlier Family Voucher to include young and adult students of the alternative and special education subsystems, and the private education system. Under this decree, the Family Voucher also integrated families from middle- and high-income strata, generating a greater imbalance in income distribution. For poor families with three children on average, who received a total of US$215.20, the voucher amount represented close to 100 per cent of their monthly income. In contrast, for the high-income stratum, this amount represented only 8 per cent of their monthly income. For poor families, the voucher covered expenses on food; for the middle-income stratum, it may have supported access to medicines; and for the high-income stratum, the voucher likely increased superfluous consumption. Thus, inequality in income distribution was legitimized by the principle of universality, which entitled every household with school-aged members to cash transfers during the pandemic, irrespective of whether or not they were in the same socioeconomic situation. The principle of universality meant that a family owning a cigarette factory received the same amount of Family Voucher as the woman who sold these cigarettes on the street, working ten or twelve hours a day without social protection. This class inequality had significant gendered and racialized implications. More than 63 per cent of women were employed in the informal sector and belonged to the low-income stratum, and 31.3 per cent of the indigenous population were living in extreme poverty. In contrast, men and non-indigenous populations in the middle- and upper-income strata had access to better employment and income (UDAPE 2021).

In order to spur consumption by injecting cash into households and thus reduce the impacts of the economic recession, DS No. 4215 of April 2020 also created the third CCTP called *Bono Universal*, or Universal Voucher, which offered a one-time grant of US$71.73 to Bolivians between eighteen and sixty years old who were not receiving the Family Basket Voucher (Ministry of the Presidency 2020c). The Universal Voucher excluded public servants, private sector workers and those receiving benefits from their pension funds or annuities.

Although there is no available data that examines the beneficiaries of these vouchers based on sex, income and ethnicity, they were characterized by implicit gendered and racist biases. Going by Agenjo's (2012) classification of gender biases in the economy, the principle of universality that marked the Covid-19 emergency vouchers contained a mercantilist bias that disadvantaged the poorest sectors and deepened the income gap by reproducing distributive inequalities in which women, and particularly indigenous women, continued to be the most disadvantaged. The Family Voucher assigned a larger amount (US$71.73) to families with school-aged children, across the economic strata. In contrast, the Family Basket Voucher, meant to benefit the poorest sectors of society, provided the smallest amount (US$57.38) and reached a limited section of its target population. In addition, beneficiaries of the Family Basket Voucher were explicitly excluded from the Universal Voucher alongside other marginalized groups. In fact, according to the Ministry of Economy and Public Finance (2020), the Universal Voucher excluded 'the most vulnerable sectors of society, elderly people who receive their *Renta Dignidad* (Dignity Pension) and do not receive any other pension or retirement, mothers who receive the Juana Azurduy Voucher, and people with moderate, severe and very severe disabilities as well as the blind'. As such, sections of the population were excluded from the benefit of the Universal Voucher despite being poor, elderly, persons with disabilities and/or women.

Those excluded from the Universal Voucher were later included in the *Bono Contra el Hambre*, or Voucher against Hunger, issued by the new MAS government through DS No. 4392 of 13 November 2020 (Ministry of the Presidency 2020d). Its beneficiaries, who received one-off payments of US$143.77 each, included Bolivian citizens who were over eighteen years as of 16 September 2020, resided in the country and belonged to one of the following groups: i) women receiving the Juana Azurduy Voucher; ii) visually impaired persons receiving the *Bono de Indigencia* or Indigence Voucher;[9] iii) persons with severe or very severe registered disabilities; iv) persons who did not receive any salary from the public or private sector; and v) independently insured people in the Integral Pension System. Despite the greater inclusiveness of the Voucher against Hunger, it granted the same monetary benefit to all recipients who fulfilled its conditionality, regardless of income level, sex, employment status and ethnicity. The failure to consider these variables, which are determinants of discrimination and inequality, reproduced implicit gendered and racist biases.

3.2 Emergency vouchers: A comparative analysis

Table 8.1 presents a comparison of the four emergency vouchers, or CCTPs, issued during the pandemic. The Family Basket Voucher aimed at the low-income stratum consisting of 4.5 million people had the lowest level of coverage, reaching 26.12 per cent of the population. This voucher was plagued by problems of distribution and reflected a lack of political will to cover all intended beneficiaries, thus disadvantaging the poorest sections of the population who also belong to racially marginalized communities. The low coverage was likely due to the concentration of governmental efforts in the cities, thus excluding people from rural areas, and corruption resulting from the lack of transparency in the management of funds.

The Universal Voucher covered just over 77 per cent of the target population. However, of its total number of beneficiaries, only 29.19 per cent (1.5 million

Table 8.1 Beneficiaries of the Bolivian Covid-19 CCTPs (2020–23)

Covid-19 emergency vouchers	Potential beneficiary population who met the conditionality by 2020 (1)	Actual beneficiary population who received transfers (2)	Individual transfer amount ($) (2)	Total transfer amount ($) (2)	Estimated coverage of target population (%)
Family Basket Voucher	45,93,418	12,00,000	57.38	6,88,66,571	26.12
Family Voucher	34,87,567	32,00,000	71.73	22,95,55,236.7	91.75
Universal Voucher	51,92,946	40,00,000	71.73	28,69,44,045.9	77.02
Voucher against Hunger	51,92,946	40,15,364	143.47	57,60,84,273.0	77.33
			Total	1,16,14,50,126.6	

(1) Source: Compiled by author based on data from INE (2023a, 2023b).
(2) Source: Compiled by author based on data from the Ministry of Economy and Public Finance (2020).

people) are estimated to be from low-income groups. Most of the low-income sections of the population had been included in the Family Basket Voucher and were thus excluded from the Universal Voucher. The Voucher against Hunger, with 77.33 per cent coverage, reached over 4 million people. We estimate that 62.24 per cent of its beneficiaries belonged to the middle- and high-income strata. Considering that 78.3 per cent and 37.7 per cent of Bolivia's rural and urban populations, respectively, are poor, the Covid-19 CCTPs, by not considering data on poverty differentiated by geographical area, reproduced implicit classist and racist biases (see Figure 8.1).

These estimates offer only a rough approximation of the inequitable distribution of resources via CCTPs during Covid-19. As the discussion above indicates, the emergency vouchers were rooted in a principle of universality that cut across income levels and geographic locations and yet did not reach the entire intended population. Rather, in their aspiration for universality, the CCTPs standardized and homogenized situations that were different and treated diverse social subjects as if they all had the same socioeconomic conditions and needs, thus reproducing biases based on class, gender, race and ethnicity.

The priority of the Covid-19 CCTPs was to inject large amounts of money into the market and boost aggregate demand, which, together with tax exemptions and the transfer of resources to the financial system, was expected to protect the reproduction of capital.[10] Accordingly, the four emergency vouchers pumped in a total of US$1.161 billion into the market but failed to prevent declines in income and employment. In 2020, the low-income population stratum increased by 1.77 per cent, the population in the middle-income stratum decreased by 2.2 per cent and the overall unemployment rate of 8.64 per cent was the highest in the last five years.

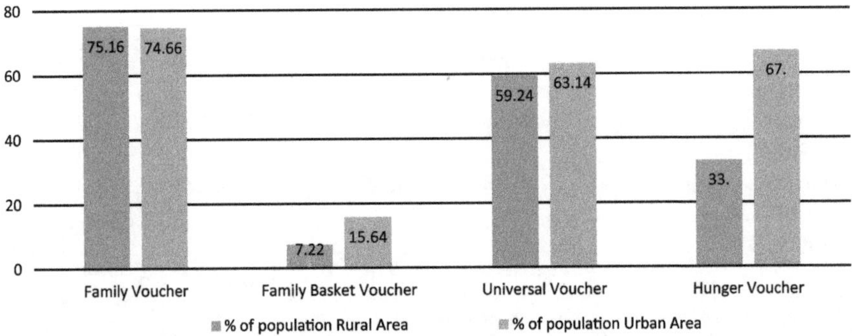

Figure 8.1 Beneficiaries of Covid-19 vouchers segregated by geographical area in Bolivia. *Source: Compiled by author based on data from the National Statistics Institute (2020) and the Ministry of Economy and Public Finance (2021b).*

4. Conclusion

This chapter demonstrated that the middle- and high-income strata benefitted the most from the implementation of the four Covid-19 emergency CCTPs due to economic behaviour marked by racialized class stratification and gender inequality. The implicit mercantilist bias of these vouchers, unfavourable to women and the poor, deepened gendered and racialized distributive inequality. The same stratification also led to different groups experiencing differentiated impacts of Covid-19 in Bolivia, exacerbated by an informal labour market, a weak social protection system and a precarious health system. In turn, social and labour precarities were deepened by the pandemic.

Our analysis of CCTPs reveals at least three characteristics that lead us to affirm that monetary transfers in Bolivia during the pandemic were instances of 'stagnant policies that depend on pre-existing trajectories' (Llavaneras Blanco and Cuervo 2021). Firstly, their primary aim was to guarantee macroeconomic stability. Secondly, the CCTPs were accompanied by significant tax relief for private companies, subsidies for basic services for citizens, moratoriums and loan payment flexibilities that mainly benefitted big capital, reductions and/or deferrals of employers' social security contributions and heavy subsidies to companies for the payment of salaries. These fiscal measures cost the government more than US$2 billion and benefitted the private sector, which had been emboldened under the transitional government. Finally, considering that more than 73 per cent of employed women work in the informal sector and the subordinate classes are largely of indigenous peasant origin, the CCTPs' reproduction of income inequalities was the result of sexism and ethnicization of the labour force as a labour policy.

The limited redistributive potential of the Covid-19 CCTPs was accentuated by the regressive effects of tax relief for private companies and indirect taxes that remained unchanged. The tax relief provided during the pandemic led to a fiscal loss of US$287 million and mainly benefitted private companies. In tandem, indirect taxes, such as the value added tax (VAT), remained the same, thus providing no relief for the poor. This policy move sheds light on the strong influence of the private sector in determining fiscal and economic policies throughout the years of the MAS government.

The universality criterion of the CCTPs treated all beneficiaries as a homogenous group and did not consider how underlying inequalities based on class, ethnicity, race and gender were biased in favour of higher-income sections. The four vouchers analysed in this chapter transferred similar amounts to all families regardless of their income levels, thus confirming that the intention behind these transfers was only to arrest further declines in consumption. In this, the Covid-19 CCTPs were an extension of the neoliberal model, which is far removed from the care and sustainability of life and instead focuses on the preservation of capital and consumption levels. The emergency measures of the pandemic reinforced the normalization of the sexual division of labour as well as the organization and functioning of regenerative and care work as a mechanism for capturing accumulated rents. The gender biases evident in the CCTPs contributed to this.

The principle of universality in social policies is a historic conquest in the peoples' struggle for human rights. These achievements were promoted by feminist movements and gender analyses. In the old, highly developed welfare states, such policies have served to level the playing field among their citizens. But in the weak welfare states and the current neoliberal economies of the global South, particularly in Bolivia, universal access to services has not been equalized and is a cultural imposition. In rural areas, services are poor for poor people. Statistics on health, education, access to drinking water and other services demonstrate disparities based on race, gender and class that cannot possibly be addressed by homogenous and homogenizing policy approaches.

When it comes to urban-rural dynamics, the forms and means of exchange shape inequalities based on the valuation of products and producers; rural products, generally agricultural and artisanal, have a lower exchange value in the market than manufactured products. A similar dynamic was observed in the situation of internal migrant domestic workers in China (Sa, this volume), which confirmed how territorial inequalities intertwine with gender, internal migration and class inequalities, and shape differential working and living conditions. Territorial disparities are related, but not limited, to class inequalities and are entangled with race and gender. In this context, the principle of universality does not level the playing field. On the contrary, it imposes a single and skewed worldview over other existing worldviews and cultures. A specific knowledge system, namely a Eurocentric worldview that is almost always made by white men and rooted in heteronormative patriarchal knowledge, is thus universalized and homogenized. Both the 2019–20 transitional government and the current MAS government followed these older trajectories and responded similarly to the challenges unleashed by the Covid-19 crisis. Both directed their best efforts to one end: to rescue an economic model through traditional fiscal policies that were stagnant and dependent on pre-existing trajectories. In the process, they failed to safeguard the poor, women and indigenous communities against the worst impacts of the pandemic.

Notes

1   In the first year of the pandemic, Bolivia had two consecutive governments, one transitional, emerging from the political conflict of 2019, and the other democratically elected in October 2020.
2   The Plurinational State is based on political, economic and democratic pluralism. It recognizes and respects the pre-existence of the native indigenous nations and peoples, community economy and democracy, and all languages.
3   The new Constitution recognizes women's rights to equality in more than fifty articles, including through the recognition of the economic value of household work.
4   *Cholas* refers to clothing worn by women of indigenous and peasant origin, mainly from the Aymara and Quechua peoples.
5   *Vivir bien* or living well is a philosophical category of Andean-Amazonian indigenous peoples inscribed in the Constitutions of Ecuador and Bolivia. It represents an outlook that is opposed to the Western conception of capitalism and development.

6   Article 1 of the UN Declaration on the Right to Development of 1986 defines the right to development as 'an inalienable human right by virtue of which every human person and all peoples are entitled to participate in, contribute to, and enjoy economic, social, cultural and political development, in which all human rights and fundamental freedoms can be fully realized'. The right to development is present in the Bolivian approach to development alongside, and in tension with, *vivir bien*.

7   The central intention of the conservative movement was to eliminate the few advances made by the indigenous nations and peoples through the 2009 Constitution. The transitional government that came to power in November 2019 unleashed heavy repression that violated the political rights mainly of the migrant indigenous peoples settled in the cities of La Paz, El Alto, Cochabamba and Santa Cruz, the country's economic and political hub.

8   These are indigenous nations in Bolivia.

9   *Bono de Indigencia* or Indigence Voucher is a pre-pandemic programme that supported visually impaired people.

10 Lena Lavinas proposes a similar analysis in which she argues that CCTPs are injections of public resources into the private sector. Lavinas elaborated on this point in the DAWN Talk, *A Financialised Life*, in November 2021, available at: https://www.youtube.com/watch?v=nRZA4vAYMns.

References

Agenjo, A. (2012), 'Deconstrucción de los sesgos de género androcéntricos en la economía', Diploma in Feminist Economics, fiscal policy and GRB, CIDES – UMSA, 2012.

Coello, R. and Fernández, S. (2014), 'Política fiscal y equidad de género en Bolivia', Bolivia, CEDLA – FADGD.

ECLAC (2019), 'Social Panorama of Latin America and the Caribbean'. Available at: https://www.cepal.org/es/publicaciones/44969-panorama-social-america-latina-2019 (accessed on 18 September 2021).

ECLAC (2020), 'Fiscal Panorama of Latin America and the Caribbean, 2020: Fiscal Policy amid the Crisis Arising from the Coronavirus Disease (COVID-19) Pandemic', (LC/PUB.2020/6-P), Santiago. Available at: https://hdl.handle.net/11362/45731 (accessed 21 November 2023)

Federici, S. (2015), *Calibán y la Bruja: mujeres cuerpo y acumulación originaria*, Traficantes de Sueños, 5th Edition, Spain.

Firestone, S. (1976), *The Dialectic of Sex: The Case for Feminist Revolution*, New York: Bantam Books (*La dialéctica sexual*, Barcelona, Kayrós, 1976).

INE (2023a), 'Encuesta de Hogares 2011–2021' Available at: https://www.ine.gob.bo/
index.php/estadisticas-sociales/empleo-mercado-laboral/encuesta-de-
hogares/#1656625678333-0d9ba6ac-46c4 (accessed 19 December 2023).

INE (2023b), 'Encuesta Continua de Empleo 2011-2019'. Available at: https://www.ine.
gob.bo/index.php/estadisticas-sociales/empleo-mercado-laboral/ (accessed
19 December 2023).

McGuire, J. W. (2013), 'Conditional Cash Transfers in Bolivia: Origins, Impact, and
Universality', Paper prepared for the 2013 Annual Meeting of the International
Studies Association, San Francisco. Available at: https://socialprotection.org/sites/
default/files/publications_files/3-11-15%20McGuire2013cBolivianCCTs.pdf
(accessed 21 November 2023).

Ministry of Economy and Public Finance (2013a), 'Memoria de la Economia Boliviana'.
Available at: https://economiayfinanzas.gob.bo/index.php/node/7577 (accessed
19 December 2023).

Ministry of Economy and Public Finance (2013b), 'Modelo Económico Social
Productivo Comunitario del Ministerio de Economía y Finanzas Públicas'. Available
at: https://repositorio.economiayfinanzas.gob.bo/documentos/2018/UCS/
materialesElaborados/publicaciones/modelo_decima_edicion.pdf (accessed
19 December 2023).

Ministry of Economy and Public Finance (2016), 'Memoria de la Economia Boliviana
2015'. Available at: https://economiayfinanzas.gob.bo/index.php/memorias-
economia-boliviana (accessed 19 December 2023).

Ministry of Economy and Public Finance (2018), 'Memorias de la Economía Boliviana
2017'. Available at: https://economiayfinanzas.gob.bo/index.php/memorias-
economia-boliviana (accessed 19 December 2023).

Ministry of Economy and Public Finance (2019), 'Memorias de la Economía Boliviana
2018'. Available at: https://economiayfinanzas.gob.bo/index.php/memorias-
economia-boliviana (accessed 19 December 2023).

Ministry of Economy and Public Finance (2020), 'Government Financial Support for
Families and Employment', Information Booklet. Available at: https://repositorio.
economiayfinanzas.gob.bo/documentos/Documentos_de_Interes/2020/cartilla_
ECONOMICA_COVID19.pdf (accessed 25 November 2023).

Ministry of Economy and Public Finance (2021a), 'Memorias de la Economía Boliviana
2020'. Available at: https://www.economiayfinanzas.gob.bo/sites/default/
files/2022-11/MEB_2020.pdf (accessed 17 April 2023).

Ministry of the Economy and Public Finance (2021b), 'Rendición pública de cuentas
inicial 2021: Reconstrucción de la economía boliviana'. Available at: https://www.
economiayfinanzas.gob.bo/sites/default/files/2022-09/Rendicion.Publica.
Cuentas.2021.1.pdf (accessed 25 November 2023).

Ministry of the Presidency (2020a). DS No 4197 of 18 March 2020 Family Voucher.
Available at: http://www.gacetaoficialdebolivia.gob.bo/normas/buscar/ (accessed
18 September 2021).

Ministry of the Presidency (2020b), DS No 4200 of 25 March 2020 Family Basket Voucher (2020), Published in the Official Gazette of the Plurinational State of Bolivia. Available at: http://www.gacetaoficialdebolivia.gob.bo/normas/buscar/ (accessed on 18 September 2021).

Ministry of the Presidency (2020c), DS No 4215 of April 2020 Universal Voucher and Extension of the Scope of the Family Voucher. Available at: http://www. gacetaoficialdebolivia.gob.bo/normas/buscar/ (accessed on 18 September 2021).

Ministry of the Presidency (2020d), DS No 4392 of 13 November 2020 Hunger Voucher. Published in the Official Gazette of the Plurinational State of Bolivia. Available at: http://www.gacetaoficialdebolivia.gob.bo/normas/buscar/ (Accessed on 18 September 2021).

Paz Arauco, V. Gray Molina, G. Jiménez Pozo, W and Yáñez Aguilar, E (2013). '¿Qué explica el bajo impacto redistributivo de la política fiscal en Bolivia?'. Available at: https://commitmentoequity.org/publications_files/Bolivia/ BoliviaResumenSeptember302013.pdf (accessed on 22 November 2023).

Picchio, A. (2009), 'Condiciones de vida perspectivas, análisis económico y políticas públicas', *Revista de economía crítica*, No 7, periodicidad anual, Spain. Available at: https://revistaeconomiacritica.org/index.php/rec/article/view/407/390 (accessed 22 November 2023).

Rivera Cusicanqui, S. (2019), *Un Mundo Ch'ixi es posible: Ensayos desde un presente en crisis*, ed TINTA LIMON Bolivia.

Stotsky, J. (2005), *Sesgos de género en los sistemas tributarios*, Instituto de Estudios Fiscales, Madrid, Spain.

Ugarte, D. and Bolívar, O. (2015), 'El Efecto de la Redistribución del Ingreso sobre la Reducción de la Pobreza en Bolivia', *Cuadernos de Investigación Económica Boliviana*, 4: 45–80. Available at: https://www.economiayfinanzas.gob.bo/sites/default/ files/2022-12/CIEB_2015_Esp_Paper_2.pdf (accessed 22 November 2023).

UDAPE (2021), Dossier of Social and Economic Statistics 2021, Ministry of Development Planning, Economic Policy Analysis Unit, Volume No. 31. Available at: https://www.udape.gob.bo/portales_html/dossierweb2021/htms/dossier31.html (accessed 17 April 2023).

UDAPE (2022), Dossier of Social and Economic Statistics 2022, Ministry of Development Planning, Economic Policy Analysis Unit, Volume No. 32. Available at: https://www.udape.gob.bo/portales_html/dossierweb2022/htms/index.html (accessed 17 April 2023).

UN Women (2020), 'Cash Transfers and Gender Equality: How to Improve their Effectiveness to Address the COVID-19 Crisis', Regional Office for the Americas and the Caribbean, BRIEF v 1.1 15.05.2020. Available at: https://lac.unwomen.org/es/ digiteca/publicaciones/2020/05/respuesta-covid-19- transferencias-monetarias (accessed 18 September 2021).

Zavaleta Mercado, R. (1979), *El poder dual en América latina: estudio de los casos de Bolivia y Chile*, Ed siglo XXI, Argentina.

Appendix

Table 8.2 Poverty and Inequality Estimated by the Poverty Line Method by Geographic Area in Bolivia (2016–21)

Geographical area and indicators	2016	2017	2018	2019	2020	2021
Bolivia						
Incidence of moderate poverty (%)	39.5	36.4	34.6	37.2	39.0	36.4
Incidence of extreme poverty (%)	18.3	17.1	15.2	12.9	13.7	11.1
Gini index	0.46	0.46	0.43	0.42	0.45	0.42
Urban areas						
Incidence of moderate poverty (%)	31.6	28.2	26.1	31.3	32.4	31.5
Incidence of extreme poverty (%)	10.0	9.3	7.2	6.4	7.2	6.1
Gini index	0.41	0.40	0.38	0.39	0.41	0.38
Rural areas						
Incidence of moderate poverty (%)	56.9	55.1	53.9	50.8	54.7	48.1
Incidence of extreme poverty (%)	36.6	34.6	33.4	27.8	28.8	23.0
Gini index	0.54	0.54	0.49	0.47	0.48	0.48

Source: Compiled by author based on UDAPE (2022) with data from INE.

Table 8.3 Poverty Indicators by Ethno-linguistic Status in Bolivia (2016–19)

Geographical area and indicators	2016	2017	2018	2019
Bolivia				
Incidence of moderate poverty (%)	43.0	42.2	39.9	37.2
Indigenous	54.0	154.1	53.4	47.2
Non-indigenous	35.1	34.7	32.5	32.1
Incidence of extreme poverty (%)	19.0	18.4	15.3	12.9
Indigenous	28.6	29.4	26.5	21.1
Non-indigenous	12.0	11.4	9.0	8.6
Gini index	0.46	0.46	0.43	0.42
Urban areas				
Incidence of moderate poverty (%)	35.6	34.4	31.4	31.3
Indigenous	42.6	40.9	38.3	36.4
Non-indigenous	32.7	32.2	29.6	30.0
Incidence of extreme poverty (%)	10.8	10.2	7.0	6.4
Indigenous	13.9	12.9	9.5	8.1
Non-indigenous	9.4	9.2	6.3	6.0
Gini index	0.41	0.40	0.38	0.39
Rural areas				
Incidence of moderate poverty (%)	59.4	59.9	59.2	50.8
Indigenous	65.0	65.0	65.8	55.6
Non-indigenous	47.2	48.3	47.0	42.6
Incidence of extreme poverty (%)	37.1	37.0	34.3	27.8
Indigenous	42.7	42.9	40.6	31.3
Non-indigenous	24.9	23.6	22.1	21.9
Gini index	0.54	0.54	0.49	0.47

Source: Compiled by author based on UDAPE (2021).

Section III

Social Organizing, Resistance and a Collective Politics of Care

9

Building a Care System in Argentina: Transformative Potential and Persistent Challenges

Cecilia Fraga and Corina Rodríguez Enríquez

1. Introduction

The advances in the construction of a care system in Argentina temporally coincided with the Covid-19 pandemic. These advances were not born out of the health emergency, but rather were the result of years of work in academia, civil society, women's and feminist movements, and public policy spaces. However, the pandemic was a crucial moment as it made visible the central and essential nature of care. It exposed the processes that reproduce inequality and highlighted an unjust social organization of care.

Broadly defined, the social organization of care is the way in which the state, households, community organizations and the market interact to meet society's care needs (Rodríguez Enríquez and Fraga 2021). In Argentina, as in most of the world, the social organization of care is marked by an emphasis on the family, a disproportionate burden on women and feminized bodies, reliance on the community and the limited presence of the state. The move towards advancing a just and fair care agenda began in the country in the 2000s and was further accelerated by the pandemic, which intensified care responsibilities. This chapter analyses the construction of Argentina's care system and argues that this process holds transformative potential even as it faces obstacles posed by entrenched political, social and cultural dynamics, and a persistent economic crisis.

The chapter is based on a desk review of existing literature on the subject, including, but not limited to, documents of the Ministry of Women, Gender and Diversity (MMGD) and the Caring with Equality Bill. It is also based on participant observations drawn from attending some virtual sessions of the

Territorial Parliaments of Care (Parlamentos Territoriales de Cuidados or PTC), which played a crucial role in the development of Argentina's care agenda and whose inputs were key in the process of drafting the Caring with Equality Bill. During these online sessions, which we attended at the invitation of the organizers, we listened to and observed the arguments and conclusions of the organizations and institutions participating in the PTCs. In this regard, it should be noted that Corina Rodríguez Enríquez, one of the authors of this chapter, was a member of the expert group convened by the government to draft the Bill, a process that is discussed later in this chapter.

The chapter is organized as follows: Section 2 describes the main characteristics of the social organization of care in Argentina. Section 3 reviews the socio-historical context that made it possible to build a care agenda in the country and how this was affected by the pandemic, both in terms of intensifying the demand for care and reinforcing the visibility of the essential nature of care. Sections 4 and 5 then look at the process put in place by the MMGD for the construction of a care system, with an emphasis on the role played by the PTCs and the drafting of the Caring with Equality Bill. The final section lays out our main conclusions.[1]

2. Social organization of care in Argentina and the pandemic impact

The social organization of care in Argentina[2] is characterized by i) a largely family-based and feminized nature with variations arising from social class, geographic location and type of care; ii) a persistent gender gap in the time spent on unpaid care and domestic work; iii) a marked socioeconomic inequality in access to care services, which stems from insufficient public provision and a market provision segmented according to the purchasing power of the population; iv) relatively more (but still deficient) public provision of care services for children than for the elderly and the disabled; v) a highly unregulated market provision of care services of very uneven quality, concentrated in large cities; and vi) a feminized and precarious paid care industry (including domestic work) that employs a high percentage of migrant workers. Paid care work is also characterized by low wages and high levels of informality, although these conditions have been improving since the enactment, in 2013, of a law to regulate care work. This legislation expanded domestic workers' labour rights to annual and maternity leave and mandated fairer compensation and working hours in line with ILO Convention 189 (ILO 2014).

With almost universal access to basic schooling in Argentina, public provision of care is concentrated in the school system, though the coverage is lower for early childhood education, particularly for children up to three years. Care provision in schools is complemented by a welfare-oriented provision that focuses on meeting the care needs of low-income households in the form of child development centres and early childhood spaces. This welfare provision is usually shared between the state, which provides funding for salaries and maintenance of infrastructure, and civil society organizations (CSOs), many of which have provided these services in the past. The quality and form of care provided in schools vary with the institution and geographic location.

The above-mentioned dimensions of the social organization of care manifest differently in urban centres, smaller cities and rural areas. They are also strongly segmented by the socioeconomic status of the population. For instance, the care needs of households living in socially vulnerable environments are fulfilled by the community and community care practices. This little-studied aspect of care work (Sanchís 2020) revolves around the actions of community organizations and offers fertile ground for studying networks as support mechanisms for care provisions (Pérez Orozco 2014).

What we now call community care is linked to the ways in which unprotected populations in Argentina have historically met their care needs. The most recent antecedent dates back to the economic, social and political crisis of 2001–02. During this period, community care was part of the organizing strategies that people applied in order to survive and meet their needs. These included autonomous community-led projects; participation in the popular, social and solidarity economies; experiences of exchange and barter; and working in recovered enterprises[3] and cooperative projects, among others. The reflections on community care presented in this chapter are shaped by these experiences, which may or may not include reconciling care demands with labour participation. For example, the community dimension of care is studied in relation to meeting children's need for food, education and play and highlighting the role of women in sustaining life, especially among vulnerable populations (Fournier 2017, Zibecchi 2014). Furthermore, care provision in the context of the popular economy is seen as an autonomous employment-generating post-crisis strategy.

The Covid-19 pandemic and the actions taken to deal with it increased care responsibilities, which had significant implications for the organization of household activities, time management and distribution of unpaid work (INDEC 2020, UNICEF 2020). In Argentina, the situation was exacerbated by an already heavy burden of care on women. According to the National Time Use Survey, women spend six hours and thirty-one minutes a day on average on unpaid work compared with three hours and forty minutes a day spent by men (ENUT 2021). This gender gap is observed in all unpaid work, including care work, support work for other households, community and volunteer work, and domestic work. Against this backdrop, the pandemic further increased the time spent on unpaid care and domestic work.

Paid care workers suffered severe consequences as they were first prevented from working and subsequently forced to work in conditions of enormous risk. At the beginning of the quarantine, the Argentinian government declared that those employed in domestic service should enjoy paid leave until the activity was reinstated.[4] However, high levels of informality and precarity in paid domestic care work meant a high incidence of job losses. The Domestic Helpers' Union (Unión del Personal Auxiliar de Casas Particulares or UPACP) estimated that between 50,000 and 55,000 domestic workers lost their jobs during this period. Those who were able to retain their jobs suffered a loss of income. According to Wlosko et al. (2020), 82 per cent of domestic workers had to stop working during the quarantine, but only 33 per cent continued to receive remuneration, in some cases, with pay cuts.

Those who continued to work due to exceptional circumstances faced an increase in the intensity of work, longer working hours and a loss of weekend breaks. This was the case for those who engaged in care activities for dependent persons, were employed on a live-in basis and, therefore, had to remain in isolation in their employers' households, or were forced by their employers to keep working. These workers were confronted with higher risks, either because the necessary safety and prevention measures were not implemented in those homes or because they were caring for sick people. Many of them saw their rights violated during this period due to the lack of sufficient information and increased exposure to violence, all of which likely affected migrant workers with greater intensity and frequency (López Mourelo 2020).

The pandemic revealed that in emergency situations, where conditions were more extreme and deprivation more marked, community networks came to the fore to guarantee the daily reproduction of life. Women in poor neighbourhoods in the urban centres were the ones who provided care in line with the solidarity mechanisms promoted by schools, clubs and social non-profit organizations. In such cases, the community responded even as the state was absent or inadequately present (Rodríguez Enríquez 2020). A similar phenomenon, namely an intensification of community care during the pandemic, was also seen in contexts beyond Argentina, such as among migrant organizations in Chile (Liberona,

Stefoni and Salinas, this volume) and paid domestic workers in Malaysia (Sreedharan and Ne Foo, this volume).

3. Consolidation of the care agenda

The issue of care has been prominently discussed in Argentina since the mid-2000s. However, the care agenda has been developing for much longer under the auspices of commitments made following the country's ratification of the Beijing Platform for Action twenty-five years ago, successive consensuses from the Regional Women's Conferences of Latin America and the Caribbean,[5] the push from academic sectors and the growing attention given by women's and feminist movements to the issue.

To start with, the care agenda promoted the generation of information to strengthen existing analyses. In addition to qualitative studies, there have been three subnational time use surveys conducted in the country, two in the city of Buenos Aires in 2005 and 2016, and one in the city of Rosario in 2010. The Permanent Household Survey of 2013 conducted by the National Institute of Statistics and Census (Instituto Nacional de Estadística y Censos or INDEC) included a module on unpaid work, which contained information, albeit insufficient, on time use at the national urban level.[6] Subsequently, the National Survey on Social Structure (La Encuesta Nacional sobre la Estructura Social or ENES), conducted between 2014 and 2015, included research and new information on care strategies.[7] Finally, in 2021, the first National Time Use Survey[8] demonstrated that, since 2005, the care agenda has been included in public statistics and social research with varying degrees of priority.

These studies and surveys, coupled with advocacy by women's organizations, gradually visibilized the unjust nature of the social organization of care and allowed a legislative care agenda to gain ground. By 2010, countless bills were brought before the national Parliament, proposing everything from the extension of care-related work leave to the construction of federal care systems for early childhood and strategies for the recognition, valuation and remuneration of domestic and unpaid care work.[9] However, none of the bills managed to advance beyond the stage of committee discussions.

Despite the challenges to advancing legislative discussions, the subject of care became part of labour negotiations and sub-national policy making. Care was incorporated into collective bargaining processes, which recognized the burden of care responsibilities on women, girls and LGBTI+ people. Through these collective bargaining processes emerged commitments to facilitate a better balance between work and family responsibilities by improving the provision of care services, offering allowances for the purchase of these services in the market and extending parental leave beyond the provisions of the employment contract law.[10] In the same vein, several subnational jurisdictions either implemented parental leave for those in provincial public employment or extended the duration of such leave to various degrees.

There were three processes that particularly accelerated the care agenda in Argentina. The first was the steady expansion of the feminist movement since 2015. The second was the coming to power in 2019 of a new federal government more receptive to feminist demands. The third was the role of the Covid-19 pandemic in making visible the essential nature of care and its implications for the unjust social organization of care.

A key milestone in the expansion of the feminist movement was the call on 3 June 2015 for a mobilization against gender-based violence, which gave rise to the *Ni una menos* (which translates to Not one less) movement. This spontaneous call for public mobilization brought thousands of people, mostly women and youth, onto the streets, thus renewing the national feminist movement. The struggle against gender-based violence converged with the longer-term demand by the National Campaign for the Right to Legal, Safe and Free Abortion for the legalization of voluntary interruption of pregnancy.[11] Violence against the bodies of women and girls and the right to decide about one's own body monopolized the debates of feminists, mass media, public policy fields and society in general.

These demands were articulated at the National Women's Meetings and other feminist spaces[12] alongside issues such as women's double and triple working days and the tensions between work and family life. In 2016, a national one-hour paid and unpaid work strike was called, and in 2017, as part of the International Women's Strike on 8 March, women from several countries organized general strikes and mobilizations against gender-based violence and for the recognition of unpaid work. This was followed by international strikes promoted by feminist movements in Argentina and Spain under the slogan 'if our lives are worthless, produce without us'. Together, these actions highlighted the urgency of acknowledging care as a problem of public order and rights.

The care agenda in Argentina also gained momentum with a change in the national government in 2019. The new administration established the MMGD, which paved the way for the institutionalization of a gender lens in public policy. This ministry inserted care in the government's agenda by proposing definitions and starting points taken from the feminist movement, which recognized care work as a source of inequalities, visibilized its importance in sustaining the social and economic system, noted the sexual division of labour that permeates care work, and pointed to the need for a fairer distribution of care, both within households as well as between the state, families, the market, and social and community organizations. Based on this understanding of care, the MMGD set up institutional spaces such as the National Directorate of Care Policies under the Secretariat for Equality Policies, with the aim of promoting cultural changes and making resources available to transform the distribution of time spent on and the work done to meet care responsibilities.

4. Towards the construction of a national care system: The essential components

With the creation of the MMGD, which coincided with the pandemic, the possibility of promoting care policies through the construction of an integrated federal care system began to take shape. From the outset, the ministry prioritized 'working for a fairer redistribution of care tasks'.[13] One of its first measures was 'the creation of the area of Care, with the understanding that it is necessary to translate the political will into concrete and tangible resources'.[14]

4.1 An inter-ministerial board on care

Given the various agencies that would be involved in care services, the regulation of care and the provision of other benefits within the social protection system, the MMGD formed an Inter-ministerial Board on Care.[15] This body brings together fourteen agencies of the National Executive Branch[16] with the aim of debating and planning policies that contribute to transforming the social organization of care. The Board has been key to formulating care policies in response to Covid-19.[17]

One of its first actions was the creation of a document that seeks to establish 'conceptual and operational agreements for the construction of a common language, a framework of meaning and a context of articulation' to guide the Board in its pursuit of 'redistributing and recognising care as a need, as a job and as a right'.[18] The document develops a conceptual framework that establishes consensus around the notion of care, the right to care and the social organization of care, and creates the first consolidated set of existing policies and those that were planned to be developed in the short term.

Another advancement in the institutionalization of the Argentinian care system was the construction of a Federal Map of Care, which i) provides information for the management of public policies and the identification of potential solutions to care demands; ii) facilitates bridging the gap between the demand and supply of care; and iii) lays the foundation for a future information system. This geo-referenced federal map offers information on the current supply of care services for children, the elderly and people with disabilities as well as on existing care training centres.[19] Open access to the first care mapping product was launched on 22 July 2021.

4.2 A campaign to generate consensus around care: The crucial role of PTCs

The other component of this process was the launch of the Caring with Equality National Campaign with two central objectives: i) to recover pre-existing conceptualizations, knowledge, know-how and practices related to care in the different territories in order to identify priorities that could be fed into the formulation of public policies on care; and ii) to promote greater awareness of care practices and policies from a comprehensive federal and gender equality perspective and advance a collective co-responsibility towards the right to care and receive care.[20]

The campaign's main component was the PTCs, which are 'spaces of confluence and dialogue amongst a multiplicity of actors in the territories'. According to the MMGD, the PTCs are 'community, institutional, academic and cultural' spaces meant to 'generate [a] collective consensus that will nourish the public agenda of care' (2020: 8). While seeking to raise awareness on issues surrounding care, these spaces facilitated learning about specific care demands, the conditions in which care systems are built, the relevant actors involved, and the consensus and tensions that could arise during the implementation and expansion of specific policies.

The PTCs are a novel place-based participatory process. They constitute the third of five stages of intervention at the provincial level of the Caring with Equality National Campaign.[21] The PTCs are preceded by the Internal Rounds of Exchange and Reflection and seek participation from various social organizations and institutions involved in the care of children, the elderly and the disabled; health and education sectors; community care networks; feminist organizations; provincial and municipal government departments; trade unions and business associations linked to care sectors; and representatives of the legislature, national bodies and universities. That makes the PTCs part of an ongoing dialogical process.

Their implementation is organized along three axes: political, cultural and communicational. Each PTC consists of five-minute interventions on each thematic area by spokespersons who present the conclusions reached in the Exchange and Reflection rounds on two questions put forth by the MMGD: how do we care today? And how do we want to care and be cared for in the future? Since this is not a decision-making initiative, there is no need for voting mechanisms or the adoption of resolutions. Instead, the PTCs allow for the coexistence of different and even contradictory positions. It is worth noting, though, that even if they are intended to be as inclusive as possible, like all participatory processes, the PTCs have limitations arising from the determination of who does and does not participate and from the unequal power of the voices involved.[22]

One aspect that emerged in all the PTCs was the normalization of domestic and care work as something that only women and feminized bodies do, underscoring the importance of making diversity visible in unpaid work (MMGD 2021b). The other aspect was the certainty that if women and LGBTI+ people did not do this work, no one else would (MMGD 2021a). This indicates that the state is perceived neither as an actor in the social organization of care nor as an interlocutor through which to demand an equitable social organization of care. While sectors with trade union organizing have made specific care-related demands on the state, such as the push for parental leave, these instances remain outliers. To underscore the limited presence of the state, PTC participants offered a detailed description of their daily lives, which are full of obstacles and where care needs are only resolved through family and community networks.

Discussions in the PTCs revealed an overarching reliance on the family in the social organization of care, signalling the need to alleviate the care burden of households through policies such as the expansion of public care services. For example, the PTC in Patagonia emphasized issues related to the provision of care services and the professionalization of care work, whereas in the northwest region, an area with more traditional and cultural imprints, the PTC stressed the need to combine care provided by extra-domestic services, for example, child development centres, with that provided by families. This reflects a cultural view that continues to situate care within families even as it demands actions to redistribute care within them (MMGD 2021b).

The importance of community care emerged alongside state-, market- and family-centric care provisions.[23] In particular, the pandemic emphasized the need to financially support and remunerate the work of women and LGBTI+ people in soup kitchens and community kitchens, which saw increased workloads because of the influx of children and older people during this time. More generally, the Covid-19 crisis prompted a rethink of the ways in which public policies can strengthen and support community spaces, possibly in conjunction with other social policies such as income support. In this regard, a challenge for the state is to devise ways to move forward with the care agenda without encroaching on or violating visions of care that uphold the communities' norms while favouring equity and guaranteeing rights.

Another issue that arose in the PTCs was the need to recognize care as a profession. Care practices related to children, the elderly and people with disabilities offer fertile grounds to establish the idea of care as work. The demand for technical and emotional training for caregivers voiced in the PTCs highlights the lack of such tools and skills. Requests were also made to address the mental health of caregivers, especially in care situations that were not chosen, and generate support networks to address this issue. The push to recognize care as work is in line with principles established by the MMGD and the Inter-ministerial Board on Care and is enshrined in the proposed Caring with Equality Bill discussed in Section 4.3. In contrast, the perception of care as a right did not emerge in the PTCs, which is in line with the lack of identification of the state as a guarantor of care. Other issues that were discussed included linking care with other rights such as access to water, health and education. While not explicitly stated in the PTCs, care could also be linked to the demand for basic infrastructure for these provisions.

The PTCs reiterated the importance of deconstructing masculinities in order to build a fairer social organization of care. This is indicative of a need to change the prevalent conflation of femininity with care and the assumption that masculinity is less associated with it. The PTCs emphasized that this cultural construct needed to be addressed in order to move towards a redistribution of care, indicating that participants likely held more progressive views than those that circulate in their social, work and family environments. It would be important to consider this possible bias of PTC participants while formulating public policies at the level of the territories and localities.

The MMGD views the PTCs as a process that recognizes and strengthens the voices of local actors in the territories. A positive outcome of this process has been the capacity building of gender equality institutions at the sub-national level based on their interactions with other areas of government as they organized meetings prior to the PTCs. By creating a deliberative space for local CSOs and sub-national gender equality institutions, the PTCs brought legitimacy to local actors, recognizing their roles and, in some cases, empowering them.

4.3 The Caring with Equality Bill: The unfinished final step in the care agenda

The last link in the process of developing a care system in Argentina was the Caring with Equality Bill. The Drafting Committee set up in October 2020 to prepare the Bill brought together a number of experts in the field with the aim of proposing a law that would provide an institutional framework for a future care system. The law was intended to establish the guiding principles, components and modes of governance of the care system, the priority population it would serve, the benefits it should include, the governmental bodies/department that would implement it and the financing mechanisms that should guarantee its operation. The executive used the proposal submitted by the Drafting Committee and added other clauses such as the extension of leave for pregnant and non-pregnant persons.[24] This culminated in the Caring with Equality Bill, which promotes the creation of the Integral System of Care Policies in Argentina (SINCA). On 2 May 2022, the President sent the proposed Bill to the National Congress.

There are ten aspects of the Bill that we are interested in highlighting:

i)   its approach, building on gender, feminist and diversity perspectives that permeate all proposed articles and principles;
ii)   the inclusion of transformative elements such as the reference to pregnant and non-pregnant persons, which replaces the traditional language on maternity and paternity;
iii) the creation of the SINCA;
iv)   the positioning of care as a right;
v)   the recognition and valuing of care work;
vi)   the special reference to paid care work and the obligation that it be carried out under decent work conditions;
vii) its reference to a set of policies for the redistribution, reconciliation and co-responsibility in the social organization of care;
viii) its extension of leave for pregnant and non-pregnant persons, which implies amendments to regulations and policies in various other sectors;
ix)   its establishment of the Inter-ministerial Board on Care Policies, which would continue the work of the existing board; and
x)   the general considerations it puts forth on financing.

These aspects of the Caring with Equality Bill herald a transformative path for the social organization of care. The Bill is in line with the outcome of the XV Regional Conference on Women in Latin America and the Caribbean held in November 2022 under ECLAC's leadership. The conference's central theme was The Care Society: Horizon for a Sustainable Recovery with Gender Equality. Specifically, the Buenos Aires Commitment[25] consolidated the importance of a care agenda for gender equality in the region by recognizing the gendered repercussions of Covid-19, and pointed to the high levels of public indebtedness in many countries in the region, which could be an obstacle to advancing this agenda.

5. A fork in the road: Emerging roadblocks in the care agenda

The Covid-19 pandemic and the way in which it brought to light the essential nature and the unfair social organization of care were expected to reinforce this transformative path. However, other trends seem to be hindering the care agenda in Argentina. To begin with, the national government has seen a decline in popular support, leading to its defeat in the mid-term legislative elections in November 2021. The government's loss of majority in the Senate affects the governing coalition's chances of approving its own projects, including the Caring with Equality Bill.

Also worrying are the political changes within the government following the electoral defeat, starting with the appointment as Chief of Cabinet of a provincial governor openly opposed to women's rights. This even as the President declared his commitment to the gender equality agenda. Another factor that raises doubts is the October 2022 appointment of Ximena Mazzina as the new Minister of Women, Gender and Diversity. Despite her support for advancing the cause of a care system in Argentina, it is worth noting that Mazzina was not part of the initial feminist movement. Her appointment comes amid rejigs in other ministries such as labour and social development. A crucial change in this regard is Sergio Massa's takeover as the new Minister of Economy in July 2022 amid debt restructuring negotiations with the International Monetary Fund (IMF) (Infobae 2023). These shifts in the Cabinet, coupled with greater fiscal restrictions, indicate a shrinkage of the policy room available to effectively implement public and social policies in general and care policies and the SINCA in particular.

The prioritization of public policies and social demands has also been hindered by the deterioration of Argentina's economic situation. High inflation has severely dampened the purchasing power of the majority of the population, a situation that was already worsened by the pandemic. The issues exposed by the Covid-19 health crisis, such as the question of care, seem to be overshadowed in post-pandemic Argentina. The urgencies of daily material survival appear in the social consensus to be disconnected from the possibility that a fairer social organization of care could provide for this same daily reproduction of life.

This, coupled with the partisan disputes arising from the electoral process, effectively vetoes the advances made in the form of the Caring with Equality Bill proposal and the broader care agenda. However, we have hope in the strength of the feminist movement to continue to be an active and demanding actor and in the ability of feminists to mobilize and push policy makers to remain loyal to this mandate.

6. Conclusion: Transformative potential with persistent challenges

The process of construction of a transformative care system in Argentina was largely due to the efforts of feminist women in public institutions who, drawing inspiration from the long road travelled by feminism, built a consensus on the need to modify the unjust social organization of care. The dialogue between academia, social organizations and political actors gained further ground during the pandemic, consolidating the care agenda and leading the way for care to become a part of public management. The Caring with Equality Bill was the first concrete step towards building a set of public policies aimed at recognizing and redistributing care work, guaranteeing the right to care, expanding care services, improving care workers' conditions and bringing about a cultural transformation in care arrangements.

Three elements of this process appear to have the greatest transformative potential. The first is the experience of the PTCs as a way to lay the foundations for social change, driven by public policies. These spaces amplified the voices of diverse actors and allowed them to engage in dialogue with each other. While not immune to tensions and errors of exclusion, the PTCs were a novel experience with great potential. Their scope will only become clear when the process matures sufficiently to reveal how many and which issues raised by the PTCs have crystallized into policies.

The second element concerns recognizing the role of the community in the social organization of care and how such arrangements can be placed at the centre of transformative care practices. The pandemic showcased the essential nature of this type of arrangement. The PTCs organized during this time foregrounded voices and experiences from the territories that revealed the existence of networks of collaborative care, thus highlighting the fact that reliance on the market is not the only way to meet care needs. In this regard, a future challenge will be to integrate community care arrangements into public policies, strengthen rights, bring about cultural and social transformation and respect the wishes and aspirations of people and communities in the territories.

The third crucial element in the process of developing a care system is the Caring with Equality Bill. Besides drawing on the academic and political work of feminisms, the proposed Bill includes several demands and concerns expressed in the PTCs such as the burden of care on feminized bodies, the recognition of care as work, the need to professionalize care, the recognition of the diverse forms of care, the importance of remunerating care work in community arrangements and the need to bring about cultural changes to foster a fairer social organization of care.

As this chapter demonstrated, the drive to develop a care agenda in Argentina started well before the pandemic, but the issues raised during the Covid-19 crisis about the fragility and injustice of care arrangements solidified the social consensus that urgent changes were necessary. Going forward, political-partisan tendencies persist, hindering long-term strategic efforts to identify and explore innovative policy and programme options over time. The current political electoral moment in Argentina, the erratic course of the economic programme, the burden of public debt and a context of economic crisis and inflation modify priorities and social consensus and cast shadows over the possibility of sustaining transformative impulses. For this reason, citizen and feminist monitoring is essential to preserve past achievements and overcome the obstacles that continually emerge in the process of seeking expanded rights and reduced inequalities.

7. Epilogue: When challenges worsened and the government's political orientation changed drastically

In August 2023, a version of the Caring with Equality Bill (Cuidar en Libertad) finally went through the parliamentary commission in charge of reviewing it but was never brought to debate in the chambers of Congress. This truncated version of the Bill focused on partially transforming the system of parental leave and did not address most of the proposals put forth by the expert group. At the time of finishing this manuscript (January 2024), a new government came to power in Argentina. With it, the growing challenges against the care agenda become a reality in ways worse than we anticipated. The new President, Javier Milei, is an emerging leader of the new radical right who came to power without a political party structure or prior experience as a public servant. His ascent to power was partly aided by his anti-gender perspectives. One of his campaign proposals was to eliminate the MMGD, and we expect that he will follow through with it.

In this context, we want to leave the reader with two final reflections. Firstly, the growing popularity of the anti-gender discourse that poses a real threat to the advances made in favour of women and sexual diversity rights is powered by historically reactionary groups. Nonetheless, it is also a reaction to the progress made towards achieving the gender equality agenda, which has questioned longstanding privileges. Significant support for the new radical right comes from young men who feel frustrated and alienated by the advancement of autonomous femininities.[26]

Thus, it is plausible to interpret the current moment as part of a process of profound change. Transformative change is never linear, and, in the case of Argentina, it makes sense to understand it as a process in which feminism and anti-feminism are at loggerheads. There are advances and backsliding – moments in which feminist mobilization is booming and times like the present, which are simultaneously characterized by the expansion of the antifeminist movement and the advance of feminist resistance. We want to focus our second reflection on this point.

It is important that the current period of pushback against the rights of women and diversity serves as an opportunity to rebuild and reorganize while examining the work done so far on the care and gender equality agenda from a critical perspective. In that light, we ask, what was missing from this agenda that would have made it more inclusive of all majorities? How can we improve the work on masculinities so as to avoid reactionary positionings? To what degree did the persistent economic crisis affect the gender and care agenda? Did we underestimate the hold of traditional gender roles on Argentinean society? How do we confront reactionary narratives that seem to take root in ways that defy common sense? Framed by a climate of libertarian reactionary individualism, how can we rebuild a progressive field of unity while recognizing and respecting differences?

The women's struggle has never been easy. All of its victories were gained after many years of progress and backsliding. We are currently in one of the latter. We have an asset in the form of feminist resistance that has produced so many achievements that are hopefully irreversible. Expanding our vision, avoiding sectarian forms of organizing and recreating resistance strategies in imaginative ways will enable us to get through this difficult time and reach a new cycle of expansion of rights for all persons.

Notes

1   We are grateful for the comments received from Yálani Zamora, Nanette Liberona and Soledad Salvador on a preliminary version of this paper.

2   Current diagnoses on the social organization of care in Argentina, with a strong focus on the survey of existing policies and a propositional component, can be found in Aulicino et al. (2015), Faur and Pereyra (2018), ILO et al. (2018), Alonso and Marzonetto (2019), Rodríguez Enríquez et al. (2019), and ELA and UNICEF (2020).

3   These are companies that were in crisis or declared bankrupt, usually after fraudulent practices by their owners. They were later taken over by workers who put them back into operation.

4   During 2020, the national government established several restrictions based on the health situation through successive decrees. Among other things, these decrees established paid leave as the responsibility of the employer. For more information on Resolution 202/2020 of the Ministry of Labour, Employment and Social Security on the suspension of duty to attend the workplace, see: http://servicios.infoleg.gob.ar/infolegInternet/verNorma.do?id=335675.

5   It was at the Quito conference (2007) that specific agreements were included for the first time in the consensus signed by countries, and this has been repeated in every consensus since then.

6   For a critical reading of the characteristics of this module and an analysis of its results, see Rodríguez Enríquez (2015).

7   For an analysis of the ENES data on the dimensions of care, see Faur and Pereyra (2018).

8   For more information on the ENUT (2021), see: https://www.indec.gob.ar/indec/web/Nivel4-Tema-4-31-117.

9   For a compilation of legislative bills on care, see Laya and Rossi (2015).

10 Laya (2015) presents a systematization of the inclusion of care clauses in collective agreements.

11 The Law on the Voluntary Interruption of Pregnancy (IVE) was passed on 30 December 2020 and enacted on 14 January 2021.

12 They have been held every year in different cities since 1986 and have brought together increasing numbers of women from all over the country and from diverse social backgrounds. For more information on these meetings, see Brugo (2019).

13 See: https://www.argentina.gob.ar/generos/cuidados.

14 ibid.

15 See: https://www.argentina.gob.ar/generos/cuidados/mesa-interministerial-de-politicas-de-cuidado.

16 The list of organizations that make up the Inter-ministerial Board can be found at: https://www.argentina.gob.ar/cuidados/mesa-interministerial-de-politicas-de-cuidado/integrantes.

17 The full set of measures taken by the national government during the pandemic can be found here: https://www.argentina.gob.ar/coronavirus/medidas-gobierno.

18 See: https://www.argentina.gob.ar/sites/default/files/mesa-interministerial-de-politicas-de-cuidado3.pdf.

19 This map can be viewed at: https://mapafederaldelcuidado.mingeneros.gob.ar. In dialogue with the other instances of the process of constructing a care system, the map can be supplied with inputs and information.

20 See: https://www.argentina.gob.ar/sites/default/files/campananacionalcuidarenigualdad.pdf.

21 The first stage consists of a round of introductions while the second stage consists of rounds of exchange and the formation of multi-sectoral provincial teams in charge of convening the sectors involved in the social organization of care in each province. The third stage involves the implementation of the PTCs, which are organized based on the provinces, with the possibility of including other territorial sub-units, for e.g., municipal government areas. The fourth stage involves a systematization of experiences and the fifth stage replicates the experience of the PTCs in a scaling-up and/or targeting exercise. For further information, see 'Notes on care. Material for rounds of exchanges and reflection towards Territorial Parliaments of Care' (MMGD 2020).

22 It should be noted that the PTCs were initially conceived as face-to-face sessions that would be organized regionally. This would have involved a selection mechanism derived from the different physical possibilities for people to mobilize to specific meeting points, which may have been especially relevant in regions that cover a larger geographical area and have a highly dispersed population. However, due to the pandemic, many PTCs were conducted virtually, which may have facilitated wider participation in some cases. There are currently no studies that analyse these dimensions of participation.

23 The reports of the PTCs of the Patagonian region, NOA region and NEA region can be found on the official website of the MMGD: https://www.argentina.gob.ar/generos/cuidados/camp-nac-cuidar-en-igualdad/informes. The points made also stem from the authors' participation in two PTCs.

24 The executive included care-related leave in the Bill against the advice of the Drafting Committee, which had recommended that it be introduced separately.

25 Available at: https://conferenciamujer.cepal.org/15/es/documentos/compromiso-
    buenos-aires.
26 It is important to note that even though young men constituted the initial core
    support of the far right leadership, this political movement also received support
    from a broad and diverse base. The reasons that may explain this are beyond the
    scope of this text. However, we want to highlight a few of them: the persistent
    economic crisis and related declining conditions of living, the crisis of the traditional
    party system and the enactment of politics in ways ever more distant from the lived
    experiences of the majority of people.

References

Alonso, V. and Marzonetto, G. (2019), 'El cuidado de personas con dependencia:
    Diagnóstico de situación y oferta de servicios estatales para adultos mayores y
    personas con discapacidad en la Argentina'. Buenos Aires: Ciepp. DT 102. Available
    at: https://www.ciepp.org.ar/images/ciepp/docstrabajo/Documento_102.pdf
    (accessed 27 November 2023).

Aulicino, C., Gerenni, F. and Acuña, M. (2015), 'Primera infancia en Argentina: políticas
    a nivel nacional'. Buenos Aires: CIPPEC, DT 143. Available at: https://www.cippec.
    org/wp-content/uploads/2017/03/1166.pdf (accessed 27 November 2023).

Brugo, N. (2019), 'Encuentro Nacional de Mujeres' en Susana Gamba (coord.) Se va a
    caer. POPOVA, Argentina.

ELA and UNICEF (2020), 'Apuntes para repensar el esquema de licencias de cuidado en
    Argentina', Buenos Aires: ELA and UNICEF. Available at: https://www.unicef.org/
    argentina/sites/unicef.org.argentina/files/2020-03/Apuntes-para-repensar-el_
    esquema-de-licencias-de-cuidado.pdf (accessed 27 November 2023).

Faur, E. and Pereyra, F. (2018), 'Gramáticas del cuidado', in (eds) Piovani, J. I. and A. Salvia,
    *La Argentina en el siglo XXI: Cómo somos, vivimos y convivimos en una sociedad
    desigual: Encuesta Nacional sobre la Estructura Social*, Buenos Aires: Siglo XXI Editores.

Fournier, M. (2017), 'La labor de las trabajadoras comunitarias de cuidado infantil en el
    conurbano bonaerense ¿Una forma de subsidio de "abajo hacia arriba"?' in *Trabajo y
    Sociedad*, n°28, Santiago del Estero, Argentina. Available at: http://www.scielo.org.ar/
    scielo.php?pid=S1514-68712017000100005&script=sci_abstract (accessed 27
    November 2023).

ILO, UNICEF, UNDP and CIPPEC (2018), 'Las políticas de cuidado en Argentina.
    Avances y desafíos', Buenos Aires: ILO, UNICEF, UNDP and CIPPEC. Available at:
    https://www.ilo.org/wcmsp5/groups/public/---americas/---ro-lima/---ilo-buenos_
    aires/documents/publication/wcms_635285.pdf (accessed 27 November 2023).

INDEC (2020), 'Estudio sobre el impacto de la COVID-19 en los hogares del Gran
    Buenos Aires. Primer informe de resultados', Buenos Aires: INDEC. Available at:

https://www.indec.gob.ar/ftp/cuadros/sociedad/EICOVID_primer_informe.pdf (accessed 27 November 2023).

Infobae (2023), 'Crisis en Argentina: el Gobierno nombró un nuevo ministro de Economía', 28 July. Available at: https://www.infobae.com/america/america-latina/2022/07/28/crisis-en-argentina-el-gobierno-nombro-un-nuevo-ministro-de-economia/ (accessed 13 December 2023).

Laya, A. (2015), 'El Derecho al Cuidado en los Convenios Colectivos de Trabajo del Sector Privado. Análisis comparativo de Convenios Colectivos en las ramas de actividades con mayor índice de feminización del sector privado', Buenos Aires: ELA, CIEPP and ADC. Public Policy and the Right to Care Working Paper Series No. 5. Available at: https://ela.org.ar/publicaciones-documentos/el-derecho-al-cuidado-en-los-convenios-colectivos-de-trabajo-del-sector-privado/ (accessed 27 November 2023).

Laya, A. and Rossi F. (2015), 'Aportes para la discusión legislativa sobre reformas necesarias en materia de cuidado', Buenos Aires: ELA, CIEPP and ADC, El cuidado en la agenda DT 6. Available at: https://ela.org.ar/publicaciones-documentos/aportes-para-la-discusion-legislativa-sobre-reformas-necesarias-en-materia-de-cuidado/ (accessed 27 November 2023).

Llavaneras Blanco, M. and Cuervo, M.G. (2021), 'The Pandemic as a Portal: Policy Transformations Disputing the New Normal', DAWN. Available at: https://dawnnet.org/wp-content/uploads/2021/04/DAWN-Discussion-Paper-32_The-Pandemic-as-a-Portal.pdf (accessed 27 November 2023).

López Mourelo, E. (2020), 'COVID-19 and Domestic Work in Argentina', Argentina: ILO. Available at: https://www.ilo.org/wcmsp5/groups/public/---americas/---ro-lima/---ilo-buenos_aires/documents/publication/wcms_765143.pdf (accessed 27 November 2023).

MMGD (2020), *Encuestas relativas a cuidados, violencia y situación de trabajadoras de casas particulares en tiempos de pandemia*, Buenos Aires: Minger.

MMGD (2021a), 'Parlamentos Territoriales de Cuidado. Región Patagonia. Informe de sistematización'. Available at: https://www.argentina.gob.ar/sites/default/files/2021/02/patagonia_informe_de_sistematizacion_aportes_federales_para_la_construccion_del_anteproyecto_de_ley_sobre_cuidados_igualitarios.pdf (accessed 4 December 2023).

MMGD (2021b), 'Parlamentos Territoriales de Cuidado. Región NOA. Informe de sistematización'. Available at: https://www.argentina.gob.ar/sites/default/files/2021/02/cuidados_parlamentosterritoriales_noa.pdf (accessed 4 December 2023).

MMGD (2021c), 'Parlamentos Territoriales de Cuidado. Región NEA. Informe de sistematización'. Available at: https://www.argentina.gob.ar/sites/default/files/2021/02/nea_informe_de_sistematizacion_aportes_federales_para_la_construccion_del_anteproyecto_de_ley_sobre_cuidados_igualitarios.pdf (accessed 4 December 2023).

Pérez Orozco, A. (2014), *Subversión feminista de la economía. Sobre el conflicto capital-vida*, Traficantes de sueños, España.

Rodríguez Enríquez, C. (2015), 'El trabajo de cuidado no remunerado en Argentina. Un análisis desde la evidencia del módulo de Trabajo no Remunerado,' Buenos Aires: ELA, CIEPP and ADC, Public Policy and the Right to Care Working Paper Series No. 2. Available at: https://ela.org.ar/publicaciones-documentos/el-trabajo-de-cuidado-no-remunerado-en-argentina-un-analisis-desde-la-evidencia-del-modulo-de-trabajo-no-remunerado/ (accessed 27 November 2023).

Rodríguez Enríquez, C., Marzonetto, G. and Alonso, V. (2019), 'Organización social del cuidado en la Argentina. Brechas persistentes e impacto de las recientes reformas económicas,' Estudios del Trabajo, No. 58: 1–31. Available at: http://www.scielo.org.ar/scielo.php?script=sci_arttext&pid=S2545-77562019000200003 (accessed 27 November 2023).

Rodríguez, C. (2020), 'Perspectiva feminista en la pandemia y más allá,' in (ed) J.P. Bohoslavsky, *Covid-19 y derechos humanos. La pandemia de la desigualdad*, Buenos Aires: Editorial Biblos.

Rodríguez Enríquez, C. and Fraga, C. (2021), 'The Social Organisation of Care: A Global Snapshot of the Main Challenges and Potential Alternatives for a Feminist Trade Union Agenda,' Public Services International. Available at: https://publicservices.international/resources/publications/the-social-organisation-of-care-a-global-snapshot?lang=en&id=12358 (accessed 27 November 2023).

Sanchís, N. (2020), 'El cuidado comunitario en tiempos de pandemia…y más allá,' Asociación LolaMora, Red de Género y Comercio. Investigación y Capacitación para la Acción, C.A.B.A. Available at: http://asociacionlolamora.org.ar/wp-content/uploads/2020/07/El-cuidado-comunitario-Publicación-virtual.pdf (accessed 27 November 2023).

UNICEF (2020), 'Encuesta de Percepción y Actitudes de la Población. El impacto de la pandemia Covid-19 en las familias con niñas, niños y adolescentes,' Tercera ola, Results Report. Argentina. Available at: https://www.unicef.org/argentina/media/11316/file/Encuesta%20de%20percepción%20y%20actitudes%20de%20la%20población.%20El%20impacto%20de%20la%20pandemia%20COVID-19%20en%20las%20familias%20con%20niñas,%20niños%20y%20adolescentes..pdf (accessed 27 November 2023).

Wlosko, M., Casas, V. and Palermo, H. (2020), 'Encuesta a trabajadore/as de casas particulares y su situación laboral en el contexto de aislamiento por la pandemia de Covid-19 en Argentina,' Buenos Aires: Ceil-Conicet and Universidad Nacional de Lanús. Research materials 6. Available at: http://www.ceil-conicet.gov.ar/wp-content/uploads/2020/05/INFORME-PRELIMINAR-ENCUESTA-TCP-difusion1.pdf (accessed 27 November 2023).

Zibecchi, C. (2014), 'Cuidadoras del ámbito comunitario: entre las expectativas de profesionalización y el "altruismo"', *Íconos. Revista de Ciencias Sociales*, No. 50, FLACSO-Ecuador. Available at: https://doi.org/10.17141/iconos.50.2014.1433 (accessed 27 November 2023).

10

Grassroots Feminist Organizing in Jamaica: Fostering Transformative Change for Domestic Workers during Covid-19

Ayesha Constable

1. Introduction

Grassroots feminist organizing has historically played a pivotal role in supporting the well being and advocating for the rights of marginalized communities. Through their focus on people-centric and localized engagements, feminist groups in Latin America and the Caribbean region have organized and led initiatives that seek to address the critical needs of women and other gender minorities and of occupational groups such as sex workers and domestic workers. During the Covid-19 crisis, feminist activists and movements once again voiced demands for fairer and more inclusive policies, equitable recovery for all from the pandemic and transformative change (AWID 2021). In Jamaica, grassroots feminist groups, such as the Jamaica Household Workers Union (JHWU), displayed exceptional leadership in agitating for an urgent response to the challenges faced by domestic workers during the pandemic.

In May 2020, the International Labour Organization (ILO) had predicted that, amid an already unequal labour market, the Covid-19 crisis could further exacerbate existing working poverty[1] and labour inequalities (ILO 2020a). Accordingly, the United Nations agency had recommended that governments tailor their support packages to save businesses and jobs, prevent layoffs and protect incomes. The ILO had also urged governments to focus on all those who work, including the self-employed, own-account workers and gig workers, whether in the formal or informal economy and whether paid or unpaid, as well as those who have no way of supporting themselves (ibid.). Yet, seasonal informal workers and especially domestic workers, who are mostly women, experienced the worst fallouts of the pandemic (UN Women 2020). In response, gender considerations reverberated in global public debates, media coverage, calls to action and official responses to Covid-19. Gender experts in international organizations set up policy roadmaps to address the adverse social and economic impacts of the global health crisis and put in place monitoring tools to track policy progress (Tabbush 2020).

In Jamaica, as in most countries across the world, the government responded to the pandemic with a raft of policy changes to stem the spread of the virus and ameliorate its pernicious effect on the economy and the labour market (ILO 2020b). Following the first confirmed case of Covid-19 in the country on 10 March 2020, the government implemented travel restrictions, school closures, nightly curfews and restrictions on public gatherings and entertainment events, among other measures (STATIN 2020, Dewi et al. 2021). The economic impacts were immediate. In April to June 2020, the Jamaican economy contracted 18.4 per cent year-on-year while employment fell 10.8 per cent in July 2020 compared to a year ago (STATIN 2020). Workers in the informal sector, including domestic workers, were the worst affected. School closures and a lack of access to digital technologies also affected domestic workers and their children.

Against this backdrop, the JHWU mobilized resources to support domestic workers across the country and demanded policy reforms to bolster workers' capacity to respond to economic shocks. The union sought to ensure fair and just working conditions and wages for household workers, protect their rights, provide them with skills training in household management and empower members to achieve their personal and on-the-job goals (Mundle 2020).

The JHWU (2022) defines a domestic worker as a female or male worker who is employed in another person's home and undertakes a number of tasks such as washing, cooking, cleaning, child rearing and geriatric care. The definition aligns with that of the ILO (2021), which further adds that a domestic worker can be categorized as live-in (residing in the home of the employer) or live-out (living in their personal residence). In Jamaica, a live-out worker is typically called a day's worker and may be employed in multiple homes. Domestic workers in the country experience high levels of poverty, long working hours (especially when they reside with employers) and limited options for alternative livelihoods due to low levels of formal educational attainment.

According to the ILO (2010), domestic work is undervalued, underpaid, unprotected and poorly regulated for several reasons, including i) the similarities between paid domestic work and the unpaid care work done by women in their own homes in the form of housework and care work for other household members; ii) the fact that domestic workers are typically not male breadwinners but women (who are often the main breadwinners for their families and themselves) and, in many countries, children; and iii) the fact that domestic workers usually belong to historically disadvantaged communities such as minority ethnic groups, indigenous peoples, oppressed-caste groups, low-income rural and urban groups, and migrants who are especially vulnerable to discrimination in employment and work (ibid). Any attempt to examine the impacts of Covid-19 on domestic workers thus requires an intersectional analysis of the historical, political and economic factors that shape national, subnational and individual-level circumstances.

This chapter highlights the complexities in the relationships between domestic workers and their employers, and the national institutional arrangements in which these workers are embedded. Using the pandemic as a point of departure, it examines the factors that make domestic workers vulnerable and pays attention to the power hierarchies and systemic inequalities that shape their life experiences (Lokot and Avakyan 2020). Against this backdrop, the chapter examines how the JHWU supported domestic workers during the Covid-19 crisis and the factors that hindered or facilitated their efforts. It uses an intersectional feminist lens to analyse how the pandemic-related policy changes affected domestic workers, who are primarily women of Afro-Jamaican descent from lower economic classes with low levels of education, and the implications of such policies for their health, income and overall well being. The chapter argues that intersecting social identities, such as gender, race, class and migrant status, work in conjunction to exacerbate the vulnerability of domestic workers to political, economic and social disenfranchisement. Since intersectionality is inextricably linked to an analysis of power, such an approach also emphasizes the political and structural inequalities experienced by domestic workers (Cho et al. 2013). A key consideration in the chapter is how gender, educational levels and the informal nature of domestic work intersect to place these workers outside the purview of national policy and decision making. Finally, the intersectional approach underlines the differential impact of the pandemic on different individuals and social groups and helps in designing policy responses that mitigate, instead of exacerbate, the unequal impact of the crisis (Maestripieri 2021).

The study takes a qualitative and mixed methods approach. It combines desk research with semi-structured phone interviews with domestic workers to discuss their work experiences before and after Covid-19 and a survey of twelve employers of domestic workers, administered via Google Forms.

2. Domestic workers in Jamaica: Colonial legacies and the pandemic context

2.1 How colonialism and slavery shape the lived experiences of domestic workers

The legacies of slavery and colonialism influence Jamaica's socioeconomic, legal and political landscape and form the backdrop to domestic workers' experiences (Bush-Slimani 1993). Prevailing views on women and the systemic barriers to their access to power in slave societies continue to shape attitudes towards and experiences of women in contemporary Caribbean societies. Colonial-era class relations and stigmas associated with domestic work not only determine the lived realities of domestic workers but also foreclose the possibility of inclusive policy responses.

According to Simms, 'in slave society, black women's lives established the blueprint for the 'universal maid'' (2011: 1). The colonial legacy of the exploitation of Black women's labour became 'a steady feature of family life' and 'evolved into the ever-present nanny and cleaning lady in the post emancipation upper-crust household' (ibid.). Many domestic workers do not experience the level of decency and respect that should be extended to every human being, yet they are central to Jamaica, which Simms describes as 'a society of domestic workers and maids' (ibid.).

Heron (2008) traces the legacy of slavery in the sharp class distinctions in contemporary Caribbean societies. While not as strict as during the colonial era, Jamaica's upper and middle classes are stratified and racially ascribed. This stratification ranges from European white; Jamaican white; near white; the middle-complexioned category of brown, Chinese and Indian; and the working-class majority of African descent or Black, resulting in a textured Jamaican society characterized by colour and class distinctions (ibid). Analyses of labour systems on plantations highlight that men held more prestigious and skilled jobs whereas enslaved women were confined to being field hands, domestics and washerwomen, leading to a sexual division of labour along racial lines (Reddock 1985, 2005; Bush-Slimani 1993). Other tasks carried out by women in the domestic space included nursing children, caring for the elderly, cooking, carrying water, cleaning and performing difficult, dirty and mundane household tasks (Johnson 2007).

French (1988) argues that the outcome of this gendered and racialized system of exploitation was the relegation of women's labour to invisibility and wagelessness. Their labour came to be seen as a natural extension of the housewife/domestic role, a perception that imbues the contemporary racialized and gendered nature of domestic work (ibid.). Such historical continuities acted as barriers to social change in the aftermath of the pandemic.

Currently, an estimated 11–18 million people are engaged in paid domestic work in Latin America and the Caribbean, of whom 93 per cent are women (UN Women 2020). On average, domestic work constitutes 10.5–14.3 per cent of women's employment in the region. Their working conditions are precarious, characterized by low wages, a lack of social benefits and reliance on family support in the event of layoffs or reduced incomes (UN Women, ILO and ECLAC 2020). According to UN Women (2018), domestic workers in the Caribbean experience high levels of informality, with 90 per cent employed without formal contracts. In particular, Haiti (99 per cent), Dominican Republic (96.5 per cent), Guyana (94.9 per cent) and Jamaica (92 per cent) see exceptionally high levels of informality in domestic workers' employment conditions. Underwaged, undervalued, uncounted and unprotected, these workers are among the most exploited in the labour market today.

2.2 Heightened precarity of domestic workers during Covid-19

The predominance of women in domestic work reflects the widely held view that care work and household tasks are a woman's work. Domestic work is often seen not as a profession, but rather as menial work, and domestic workers face (mis) treatment seen as commensurate with their job status. It is unsurprising that the health, social and economic crises triggered by the Covid-19 pandemic and the associated lockdowns impacted female domestic workers in particular (UN Women, ILO and ECLAC 2020). Even as the crisis magnified the importance of care work, there were widespread reports that domestic workers experienced the loss of jobs and, consequently, incomes (ILO 2020, Hutchinson 2022, Daley 2021).

2.2.1 A drastic decline in incomes

In Jamaica, employers of domestic workers were unsympathetic to the repercussions workers and their families faced during the pandemic, as their working hours were reduced or work agreements terminated as a preventative measure (Cooper 2020). Employers surveyed for this study revealed that their key concern was that household members could contract the virus from workers. As a result, some employers asked domestic workers to stop coming to their homes or reduced the number of working days.

Sharon,[2] a domestic worker who used to work in four households in the capital city of Kingston, was down to three during the pandemic due to the comorbidities of one employer. Her working hours in the remaining households were reduced because she took breaks of varying lengths at the height of the Covid-19 crisis, both for her own safety as well as that of her employers. Cynthia, another domestic worker who was also a research participant for this study, said at the time of the interview that she was only left with one elderly employer after being let go of by two others. This drastically reduced her weekly income.

Paradoxically, domestic workers were tasked with caring for patients with Covid-19 and simultaneously held responsible for ensuring that the entire household did not contract the virus. Like other poor people who suffered higher risks of infection due to precarious working conditions and housing, domestic workers became the target of a 'racism of class' (Pleyers 2020) that resulted in further loss of employment and unfair treatment.

Where domestic workers continued to work, their incomes were impacted by additional expenses incurred as precautionary measures to reduce their exposure to the virus. Some employers reported asking domestic workers to stop taking public transportation while others offered to transport them for at least a part of their journey. Sharon explained that she limited her exposure to Covid-19 by taking taxis instead of public buses, which increased her weekly transportation bill by at least 1,000 Jamaican dollars (JA$) (US$7), a significant sum for workers already beset by economic hardship. The expense was higher than usual as taxi operators hiked fares during curfew hours to capitalize on increased demand for their services. Sharon was forced to dip into her meagre savings and rely on remittances from family and friends overseas. Maxine, another domestic worker, pointed out that with one day's cleaning work for a three-member household, she was only able to afford food for her family for one day and cover transportation costs for that day. Maxine's husband's income was disrupted, forcing her to single-handedly shoulder the financial burden of the household.

In instances where domestic workers were dismissed, their payouts were at the discretion of employers, leaving most of them without an income and with limited savings. One of the domestic workers interviewed for this study was uncertain whether her work with two employers, suspended during the pandemic, would resume in the future. She received no compensation to plug the financial gap created by the loss of her jobs while the dent in her income was worsened by the increased cost of living due to growing inflation in the Jamaican economy. Another domestic worker argued that some employers were simply using Covid-19 as an excuse to get rid of workers. Others complained that while they were temporarily relieved by employers, gardeners were allowed to come to work. While employers justified this on the basis that gardeners were not directly interacting with household members, some domestic workers saw this as an extension of the gender bias prevalent in domestic service, as gardeners, who are typically men, were allowed to keep their jobs while they, as women, were laid off, rendering them vulnerable.

2.2.2 Intensified workloads, paid and unpaid

Women, who provide most of the unpaid care work within families, experienced a disproportionate increase in their care burden during the pandemic (Al-Ali 2020). This was felt more sharply by women belonging to lower-income categories (Zheng 2021). The increase in unpaid domestic and care work due to Covid-19 also made them more likely to lose their jobs because of traditional expectations surrounding women's role in the household (Daley 2021).

Women in paid domestic work faced heightened time poverty. Reduced workdays, something most employers surveyed for this study admitted to applying, intensified domestic workers' workloads, forcing them to complete more tasks in less time. But even as workloads increased, wages declined. Maxine voiced her resentment at what she saw as a devaluation of her work, which she believed was comparable to that of all frontline workers. The ad hoc adjustments in daily and weekly payments pointed to weak legislation on domestic workers' wages and the lack of structured and enforced regulation.

One domestic worker, Cynthia, explained that the burden of unpaid work had increased at home, particularly with the need to help her children with online learning following school closures as well as additional washing, cooking and cleaning as family members stayed at home full time. The challenge of supervising children's learning was worsened by little or no access to gadgets and the internet and low levels of literacy among parents, demonstrating how poverty and low educational attainment exacerbated the impacts of the pandemic on domestic workers and their families. The impact of digital inequality as a barrier to improving the situation of domestic workers is explored further in Section 3.

Social stigma and bias, which have historically led to the ill-treatment of domestic workers, also worsened during the pandemic. Research participants pointed out that protective gear was provided to other frontline workers but not to them. They also spoke of increased disrespect and scrutiny from their families and employers. These reactions, coupled with greater isolation, affected the mental health of domestic workers. Sharon reported high levels of anxiety and stress due to the pandemic. Stacy, another domestic worker, said she experienced heightened emotional and psychological stress, which sometimes triggered domestic disputes at home. Multiple studies have pointed to the increased incidence of gender-based violence during the pandemic (Al-Ali 2020, Cockayne 2021, Michaelsen et al. 2021). In Jamaica, activists lambasted the government for the lack of measures to help victims of abuse. Interestingly, it was another grassroots feminist organization, Sistren Theatre Collective,[3] that intervened to help women suffering abuse under lockdown.

The impact of Covid-19 on domestic workers was thus the result of intersectional and pre-existing inequalities, leading to heightened risks and vulnerabilities. Against this backdrop, grassroots feminist groups like the JHWU demanded an urgent response from the state to the needs of domestic workers.

2.3 Gender-blind and non-inclusive policy making

Following the onset of the pandemic, the Jamaican government swiftly implemented several stabilization measures to protect people and businesses (IMF 2020, KPMG 2020). It cancelled all large public and private events, shut down schools and quarantined entire communities. It instituted protocols for visitors arriving in the country, including pre-arrival documentation, in-airport screening and risk assessment followed by a risk-based approach to quarantine and movement limitations. It also issued guidelines on the reopening of beaches, rivers and theme parks, which are key tourist attractions; safe capacity limits for social gatherings (e.g., weddings and funerals); and operation protocols for gyms, barbershops and hair salons (IMF 2021).

These actions were in keeping with the ILO's recommendations for tackling the social, economic and employment-related consequences of this crisis through judicious policy sequencing (ILO 2020a). Researchers at the Oxford Coronavirus Government Response Tracker placed Jamaica's Covid-19 response at a stringency index of 66.7 per cent, where 100 per cent indicates the strictest level of response.[4] Though somewhat effective in curtailing the spread of the virus, these measures did not address the needs of all communities and, in some instances, exacerbated the challenges for groups such as domestic workers.

For instance, amendments to the Disaster Risk Management Act, which was used as a framework of reference in the absence of specific work-from-home guidelines/laws, were either disadvantageous to or failed to address the concerns of domestic workers. As part of these amendments, the Ministry of Labour and Social Security (MLSS) encouraged employers to provide sick leave and time off with pay during the quarantine as far as possible. Employers and workers were also encouraged to explore work-from-home and other innovative options, including, but not limited to, staff rotation, reduction in working hours, review of tasks and remote client services to address income and job security concerns. However, the nature of domestic work did not allow this group of workers to benefit from such allowances.

School closures, restrictions on public passenger vehicles (which made it difficult to travel to work), night curfews and limitations on gatherings also proved harmful to domestic workers. Some of these measures, such as the halt on church events, limited their access to forms of social gathering that have historically allowed them to build and experience a sense of community. Such spaces are important for informal collectivizing and information sharing (Hondagneu-Sotel 1994) and for the creation of 'communities of coping' (Jiang 2018).

2.3.1 *Non-enforcement of labour laws related to domestic workers' rights*

In theory, domestic workers in Jamaica are covered by national laws and qualify for most benefits except for those based on contributions to the National Insurance Fund (NIF). Most labour laws apply to all household workers and, in that sense, include domestic workers.[5] These laws entitle workers to a contract, sufficient daily and/or weekly rest, a salary no lower than the minimum wage, public holidays, paid annual leave, compensation for overtime work and social security contributions. The cost of insurance is mandated to be shared between employee and employer.

There are, however, no laws specific to the category of domestic workers, and especially during the pandemic, existing laws failed to protect them (Walker 2003). For instance, the Holidays with Pay Act, 1974, which regulates the granting of vacation and sick leave with pay, was not adhered to in the case of domestic workers. Another key legislation that was infringed upon was the Minimum Wage Act, 1938, which establishes the legal minimum that must be paid in wages. In March 2018, the minimum wage was set at JA$6,200–7,000 (US$42–47) per week. Domestic workers reported that employers arbitrarily cut working hours and reduced wages below this level.

The lack of legally mandated labour rights for domestic workers results in a lopsided power relationship between domestic workers and their employers, in which attempts to seek redress could result in termination. The limitations in the implementation of existing legislation led domestic workers to suffer devastating impacts during the pandemic.

3.　JHWU and grassroots organizing

Feminist organizations and activists have frequently been at the centre of anti-authoritarian and anti-corruption movements in the global South. More recently, they have been at the forefront of challenging the gender blindness of government interventions and responses to the Covid-19 pandemic (Al-Ali 2020). In many instances, grassroots feminist organizations responded to serve the needs of communities on the ground and plug the gaps resulting from states' inaction. In the wake of the pandemic, the JHWU organized several initiatives to help domestic workers cope with the economic fallout in particular. The union provided food packages to families of domestic workers, acquired and distributed tablets to their children to facilitate online learning, and offered financial relief to select domestic workers. It also implemented a project to support the formalization of domestic workers, which included providing them with identification cards and encouraging employers to integrate measures for record keeping and documentation, such as registers, as part of the union's push for social dialogue and capacity building (ILO 2020c).

As in Trinidad and Tobago (Roopnarine and Brizan, this volume), the Jamaican government implemented an emergency cash transfer programme called the Covid-19 Allocation of Resources for Employees (CARE), which was managed by the National Insurance Scheme (NIS). The programme offered a one-time cash package to beneficiary workers to compensate them for the loss of income arising from injury on the job, sickness, retirement or death. However, according to Shirley Pryce, president of the JHWU, a majority of domestic workers were unable to access the CARE package as they were not registered with the NIS. The unstructured nature of their employment, which makes incomes unregulated and sporadic, has historically hindered domestic workers' ability to contribute to the NIS. This meant that only a small number of workers were eligible for fortnightly payments under the government's relief programme during the pandemic (Clarke 2020). Besides, to receive the relief funds, potential beneficiaries had to have access to the online NIS system and separately register on the online CARE portal. Both requirements did not account for gender- and class-based digital inequalities. The JHWU responded to these gaps by demanding a policy change that would take a more intersectional approach. Their success, however, was stymied by factors such as negative stereotypes about domestic work, exclusionary national policies, limited access to technology and restrictive Covid measures.

3.1 Barriers hindering JHWU's efforts

3.1.1 Vaccine hesitancy and its implications for labour organizing and access to work

Jamaica did not implement a mandatory vaccination policy during the Covid-19 pandemic. While some stakeholders called for a single policy requiring vaccination for all Jamaicans, Prime Minister Andrew Holness said 'he respects the right and freedom of Jamaicans and believes that there must be a period of reasoning with Jamaicans to ensure they recognise that their freedom is not without obligation and responsibility' (JIS 2021). Jamaica recorded one of the highest rates of vaccine hesitancy in the Caribbean region. A survey conducted by Johns Hopkins Centre for Communication Programs reported that 72 per cent of Jamaicans would not accept the Covid-19 vaccine (Babalola et al. 2020). High levels of scepticism were also reported among medical personnel in Jamaica's main public hospitals (Cross 2020). In fact, research suggests that religious leaders were more successful than health care workers in influencing increased vaccine uptake in the country (Wynter-Adams and Thomas-Brown 2023).

Vaccine hesitancy was especially high among domestic workers. One respondent to this study said that she anticipated employers requesting her to be vaccinated and was prepared to quit and 'trus' God fi work tings out fi me an' mi family'.[6] She attributed her aversion to her own health challenges. Some employers surveyed said they were not willing to hire an unvaccinated domestic worker while the majority were either willing or undecided. The reference to God by the above-mentioned domestic worker highlights the relationship some may have with religion and the church, which reiterates our earlier assertion on the psychosocial implications of bans on religious gatherings during the pandemic. The government's vaccination campaign and the national responses to it (Smith 2023) led to increased distrust of government actors by domestic workers and interfered with the JHWU's efforts to promote dialogue as a step towards transformative change.

3.1.2 Digital inequalities as a barrier to information and relief support

Globally, deeply rooted and digitally enhanced networks drove an unprecedented response to the Covid-19 outbreak. At the same time, the pandemic highlighted the extent of unequal access to digital technologies and the lack of parity in participation in the digital civic sphere, resulting in the denial of digital citizenship to large sections of the global population (Henry et al. 2021). In Jamaica, digital inequality affected domestic workers' ability to access support services and relief packages, including cash transfers, and hindered the continuation of their children's schooling.

Cellphone use in the country is relatively high at 83 per cent, which is comparable to the global average of 87 per cent. At 70 per cent, internet usage in the country exceeds the global average by 10 per cent. However, fixed broadband subscriptions and download speeds are a little more than 50 per cent of the global average, underscoring the need to improve the infrastructure of and access to information and communication technologies (ICTs) (USAID n.d.).

As with many lower-income households, domestic workers lamented the fact that their children were unable to participate in online learning. For some parents, the arrangements for online schooling were not in place to allow their children to participate, thus threatening to create long-term gaps in the education of girls in particular (Al-Ali 2020). Some households had no gadgets (tablets or smartphones) for children to use. In others, there were not enough gadgets for all children or parents were unable to afford data plans.

These challenges also prevented many domestic workers from accessing financial relief monies under the CARE programme, which required online applications. This process proved difficult for many domestic workers who did not have access to the internet or were unable to fill out the form, as pointed out by the JHWU president. Additionally, those who had smartphones and could purchase internet data packages did not find them sufficient for the time required to complete the online form. To address these challenges, the JHWU started providing support to domestic workers in accessing the CARE portal and filling out application forms. However, Pryce pointed out that, due to high demand, 'the website to register for CARE funding crashed', further impacting accessibility (IDWFED 2020). In these ways, the CARE programme exacerbated existing socio-technical discrepancies, including digital inequality.

A complex web of interconnected factors limited and, in some instances, barred grassroots groups from organizing and domestic workers from benefitting from relief opportunities. Multiple forms of inequalities intersected to shape the experiences of domestic workers and undermine efforts to bring about change. In tandem, the JHWU's efforts were bolstered by global policies that fostered an enabling environment and allowed for national and transnational engagement.

3.2 Factors facilitating JHWU's efforts

3.2.1 Global policy as a pathway for grassroots action

In 2011, the adoption of the ILO Convention on Domestic Workers (No. 189) established the first global standards for domestic workers (Human Rights Watch 2011). It laid out guidelines for states to guarantee rights and social protections for domestic workers and established that all domestic workers have the right to a safe and healthy work environment. To date, the Convention has been ratified by only 30 countries, including Jamaica, which signed it in 2016. This ratification provided legitimacy and a basic framework for labour organizing for domestic workers. Subsequently, the pandemic highlighted the urgency of creating an enabling framework for the implementation of the Convention in Jamaica, and the JHWU used it as the basis in its engagements with various stakeholders, including employers of domestic workers.

3.2.2 Foreign funding as a tool for domestic action

Despite seeming increases in the availability of funds for women's rights and feminist organizations, 99 per cent of development aid and foundation grants do not directly reach such groups and only 0.42 per cent of such grants are allocated towards women's rights (AWID 2021). Data shows that the severe under-resourcing of grassroots feminist organizations, limited access to domestic sources of funding and continued reliance on foreign funding have led to the alienation and fragmentation of some national organizations (Jalali 2013).

Like many grassroots organizations, the JHWU relies on external funding to finance its operations. Especially since the union challenges the bureaucratic and hierarchical nature of the state, it rarely qualifies for government funding (Reinelt 1994). As such, it has traditionally depended on funds from private foundations and international non-governmental organizations.

During the pandemic, the JHWU received a grant from the Open Society Foundations (OSF) to develop a project that would help domestic workers cope with the impacts of the pandemic and support efforts to formalize domestic work. Though activity-based, the funding was tailored to the needs of the union and its target community of domestic workers. It allowed the union to make small cash payouts to domestic workers and provide them with identification cards. The OSF grant thus provided the JHWU with the resources to fund the immediate needs of workers and advocate for transformative change. This situation highlighted the need for more flexible and responsive funding processes and underscored the importance of funding entities establishing a stream of rapid response or crisis funding to allow more ready access in times of crisis.

3.2.3 *Digital technology as a tool for communication and transformation*

In the wake of the pandemic, longstanding transnational feminist networks that work outside formal institutional spaces galvanized to coordinate online protests demanding international and state action (Tabbush 2020). Digital organizing became the main mode of mobilization as physical gatherings were banned (Pleyers 2020). Under such circumstances, digital tools allowed for quick decentralized responses and global collective action.

In Jamaica, the JHWU, despite having limited technical support, leveraged the support of its partners to share information via social media and text messages with domestic workers in campaigns for popular education. The union also provided small monetary allocations to some domestic workers' households to facilitate internet access for online learning. As in the case of Malaysia (Sreedharan and Ne Foo, this volume), these instances demonstrate that digital access was a key determinant of successful organizing in Jamaica and highlight the need to improve the ICT infrastructure available to lower-income communities and enhance the digital literacy of these groups. The union's use of digital tools suggests that an intersectional, multilayered and feminist approach is needed when assessing exclusionary digital practices. Such an approach can catalyse a feminist democratic project of transformation and empowerment.

4. Conclusion

Domestic workers were among those most adversely impacted by Covid-19 due to various interlinked socioeconomic factors that characterize their occupational group. The Jamaican government's response to the pandemic highlighted the need for formal employment arrangements for domestic workers in the form of contract arrangements, income stability, access to social security and accessible cash transfer programmes. In addition, an intersectional and gender-responsive perspective suggests that domestic workers would have gained from unemployment benefits and access to social protection coverage. Guided by ILO Convention 189, the JHWU advocated for these measures to support domestic workers in the absence of significant state action.

Digital access proved to be an important factor, both as a barrier and as a pathway to change during the pandemic. Yet, access to and the ability to use digital tools were not uniformly available to all. The Jamaican experience highlights the need for an intersectional approach in assessing how women and other marginalized groups access and engage in digital spaces, recognizing the weight of digital inequality (Henry, Stefani and Witt 2021). While it is helpful to map the obvious and visible divides, it is worth noting that digital inequality is closely entangled with the location of individuals within multiple systems of power such as race, colour and class (Zheng 2021).

The pandemic highlighted the need for urgent and deliberate actions to plug the legislative and policy gaps that leave domestic workers vulnerable. It also fostered the emergence of creative feminist responses, initiatives and solidarities at the local and transnational levels (Al-Ali 2020). Yet, as Pleyers (2020) notes, transformative actions often coexist with reactionary institutions and processes, which uphold the status quo or, worse, further exacerbate intersectional inequalities. In the case of grassroots movements such as the JHWU, efforts towards transformative change in the pandemic conjuncture were shaped by gendered, racialized and class inequalities. The union's organizing efforts need to be urgently complemented by further action by the state and other civil society actors to expand the rights of domestic workers.

Notes

1 Defined as people who are living in poverty despite being employed.
2 Names of all domestic workers quoted in this chapter have been changed to protect their identity.
3 More information on the collective here: https://uwispace.sta.uwi.edu/dspace/handle/2139/45158.
4 The index is a composite measure that uses nine responses, including cancellation of public events, restrictions on public gatherings, closures of public transport, stay-at-home requirements and public information campaigns. See more at: https://ourworldindata.org/covid-stringency-index.
5 See more at: https://jhwu.org.
6 English translation: 'Trust God to work things out for me and my family'.

References

Al-Ali, N. (2020), 'COVID-19 and Feminism in the Global South: Challenges, Initiatives and Dilemmas', *European Journal of Women's Studies*, 27(4): 333–347. doi: 10.1177/1350506820943617 (accessed 12 August 2021).

AWID (2021), 'Where is the Money for Feminist Organizing? Data Snapshots and A Call to Action'. Available at: https://www.awid.org/sites/default/files/2022-01/AWID_Research_WITM_Brief_ENG.pdf (accessed 27 November 2023).

Babalola, S., Krenn, S., Rimal, R., Serlemitsos, E., Shaivitz, M., Shattuck and D., Storey, D. (2020), KAP COVID Dashboard, Johns Hopkins Center for Communication Programs, Massachusetts Institute of Technology, Global Outbreak Alert and Response Network, Facebook Data for Good. Available at: https://ccp.jhu.edu/kap-covid/ (accessed 14 December 2023).

Bush-Slimani, B. (1993), 'Hard Labour: Women, Childbirth and Resistance in British Caribbean Slave Societies', *History Workshop*, 36: 83–99. Available at: https://www.jstor.org/stable/4289253 (accessed 27 November 2023).

Cho, S., Crenshaw, K.W. and McCall, L. (2013), 'Toward a Field of Intersectionality Studies: Theory, Applications, and Praxis', *Signs*, 38: 785–810. Available at: https://www.jstor.org/stable/10.1086/669608 (accessed 27 November 2023).

Clarke, P. (2020), 'Domestic Workers Cry for Help – Pryce', *The Gleaner*, 11 April. Available at: https://jamaica-gleaner.com/article/lead-stories/20200411/domestic-workers-cry-help-pryce (accessed 25 January 2024).

Cockayn, D. (2021), 'The Feminist Economic Geographies of Working from Home and "Digital by Default" in Canada Before, During, and After COVID-19', *The Canadian Geographer*, 65(4): 499–511. Available at: https://doi.org/10.1111/cag.12681 (accessed 27 November 2023).

Cooper, C. (2020), 'Household Workers Dying for Lockdown Pay', *The Gleaner*, 26 April. Available at: https://jamaica-gleaner.com/article/commentary/20200426/carolyn-cooper-household-workers-dying-lockdown-pay (accessed 12 August 2021).

Cross, J. (2020), 'COVID Jab Fear: Resistance from Front-line Staff Could Hurt Vaccine Campaign, *The Gleaner*, 14 December. Available at: https://jamaica-gleaner.com/article/lead-stories/20201214/covid-jab-fear-resistance-front-line-staff-could-hurt-vaccine-campaign (accessed 12 August 2021).

Daley, J. (2021), 'COVID Household Care Slashes Women's Incomes', *The Gleaner*, 21 April. Available at: https://jamaica-gleaner.com/article/lead-stories/20210421/covid-household-care-slashes-womens-incomes (accessed 12 August 2021).

Dewi, A., Nurmandi, A. Rochmawati, E., Purnomo, E.P., Rizqi, M.D., Azzahra, A., Benedictos, S., Suardi, W., Dewi, D.T.K. (2021), 'Global Policy Responses to the COVID-19 Pandemic: Proportionate Adaptation and Policy Experimentation: A Study of Country Policy Response Variation to the COVID-19 Pandemic', *Health Promotion Perspectives*, 10(4): 359–365. doi: 10.34172/hpp.2020.54 (accessed 12 August 2021).

French, J. (1988), 'Colonial Policy Towards Women After the 1938 Uprising: The Case of Jamaica', *Caribbean Quarterly*, 34(3–4): 38–61. doi: 10.1080/00086495.1988.11829432.

Henry, N., Stefani, V. and Witt, A. (2021), 'Digital Citizenship in a Global Society: A Feminist Approach', *Feminist Media Studies*, 22(8): 1972–1989. doi: 10.1080/14680777.2021.1937269 (accessed 12 August 2021).

Heron, T. (2008), 'Political Advertising and the Portrayal of Gender, Colour and Class in Jamaica's General Elections 2007', in (eds) Dunn, L. and Wedderburn, J., IGDS Working Paper Bo. 5: Gender and Governance: 59–104, Kingston: The University of the West Indies and the Friedrich Ebert Stiftung.

Human Rights Watch (2011), 'The ILO Domestic Workers Convention: New Standards to Fight Discrimination, Exploitation, and Abuse'. Available at: https://www.hrw.org/sites/default/files/related_material/2013ilo_dw_convention_brochure.pdf (accessed 12 April 2023).

Hutchinson, B. (2022), 'Pandemic Pivot', *Jamaica Observer*, 11 October. Available at: https://www.jamaicaobserver.com/news/pandemic-pivot/ (accessed 27 November 2023).

IDWFED (2020), 'Jamaica: COVID-19 Can Quarantine us, but Domestic Workers' Rights Are not to Be Quarantined!'. Available at: https://idwfed.org/en/covid-19/domestic-workers/stories/jamaica-covid-19-can-quarantine-us-but-domestic-workers2019-rights-are-not-to-be-quarantined?fbclid=IwAR1ZlNxPfGVOIP7tTasT-rQ5tY9Cd2RJF4DP3hrEsRA-3SAOydfTvwJnGec (accessed 12 April 2021).

ILO (2010), 'Decent Work for Domestic Workers: Fourth Item on the Agenda', International Labour Conference, 100th Session, 2011. International Labour Office. Available at: https://www.ilo.org/wcmsp5/groups/public/---ed_norm/---relconf/documents/meetingdocument/wcms_143337.pdf (accessed 12 August 2021).

ILO (2020a), 'A Policy Framework for Tackling the Economic and Social Impact of the COVID-19 Crisis'. Available at: https://www.ilo.org/global/topics/coronavirus/impacts-and-responses/WCMS_745337/lang--en/index.htm (accessed 12 August 2021).

ILO (2020b), 'Beyond Contagion or Starvation: Giving Domestic Workers Another Way Forward'. Available at: https://www.ilo.org/wcmsp5/groups/public/---ed_protect/---protrav/---travail/documents/publication/wcms_743542.pdf (accessed 27 November 2023).

ILO (2020c), 'COVID-19, the Future of Work and Trade Unions: Strengthening Social Dialogue Through the Crisis'. Available at: https://www.ilo.org/caribbean/newsroom/WCMS_763469/lang--en/index.htm (accessed 16 August 2021).

ILO (2021), 'Domestic Workers'. Available at: https://www.ilo.org/global/topics/domestic-workers/lang--en/index.htm (accessed 11 August 2021).

IMF (2020), 'Jamaica Ramps up Social and Economic Support in COVID-19 Response'. Available at: https://www.imf.org/en/News/Articles/2020/05/27/na052720-jamaica-ramps-up-social-and-economic-support-in-covid-19-response (accessed 27 November 2023).

IMF (2021), 'Policy Responses to COVID-19'. Available at: https://www.imf.org/en/Topics/imf-and-covid19/Policy-Responses-to-COVID-19#J (accessed 27 November 2023).

Jalali, R. (2013), 'Financing Empowerment? How Foreign Aid to Southern NGOs and Social Movements Undermines Grass-Roots Mobilization', *Sociology Compass*, 7(1): 55–73. doi: 10.1111/soc4.12007 (accessed 12 August 2021).

JHWU (2022), 'A Manual for Household Workers and Employers in Jamaica: Know Your Rights and Obligations'. Available at: https://jhwu.org/jhwu-manual-for-jamaica (accessed 25 January 2024).

Jiang, J. (2018), 'Organizing Immigrant Workers Through "Communities of Coping": An Analysis of Migrant Domestic Workers' Journey from an Individual Labour of Love to a Collective Labour with Rights', in (eds) Atzeni, M., Ness, I., *Global Perspectives on Workers' and Labour Organizations, Work, Organization, and Employment*: 23–42, Singapore: Springer. Available at: https://doi.org/10.1007/978-981-10-7883-5_2 (accessed 14 December 2023).

JIS (2021), 'New Vaccination Policy Coming Soon – Prime Minister Holness'. Available at: https://jis.gov.jm/new-vaccination-policy-coming-soon-prime-minister-holness/ (accessed 5 November 2021).

Johnson, M.A. (2007), 'Women's Labours in the Caribbean', *Atlantis*, 32(1): 172–183. Available at: https://journals.msvu.ca/index.php/atlantis/article/view/1160 (accessed 27 November 2023).

KPMG (2020), 'Jamaica: Government and Institution Measures in Response to COVID-19'. Available at: https://home.kpmg/xx/en/home/insights/2020/04/jamaica-government-and-institution-measures-in-response-to-covid.html (accessed 10 August 2021).

Lokot, M., and Avakyan, Y. (2020), 'Intersectionality as a Lens to the COVID-19 Pandemic: Implications for Sexual and Reproductive Health in Development and Humanitarian Contexts', *Sexual and Reproductive Health Matters*, 28:1. doi: 10.1080/26410397.2020.1764748 (accessed 10 August 2021).

MacKinnon, C.A. (2013), 'Intersectionality as Method: A Note', *Signs*, 38(4): 1019–1030. Available at: https://doi.org/10.1086/669570 (accessed 14 December 2023).

Maestripieri, L. (2021), 'The Covid-19 Pandemics: Why Intersectionality Matters', *Frontiers in Sociology*, 6. Available at: https://doi.org/10.3389/fsoc.2021.642662 (accessed 14 December 2023).

Michaelsen, S., Nombro, E., Djiofack, H., Ferlatte., O., Vissandjee, B., Zarowsky, C., (2022), 'Looking at COVID-19 Effects on Intimate Partner and Sexual Violence Organizations in Canada Through a Feminist Political Economy Lens: A Qualitative Study', *Canadian Journal of Public Health*, 113: 67–877, doi: 10.17269/s41997-022-00673-1 (accessed 10 August 2021).

Mundle, T. (2020), 'Labour Ministry and Household Workers' Union Sign MOU', *Jamaica Information Service*, 15 October. Available at: https://jis.gov.jm/labour-ministry-and-household-workers-union-sign-mou/ (accessed 12 August 2021).

Pérez, L.M. and Gandolfi, A. (2020), 'Vulnerable Women in a Pandemic: Paid Domestic Workers and COVID-19 in Peru', *Bulletin of Latin American Research*, 39(S1): 71–83. doi: 10.1111/blar.13212 (accessed 10 August 2021).

Pleyers, G. (2020), 'The Pandemic is a Battlefield. Social Movements in the COVID-19 Lockdown', *Journal of Civil Society*, 16 (4): 295–312. doi: 10.1080/17448689.2020.1794398 (accessed 10 August 2021).

Reddock, R.E. (1985), 'Women and Slavery in the Caribbean: A Feminist Perspective', *Latin American Perspectives*, 12(1): 63–80. Available at: http://www.jstor.org/stable/2633562 (accessed 10 August 2021).

Reddock, R. (2005), 'Women Workers' Struggles in the British Colonial Caribbean: The 1930s', in (ed) Sutton, C., *Revisiting Caribbean labour: Essays in honour of O. Nigel Bolland*: 19–40, Kingston: Ian Randle Publishers.

Reinelt, C. (1994), 'Fostering Empowerment, Building Community: The Challenge for State-Funded Feminist Organizations, *Human Relations*, (47) 6: 685–705. doi: 10.1177/001872679404700606 (accessed 10 August 2021).

Simms, G. (2011), 'Of Maids and Monsters', *The Gleaner*, 26 June. Available at: https://jamaica-gleaner.com/gleaner/20110626/focus/focus6.html (accessed 12 August 2021).

Smith, A. (2021), 'Jamaica to Submit First Report on ILO's Domestic Workers Convention'. *Jamaica Observer*, 12 March. Available at: https://jis.gov.jm/jamaica-to-submit-first-report-on-ilos-domestic-workers-convention/ (accessed 10 August 2021).

Smith, A. Y. (2023) 'Contested Bodies and Delayed Decisions: Attitudes to Covid-19 Vaccines Among Jamaicans', *Opera*, 32: 185–207. Available at: https://doi.org/10.18601/16578651.n32.10 (accessed 27 November 2023).

STATIN (2020), *Jamaican Labour Market: Impact of COVID-19*, Kingston: Statistical Institute of Jamaica.

Tabbush, C. and Friedman, E. (2020), 'Feminist Activism Confronts COVID-19', *Feminist Studies*, 46(3): 629–638. doi: 10.15767/feministstudies.46.3.0629 (accessed 10 August 2021).

UN Women (2020), 'The Economic Impact of COVID-19 on Women in Latin America and the Caribbean'. Available at: https://lac.unwomen.org/en/noticias-y-eventos/articulos/2020/11/impacto-economico-covid-19-mujeres-america-latina-y-el-caribe#:~:text=and%20self%2Dmanagement-,It%20is%20estimated%20that%20the%20pandemic%20will%20leave%20118%20million,replace%20the%20overall%20daily%20income (accessed 27 November 2023).

UN Women, ILO, and ECLAC (2020), 'Domestic Workers in Latin America and the Caribbean During the COVID-19 Crisis'. Available at: https://www.ilo.org/wcmsp5/groups/public/---americas/---ro-lima/documents/publication/wcms_751773.pdf (accessed 27 November 2023).

Walker, N-N. (2003), 'Domestic Workers in Jamaica', *Gender Dialogue*, 10. Available at: https://repositorio.cepal.org/server/api/core/bitstreams/4f6045d0-bb18-481f-bea3-14c4b8384c73/content (accessed 14 December 2023).

Williams, R. (2023), 'National Minimum Wage Moves to $13,000 June 1'. *Jamaica Information Service*, 17 March. Available at: https://jis.gov.jm/national-minimum-wage-moves-to-13000-june-1/ (accessed 29 April 2023).

Wynter-Adams, D. and Thomas-Brown, P. (2023), 'COVID-19 Vaccine Hesitancy in a Developing Country: Prevalence, Explanatory Factors and Implications for the

Future', *Public Health*, 217: 146–154. Available at: https://doi.org/10.1016/j.
    puhe.2023.01.031 (accessed 25 January 2024).
Zheng, Y. and Walsham, G. (2021), 'Inequality of What? An Intersectional Approach to
    Digital Inequality under Covid-19', *Information and Organization*, 31(1). doi:
    10.1016/j.infoandorg.2021.100341 (accessed 10 August 2021).

11

Collective Care to Confront the Pandemic: Migrant and Pro-migrant Activism in Chile

Nanette Liberona Concha, Carolina Stefoni and
Sius-geng Salinas Pérez

1. Introduction

The situation of the migrant population in Chile in 2020 was marked by three central events: i) the Covid-19 pandemic and its health, economic and social consequences, which hit migrants the hardest; ii) the social upheaval of October 2019, which transformed the country's political scenario by questioning the neoliberal economic model inherited from the Augusto Pinochet dictatorship (1973–90) and reinforced by successive democratic governments (Araujo 2020); and iii) the parliamentary discussions on a new migration Bill that was submitted to Congress by President Sebastián Piñera at the beginning of his government's term in 2018. The Bill was enacted into law in April 2021 (Law No. 21,325 on Migration and Foreigners) following a period of discussion that saw limited participation from migrant and pro-migrant organizations.

The interlinked impacts of these events deepened the vulnerability of Chile's migrant population. The government's repressive response to the social outburst and its implementation of new restrictions following the pandemic contributed to a normalization of state control over the population. Border closures implemented with the purported objective of 'stopping' the spread of the novel coronavirus strengthened policies restricting the entry of migrants. The parliamentary debate on the new migration Bill took place in an environment of growing criminalization of migration, an acute economic crisis and an increase in irregular entries as a result of border closures. This scenario was compounded by an increase in racist and xenophobic discourse, limitations on access to social assistance during the pandemic and a series of administrative difficulties that slowed down the process of regularizing migrants.

The flip side of this repressive situation was a flourishing of resistance and solidarity movements led by women, including migrant women, who fought hard to survive, often at the cost of exposing themselves to the virus. In so doing, they demonstrated their links with the feminist movement and their capacity to exert agency in difficult situations. Their mobilization was a response to the shortcomings of the state (Gavazzo and Nejamkis 2021) and revealed the central role of care in political action. Even though economic and social inequalities persist among the migrant population, the strategies of resistance to this reality are diverse and allow for community efforts and collaborative work between migrant and feminist organizations, with social reproduction and care at their core. In the fieldwork for this chapter, too, care emerged as a key element, which we emphasize in our analysis.

This chapter examines Chile's harsh migration regime at the height of the Covid-19 pandemic, its impact on the migrant community's ability to carry on the work of social reproduction, and the resistance and survival strategies that emerged in the face of repression. In light of the four scenarios put forth by Llavaneras Blanco and Cuervo (2021) in an earlier paper and Llavaneras Blanco and Gock in the introduction to this volume, we argue that the pandemic favoured an increase in entry restrictions and biopolitical control, broadening the state's authoritarian tendencies. We analyse the differentiated impacts of the pandemic and the restrictive measures adopted with regards to the migrant population through an intersectional feminist lens. Such an approach allows us to identify the violations and violence experienced by migrant women and their families, residents and those in transit.

The chapter is based on the authors' ongoing research and was bolstered by ethnographic work conducted in the cities of Santiago and Iquique between May and July 2021. These cities were chosen for specific reasons. Chile's capital, Santiago, has the largest concentration of migrants in the country while Iquique, the capital of a border region and the country's seventh largest city, is the site where Venezuelan migrants enter through unauthorized crossings. We conducted interviews in both cities with migrant women of Peruvian, Bolivian, Venezuelan and Ecuadorian nationalities, including two activists. In addition, we undertook a systematic review of media reports published between March 2020 and May 2021, focusing on migration policy, irregular entries, expulsions and other responses of authorities and citizens to migration. Finally, we collaborated with migrant organizations through joint actions, such as by drafting and disseminating statements, in order to lend greater visibility to their issues.[1]

The chapter starts with a brief background on the social outburst of 2019, the conditions that led to the passage of the new migration law and other related policies, and the impacts of the pandemic on the migrant population, especially since the border closures. This section also analyses the Chilean government's migration policies, particularly those implemented during the pandemic, from a gender perspective. Thereafter, Section 3 offers an account of the collective resistance and survival strategies deployed by migrant women, who placed care provisions at the centre of their efforts. The chapter ends with some brief conclusions on collective care.

2. Context

2.1 Political scenario: Power in the streets before the pandemic

On 18 October 2019, Chile experienced a moment of transformative change. The day marked the start of massive mobilizations that continued for over four months despite the heavy deployment of police forces, which systematically repressed all demonstrations. This moment laid bare the executive's long history of unwillingness to tune in and listen to citizens' demands.[2] The social outburst began as student protests against a hike in the price of a ride on the capital's metro system by 30 pesos. Soon, many sections of the population, tired of waiting for solutions to the inequalities and injustices generated by the neoliberal era, joined the demonstrations (Gutiérrez 2020). The slogan, 'it's not 30 pesos, it's 30 years', reverberated throughout the country, reflecting a deep desire and demand for social transformation (Araujo 2020).

Around this time, the feminist movement had been gaining momentum with the *Ni una menos* (which translates to Not one [woman] less)[3] and #MeToo movements. In the months leading up to the October protests, women students had taken over several universities across the country, demanding policies against harassment in classrooms. They also mobilized to push for a parliamentary discussion on decriminalizing abortion beyond the three grounds currently established in Law 21030/2017.[4] Women took a leading role in these mobilizations, which was reflected, for example, in the worldwide reception of the performance *Un violador en tu camino* (A rapist in your way) by the Las Tesis collective.[5]

The social outburst of October 2019 succeeded in bringing together multiple actors who mainstreamed their demands. The result of this process was the call for a plebiscite on 25 October 2020 to approve or reject the need for a new

Constitution. The verdict was categorical: 78.27 per cent of voters approved of the need for change. Months later, elected representatives voted to form the Constitutional Convention, a process that stood out internationally for its establishment of gender parity and reserved quotas for indigenous peoples.

Among the citizens' demands was the call by migrant and pro-migrant organizations to recognize the right to migrate and the need to regularize migration (SJM 2020a). This demand was supported by social organizations such as La Coordinadora 8M, Anamuri and the Confederación de Trabajadores Mineros (Mine Workers' Confederation). In addition, feminist organizations incorporated issues such as the femicide of migrants and the death of migrant women at the border as part of their own struggles.[6]

Unfortunately, the citizen-led revolutionary impetus waned after the economic and social crisis experienced between 2020 and 2021. In September 2022, when the new Constitution was submitted to the popular vote in a new referendum, the result was the complete opposite of what was expected by groups that had mobilized for social and gender justice for the migrant population. The proposal for a new Constitution was rejected by a large majority, leaving the rights of broad sectors of society postponed once again.

2.2 Legislative scenario: The new migration law as an instrument of control and restriction

The coming to power of Piñera as Chile's President for the second term in 2018 was marked by a shift in migration policy. Shortly after taking office, Piñera sent to Congress a Bill for a new immigration law, which had been a long-standing demand from civil society. However, several migrant, pro-migrant and human rights organizations questioned the way the government handled the process of passing this Bill. Though it had certain positive aspects, such as the creation of a new institutional framework and the recognition of international agreements on human rights, the Bill restricted entry into the country by requiring a migration visa before arrival (SJM 2020b). It also facilitated administrative expulsions and established restrictions on tax-bearing benefits (ibid.).

The discussion process was also controversial. Between 2018 and 2019, members of civil society were called to different commissions in Congress to present their positions on various aspects of the Bill, but such instances of participation were greatly reduced in the final stages of its formulation following the events of October 2019 (Stang 2020).[7] The new migration law (Law No. 21,325) was finally promulgated in April 2021 in the city of Iquique and came into force in February 2022.

In discursive terms, Piñera's government installed the ideologeme of 'putting the house in order',[8] a phrase he first used to distance himself from the previous administration led by Michelle Bachelet and later to advance the idea of combating irregular migration. The *Plan Frontera Segura* (Secure Border Plan) was implemented in this context with the purported aim of safeguarding national borders against external threats (Dufraix, Ramos and Quinteros 2020; Stefoni and Brito 2019). The measure was announced in 2018 along with others that introduced new types of visas for the Haitian and Venezuelan populations.[9] Venezuelans, for instance, had to request a Democratic Responsibility Visa at the Chilean consulate in Venezuela in order to be allowed to enter Chile in an expeditious manner. The problem was that the visa had a low acceptance rate, with only 25 per cent of applications accepted and granted (Stefoni et al. 2021). As such, the Democratic Responsibility Visa was not an effective solution for Venezuelans facing forced displacement. Thereafter, as of 5 April 2021, the government suspended the processing of this visa, citing border closures due to the pandemic.

In addition, two extraordinary regularization processes were carried out during the Piñera administration. The first was part of the 'administrative measures of immediate application' implemented by the president as soon as he took office in 2018. Its main objective was to send a strong signal about the new migration policy to be introduced by his government. The second began in April 2021 with the passage of the new migration law, under which all persons who had entered Chile before 18 March 2020 through authorized crossing points and had irregular migration status became eligible to apply for residency. Those who applied for this regularization were expected to desist from any ongoing residency applications and administrative appeals. If their application was approved, they were granted a temporary visa that cost US$90 for those over eighteen years of age. Applicants needed a valid police background certificate from their country of origin at the time of application (legalized or apostilled), a valid passport (in the case of Venezuelans, an expired passport from 2013 onwards was accepted) and a tourist card or stamp of the last visa. The application had to be made online (ImmiChile 2021).

According to the migrant women leaders interviewed for this study, the process was both difficult and restrictive. One of the interviewees, P.L. from the Corporación Colectivo Sin Fronteras (Collective Without Borders Corporation) in Santiago, pointed out that the process, while benefitting a significant number of migrants, excluded those in more vulnerable situations. For example, migrants from Haiti and Venezuela found it challenging to obtain police background certificates and passports.

Moreover, many migrants found it hard to follow the online procedures and the platform itself threw up more problems. Certain groups, such as women living in rural or far-flung areas, faced difficulties in accessing the internet and computers, reflecting a digital gap based on gender, class and age. Many migrants had to bear the cost of having the forms filled out for them by those familiar with the online procedures. Needless to say, there was no state support system for families looking to carry out the regularization process. Another problematic aspect was the application fee for regularization, which had to be paid digitally from a bank account, something that migrants without regular status could not access. L.Z., leader of the Asamblea Abierta de Migrantes y Promigrantes de Tarapacá or AMPRO (Open Assembly of Migrants and Pro-migrants from Tarapacá) in Iquique, said:

> In some way, it [the process] forces migrants to have someone else pay for the regularization of their migration status. And even though [it is known that] at the border, irregular migrants pay the coyotes, we believe that those people who are processing migrants' applications are 'processing coyotes' because they charge figures that make no sense, 90,000-100,000 Chilean pesos (US$104-115) to regularize you, whether children, adults or the elderly.

These situations cast a shadow over the spirit of this regulation. P.L. from the Corporación Colectivo Sin Fronteras remarked that the issues thrown up by the regularization process posed significant difficulties for the families involved. For various reasons, migrants experienced this regularization as a scam linked to increased control and migration restrictions by the government.

2.3 Socioeconomic scenario: Impoverishment of the migrant population and the impact of pandemic border closures

The mobilizations that began on 18 October 2019 came to an end in March 2020, when the pandemic was declared in Chile. The national borders were closed and the country entered a long and uncertain quarantine. The economic consequences were immediate, starting with an intensification of the already high levels of socioeconomic inequalities in the country (Castillo 2021). According to the National Socioeconomic Characterization Survey (Caracterizacion Socioeconomica Nacional or CASEN), while the poverty rate rose for both Chileans and foreigners between 2017 and 2020, it did so unequally. The poverty rate for migrants jumped from 10.9 per cent in 2017 to 17 per cent in 2020 while that of the local population rose from 8.4 per cent to 10.4 per cent in the same period (CASEN 2021). At the national level, the increase in poverty is largely explained by job losses, although the difference between migrants and the local population is not necessarily explained by this variable. Job losses carried a heavier cost for migrants, for whom it meant the interruption of their regularization process. In the case of women, job losses also meant their exit from the labour market for the foreseeable future, as they had no one to leave their children with amid the pandemic-related mobility restrictions.

A report by the Servicio Jesuita a Migrantes or SJM (Jesuit Migrant Service) points out that the difference in poverty levels between the two groups had nothing to do with unemployment, job informality or the length of stay in the country. While the unemployment rate increased for both, migrants experienced relatively higher employment. Informal employment was higher among the Chilean population at 28 per cent compared with 24 per cent for migrants (SJM 2021). Finally, the length of settlement did not explain the greater increase in poverty among the migrant population either, as there was no significant statistical difference between the incidence of poverty among those who had been in Chile for more than five years (19 per cent) compared with those who had been in the country for a shorter period (16 per cent). The SJM study concludes that the possible explanation for the higher poverty among migrants, 'rather than [being] an issue of labour insertion and formality, or the characteristics of the current migration pattern, is due to a lower presence of institutional support networks' (ibid.: 4). This means that migrants were unable to access the support and assistance systems managed by the government. Stefoni et al. (2021) arrive at a similar conclusion, observing that only 20.8 per cent of the respondents to their study had access to unemployment insurance, 35.2 per cent to family shopping baskets and 3.1 per cent to the Covid voucher.[10]

Migrants' low access to institutional networks and support could explain the greater increase in poverty among them. This exclusion could be attributed to: i) the lack of migratory regularization, since it is not possible to access social benefits without a RUT (tax identification number); ii) the fact that few migrants are registered with the Social Registry of Households, which determines eligibility for social benefits and aid; and iii) the way the score is calculated to determine who is deserving of aid is not in line with migrants' socioeconomic reality (for example, having a university qualification deducts points in the determination of qualification for support).

It is also important to remember that the distribution of poverty across the country does not follow a linear pattern. In the northern macro-zone (of the Tarapacá region, where Iquique is located), poverty among Chileans increased from 5.3 per cent in 2017 to 8.8 per cent in 2020 while poverty among migrants increased from 14.8 per cent to 27.8 per cent in the same period (SJM 2021). During this time, the Tarapacá region went from being the region with the twelfth highest percentage of poverty in the country to the third (ibid., Cárdenas 2021). In terms of gender, poverty affects migrant women more strongly. Chilean women have a marginally higher poverty rate (10.6 per cent) than men (10.2 per cent) while female migrants have a poverty rate of 17.7 per cent compared with 16.1 per cent for male migrants (SJM 2021).

The closure of borders as a health measure to prevent the spread of the Covid-19 virus had enormous consequences for the migrant population. Firstly, while the flow of migrants did not stop, many (mainly Venezuelan nationals) had to resort to irregular crossings. Greater risks awaited those entering through unauthorized crossing points and on foot due to the altitude and extreme temperatures of the Altiplano. Likewise, the incipient growth of an informal migration industry (consisting of coyotes and other informal networks that 'help' people cross) made this route more expensive and led to the emergence of new risks such as abandonment by coyotes (Sørensen and Gammeltoft-Hansen 2013, Liberona et al. 2021). This led to a significant increase in deaths at the border.

Secondly, the border closures triggered the emergence of a criminalizing discourse on irregular migration. Amid an already repressive and violent global migration control regime, the increase in irregular entries brought with it a further intensification of restrictive measures to stop the flow of migrants (Domenech 2017). The militarization of the border began with Piñera's signing of a modification to Decree 265, which allowed the armed forces to support border control not only in tackling drug trafficking and organized crime but also in controlling migration (Rivas 2021). This contributed to the association of irregular entries with crime. In the words of P.L.:

> The pandemic brought about certain conditions that perhaps [...] facilitated [...] this government's political will to install the migration issue in its agenda as a tool for managing public opinion, [...] instrumentalizing it for the purpose of validating itself (9 July 2021).

The third consequence of the border closures was the absolute exclusion of migrants from political rights, leaving them with only two possible options to cross the border. They could either make a Voluntary Declaration of Clandestine Entry, also known as 'self-denunciation', after entering the country irregularly, subjecting themselves to control measures exercised by the migration authorities in the process (UNHCR n.d., PDI n.d.), or they could circumvent controls to avoid being detained and deported but remain without authorized migration status. According to the Policía de Investigaciones de Chile or PDI (Investigative Police), the year 2020 saw 13,000 irregular entries into the country (Nuevo Poder 2020). The situation worsened in 2021 with an even greater presence of Venezuelan men, women, children and adolescents.[11] Pandemic measures required all persons entering the territory to undergo a PCR test and quarantine in a sanitary residence[12] in Iquique, about three hours away from the Colchane border crossing by car. Government authorities provided transport from the Colchane border crossing to only those who had made a self-denunciation to the PDI. Migrants were caught between a rock and a hard place: those who did not make the self-denunciation could not get on the bus and had to walk 237 km to Iquique without the possibility of entering the sanitary residences, and those who did were subject to administrative expulsion.

Finally, the growth of xenophobia among and discrimination by local communities was yet another impact of the border closures. The media and state authorities contributed to these negative reactions by describing irregular migrants as invaders, criminals and carriers of the virus. The government insisted on calling them 'illegal' and political discourse focused on demanding order and security. In the aftermath of such rhetoric, the Venezuelan population began to experience significant stigmatization, which not only disregarded their rights but also stripped them of dignity as human beings.[13] This rhetoric created the conditions for collective deportations of migrants. In February 2021, the Chilean state arranged the first of several flights to deport migrants. The majority of the 138 people forced to return in this operation were in sanitary residences (Díaz 2021). The collective nature of this deportation made it illegal. While the Writ of Amparo,[14] a remedy for the protection of constitutional rights, was active during this time, the Chilean government's decision was made public only after the expulsion was carried out. In March 2021, the Iquique Court of Appeals declared the expulsion illegal, and thereafter, the Supreme Court rejected the government's appeal against this decision. The court had referred to Resolution 2/18 of the Inter-American Commission on Human Rights on Forced Migration of Venezuelan Persons (El Desconcierto, 2021), which was deemed sufficient precedent to apply the universal principle of welcoming protected persons in Chile on the basis of the Cartagena Declaration on Refugees of 1984.

Despite these statements, collective expulsions persisted. The second operation took place in April 2021, involving fifty-five migrants of Venezuelan nationality. In May, another fifty-six migrants were deported, followed by twenty-five on 6 June. The main nationalities were Venezuelan (40 per cent), Colombian

(22 per cent) and Bolivian (21 per cent). According to data provided by the PDI, 26 per cent of those deported in this manner were women. In the words of the migrant leader P.L., the government simply did not recognize their rights:

> [. . .] the subsequent border closures and all the actions that followed, and the latest and most serious actions that we are seeing with the collective expulsions, all respond to a government that has permanently insisted on refusing to recognize migrants as subjects of rights (9 July 2021).

3. Migrant women's heightened vulnerabilities and collective coping strategies

Taking an intersectional approach makes it clear how inequalities based on gender, class and race[15] interact with migration status to create specific vulnerabilities. We are interested in observing how such intersecting inequalities were exacerbated by the laws and measures implemented by the Chilean state, especially in the context of the health crisis, and affected migrant women in particular.

As early as 2017, the ILO noted that female migrants experienced a number of vulnerabilities in their countries of origin, en route and on arrival in the receiving country (Lupica 2017). In the same report, the ILO observed that in Latin America, many women emigrate to escape domestic and gender-based violence in their countries of origin. Furthermore, these women may experience sexual violence during their journeys, especially at border crossings or when they run into smugglers (Salinas and Liberona 2021) and trafficking networks. Once at their destination, they face discrimination and entry restrictions in the receiving country as well as a lack of access to work and social protections (Lupica 2017).

During the pandemic, these vulnerabilities increased. The high concentration of migrant women in the care sector (domestic work, care for the sick and the elderly, cleaning, etc.) meant that job losses were frequent. Yet, in a health crisis, care work also multiplied, resulting in long hours of paid and unpaid work in households (UN Women 2020). Against this backdrop, migration policies failed to pay attention to the greater vulnerabilities faced by migrant women and limited their access to key services that facilitate social reproduction. Such exclusions exacerbated the precariousness of especially those women who had fewer resources and had undertaken irregular crossings.

3.1 The role of care in migrant women's resistance and survival strategies

The unequal distribution of care work and social reproduction is the basis of a capitalist economy (Fraser 2016, Arruzza 2016). The invisibilization of social reproductive labour in households and other private spaces deepens the crisis of social reproduction, whereby sustaining everyday life becomes increasingly difficult. This conflict at the heart of capital accumulation (Fraser 2016, 2018) is deeply unequal and affects subjects differently based on their gender, sexuality, race, class and migration status.

Even as political interests shy away from incorporating a gender perspective in migration and care policies, it is important to highlight women's resistance to such policy gaps. As Pinto and Cisternas (2020) point out, it is also crucial to unveil and understand the capacity for agency that women exhibit when faced with hostile situations. In Argentina, for instance, community care practices undertaken mainly by women were key in coping with the precarity of life during the pandemic and other structural crises (Fraga and Rodríguez Enríquez, this volume). Care is central to confronting the absence of the state, and migrant women, because they are typically excluded from government policies, are often the protagonists of networks of care and resistance that sustain the social reproduction of their families (Gavazzo and Nejamkis 2021, Herrera Mosquera 2013).

Such efforts were seen in Chile in the face of public policies that did not address the issues faced by migrant women. The struggle for survival manifested in a series of collective actions of solidarity as migrant women applied their historical and socially ascribed role in organizing care provisions. Migrant organizations, such as AMPRO, focused on fundraising and food campaigns with the aim of setting up soup kitchens, some of which allowed them to deliver more than a hundred meals per day. Hundreds of boxes of goods and grocery packages were also distributed in camps and informal settlements. To organize themselves, AMPRO activists held virtual meetings, usually after they had finished the household chores and care work for their own families. At these meetings, they discussed where to distribute the donations and then handed them out and verified that the local leaders distributed them equitably and to those most in need, keeping photographic records. Much like migrant domestic workers in Malaysia (Sreedharan and Ne Foo, this volume), in times of full quarantine, these organizations obtained special permits from the municipality to move within cities, as the presence of military and police checkpoints significantly restricted mobility.

While these organizations are composed of people with diverse gender orientations, it is mainly (migrant and non-migrant) women who led the initiatives aimed at covering care needs, such as food, either through virtual campaigns or through their physical networks. A joint initiative by academics from a public university and AMPRO stands out in this regard. This particular campaign addressed the needs of incarcerated migrant women, mainly indigenous women from Bolivia, who had no visitors because they were not Chilean residents. As a result, they had little or no access to hygiene and intimate care products, a gap that was filled by AMPRO activists. Another significant example was a sexual and reproductive health campaign co-led by pro-migrant feminist organizations such as Aquelarre Feminista Iquique (Ampro Tarapacá 2021).[16] The initiative collected sexual and reproductive goods, such as condoms and sanitary napkins, and distributed them among migrant communities. Most significantly, it brought together various social and health professionals who shared their knowledge and expertise. Another initiative by Apañales, an organization dedicated to the promotion and donation of ecological washable nappies, supported families, especially mothers, who had very little or no income and found it difficult to buy nappies for their babies.

Illustration 11.1 Community pot to assist Bolvian migrants stranded on the Chile-Bolivia border. *Photo by AMPRO Tarapacá Archive.*

With the entry of large numbers of Venezuelan migrant families, migrant organizations focused on providing aid in the form of water, food, clothing, work and housing; dealing with expulsions; and demanding migration regularization. Thousands of families arrived between mid-2020 and mid-2021, settling on the streets of border towns and cities such as Iquique. Women migrant leaders began to lend a hand to these families who were criminalized daily and subjected to police abuse and anti-immigrant racism. Migrant leaders took turns, in an office or on the ground, attending to people seeking to regularize their immigration status, and orienting and guiding them towards relevant institutions.

Networking was also a characteristic observed among migrants organizing in Santiago. To support migrant families who were often accompanied by children and had no place to stay,[17] organizers began to establish relationships with a wide spectrum of public institutions, social movements and civil society organizations (CSOs). According to P.L., 'working together with institutions for the defence of human rights during the pandemic made us link up with the Children's Ombudsman's Office on issues [...] affecting children who faced serious rights violations' while living on the streets, in front of consulates or other accommodations improvised for them. She also stated that there was significant solidarity between grassroots CSOs in general and feminist and migrant organizations. 'We mobilized and worked very closely with the feminist movement, with the Coordinadora 8M and with other feminist organizations to provide social support', she explained.

These actions were opportunities to incorporate and make visible the struggles of migrant women and dissidents within the feminist movement in Chile. The leaders of these movements and organizations were women who were able to recognize the needs of other women. They generated networks of resistance and support for migrant families and communities trying to sustain their lives in a context of extreme economic and legal precarity.

There are two primary ways in which care became visible in the context of migrant lives in Chile during the pandemic. The first was the patent lack of care and social protection policies for migrants due to repressive and exclusionary government policies. The second was how care became a central part of collective and collaborative resistance strategies, and a political act led by migrant and non-migrant women and feminist organizations in response to the Covid-19 crisis. These aspects of collective community care and mobilization can also be seen in other contexts among migrants, community organizations, diasporic networks and other marginalized groups that faced structural constraints exacerbated by the pandemic and, in response, generated social organizing and resistance.

4. Conclusion

This chapter highlighted the political transformations that took place in Chile during the pandemic, including authoritarian attitudes towards migration, culminating in heightened biopolitical control. We used an intersectional approach to analyse how these forms of state control affected migrant women, as their gender, race, class and migrant status rendered them particularly vulnerable. Issues of migration, poverty and health overlapped to expose them to vicious forms of stigmatization and rejection. In particular, the health argument was used to close the nation's borders and purportedly safeguard the country against migrants who were constructed as possible agents of contamination, generating fear and resentment against them among the local population.

In this regard, we noted the variety of positions adopted by the various branches of the state, specifically the differences between the executive and the judiciary, on the subject of migrant deportations. This was demonstrated in court rulings on the expulsion of Venezuelan migrants by the government. It is clear that there was no homogenous state response, but rather contradictory institutional responses. One can hope that a better balance between the various branches of the state will help avoid the rights violations evidenced by collective deportations.

Despite a repressive state and the risk of exposure to the Covid-19 virus, migrant women leaders strove to build and maintain collective care strategies in a supportive and selfless manner, seeking to counteract the multiple attacks that migrant communities faced from a patriarchal, capitalist and racist system. Migrant women demonstrated their agency by deploying collective care strategies as a form of resistance in which the community sphere became a space for feminist politics linked to the sustenance of everyday life. They used care as a mode of survival in response to the hyper-vulnerability and precarity that permeate migrant lives and the stigmatization and racism faced by them. Migrant women also formed broad coalitions rooted in anti-patriarchal, anti-capitalist and anti-racist feminism. In fact, solidarity among migrants and non-migrants was central to challenging the adverse circumstances generated by anti-migrant policies and compounded by the pandemic.

The challenge, going forward, is to further alliances with the feminist movement in Chile, extending solidarities to the issue of sexual dissidence. This political alliance between migrants and feminists illustrates a solidarity that we believe holds the promise of new responses to the political conjunctures shaped by the pandemic.

Notes

1 Previous projects which provide us with theoretical and empirical material are: i) 'Routes and trajectories of Venezuelan migrants throughout South America. When the doors begin to close. 2020–2024' (FONDECYT 1201130); (ii) 'Migrants during the pandemic. Immobility at the margins of inclusion. 2020–2021'. COES (ANID/FONDAP/1523A0005).

2 According to the National Institute of Human Rights, thirty-three people lost their lives in these demonstrations, more than 300 were victims of eye trauma, and thousands were detained, beaten, abused and raped in police barracks (Resumen 2020). A state of emergency was declared, a night curfew was imposed and the military patrolled the streets, evoking memories of military dictatorship for many citizens (ibid.).

3 This was also a key moment that shaped feminist mobilizations in Argentina, as explained by Fraga and Rodrìguez Enríquez in their chapter in this volume. See: https://www.efe.com/efe/america/sociedad/ni-una-menos-cumple-seis-anos-de-lucha-contra-los-feminicidios-que-no-cesan/20000013-4553491.

4 Danger to the woman's life, pregnancy resulting from rape and lethal fetal non-viability.

5 Women of all ages appropriated the performance, defying the impotent gaze of those who represent and sustain the patriarchal system. See: https://www.youtube.com/watch?v=7xqwy3ELlbY.

6 See: https://www.facebook.com/coordinadorafeminista8M/posts/3218935841666511; https://www.instagram.com/p/CHrSlYqDRu3/?utm_medium=copy_link.

7 The President of the Republic, through Supreme Decree No. 104 of 18 March 2020 of the Ministry of the Interior and Public Security, declared a constitutional state of emergency for a period of ninety days, citing public calamity throughout the national territory. The measure was in place at the time of writing this chapter.

8 EFE (2020), 'Piñera Assures that He Wants to "Put the House in Order" in View of the Immigration Bill', 21 August. Available at: https://www.efe.com/efe/america/politica/pinera-asegura-querer-ordenar-la-casa-ante-proyecto-de-ley-migratoria/20000035-4324177.

9 Since 16 April 2018, Haitian nationals have required a consular tourist visa to enter Chile while Venezuelan nationals needed the same from 22 June 2019.

10 The Covid voucher was an emergency cash transfer policy for vulnerable families during the pandemic (See: https://bonocovid.cl/).

11 See: https://www.elperiodista.cl/2021/09/migracion-irregular-a-chile-efecto-bumeran-de-politicas-restrictivas/; https://www.facebook.com/169781943633864/posts/914466135832104/?d=n.

12 The sanitary residences aim to offer safe and effective quarantine or isolation in accordance with regulations to people who require it.

13 Sreedharan and Ne Foo (this volume) refer to similar anti-migrant rhetoric and practices in Malaysia, which also saw mass arrests and expulsions of migrants during the pandemic.

14 The function of the Writ of Amparo is to give persons (both individuals and juridical persons) an instrument to challenge acts of authorities (including administrative, judicial and legislative acts) that are contrary to the fundamental rights enshrined in the Constitution. See: https://oxcon.ouplaw.com/display/10.1093/law-mpeccol/law-mpeccol-e200.

15 Race is not a natural condition but a social construct.

16 Ampro Tarapaca [@Ampro_tarapaca] (2021), 'Sexual operation for migrant population [Photography]'. Instagram, 26 February. Available at: https://www.instagram.com/p/CLrTuv7q95i/.

17 What was demanded in the context of the pandemic was humanitarian return based on a return plan promoted by the government in 2018. In this case, the request of humanitarian return was made by migrants who were left unemployed because of the pandemic. See here: https://msgg.gob.cl/wp/2018/10/18/comenzo-inscripcion-en-que-consiste-el-plan-de-retorno-humanitario-para-migrantes/ and here: https://incami.cl/retorno-humanitario/.

References

Araujo, K. (2020), *Hilos Tensados. Para leer el Octubre chileno. Colección Idea*, University of Santiago, Chile.

Arruzza, C. (2016), 'Reflexiones degeneradas: Patriarcado y capitalismo', Marxismo Crítico. Available at: https://marxismocritico.files.wordpress.com/2016/03/reflexiones-degeneradas-patriarcado-y-capitalismo.pdf (accessed 4 December 2023).

Cárdenas, R. (2021), 'Casen Survey: Tarapacá was the region that most increased its poverty rate due to a fall in labour income', *La tercera*, 6 July. Available at: https://www.latercera.com/pulso-pm/noticia/encuesta-casen-tarapaca-fue-la-region-que-mas-aumento-su-tasa-de-pobreza-por-caida-de-ingresos-del-trabajo/BTR6RQAUYNFBNNTUQSKN6PEGDI/ (accessed 17 December 2023).

CASEN (2021), Encuesta de Caracterización Socioeconómica Nacional, Ministerio de Desarrollo Social y Familia, Gobierno de Chile'. Available at: https://ghdx.healthdata.org/record/chile-national-socioeconomic-characterization-survey-2017-2018 (accessed 17 December 2023).

Castillo, P. (2021), 'Desigualdad, pandemia y digitalización', *El Mostrador*, 26 July. Available at: https://www.elmostrador.cl/noticias/opinion/columnas/2021/07/26/desigualdad-pandemia-y-digitalizacion/ (accessed 17 December 2023).

Díaz, A. (2021), 'Chile lleva a cabo la mayor expulsión de migrantes irregulares en un solo día', *RT*, 10 February. Available at: https://actualidad.rt.com/actualidad/383112-chile-expulsion-inmigrantes (accessed 17 December 2023).

Domenech, E. (2017), 'Las políticas de migración en Sudamérica: Elementos para el análisis crítico del control migratorio y fronterizo', *Terceiro Milênio Revista Crítica de Sociologia e Política*, 8(1): 19–48. Available at: https://ri.conicet.gov.ar/handle/11336/58156 (accessed 4 December 2023).

Dufraix, R., Ramos, R. and Quinteros, D. (2020), '"Ordenar la casa": Securitización y producción de irregularidad en el norte de Chile', *Sociologias*, 22(55): 172–196. Available at: https://doi.org/10.1590/15174522-105689 (accessed 4 December 2023).

El Desconcierto (2021), 'Setback for the Government: Supreme Court Declares Illegal Expulsion of Venezuelans Citing Duty to Protect Refugees', 2 March. Available at: https://www.eldesconcierto.cl/nacional/2021/03/02/reves-para-el-gobierno-suprema-declara-ilegal-expulsion-de-venezolanos-aludiendo-al-deber-de-proteccion-a-refugiados.html (accessed 4 December 2023).

Fraser, N. (2016), 'El capital y los cuidados', *New Left Review*, 100: 111–132. Available at: https://newleftreview.es/issues/100/articles/nancy-fraser-el-capital-y-los-cuidados.pdf (accessed 4 December 2023).

Gavazzo, N. and Nejamkis, L. (2021), '"Si compartimos, alcanza y sobra". Redes de cuidados comunitarios entre mujeres migrantes del Gran Buenos Aires frente al COVID-19, *Remhu*, 29: 97–120. Available at: https://doi.org/10.1590/1980-85852503880006107 (accessed 4 December 2023).

Gutiérrez, O. (2020), 'Razones del levantamiento social en Chile. Necropolítica como paradigma de Estado', *Universum*, 35(1): 104–26. Available at: https://www.scielo.cl/pdf/universum/v35n1/0718-2376-universum-35-01-104.pdf (accessed 4 December 2023).

Herrera Mosquera, G. (2013), 'Gender and International Migration: Contributions and Cross-Fertilizations', *Annual Review of Sociology*, 39: 471–489. Available at: https://doi.org/10.1146/annurev-soc-071811-145446 (accessed 12 January 2024).

InmiChile (2021), 'Comienza el proceso de regularización extraordinario 2021'. Available at: https://immichile.cl/comienza-el-proceso-de-regularizacion-extraordinario-2021/ (accessed 6 January 2023).

Liberona, N., Piñones Rivera, C.D. and Dilla Alfonso, H. (2021) 'De La migración Forzada Al tráfico De Migrantes: La migración Clandestina En tránsito De Cuba Hacia Chile', *Migraciones Internacionales*, 12. Available at: https://doi.org/10.33679/rmi.v1i1.2319 (accessed 4 December 2023).

Llavaneras Blanco, M. and Cuervo, M.G. (2021), 'La pandemia como portal: Transformaciones (de) politicas que disputan la nueva normalidad', DAWN. Available at: https://bit.ly/3oBW8Xm (accessed 4 December 2023).

Nuevo Poder (2020), 'PDI has Denounced 13,000 People for Illegal Entry into Chile', *Nuevo Poder*, 31 December. Available at: https://www.nuevopoder.cl/pdi-ha-denunciado-a-13-mil-personas-por-ingreso-ilegal-a-chile/ (accessed 4 December 2023).

PDI (n.d.), Declaración voluntaria de ingreso clandestino, Available at: https://pdichile.cl/tr%C3%A1mites-online/denuncia-por-ingreso-clandestino (accessed 4 December 2023).

Pinto, C. and Cisternas, N. (2021), 'Reflexiones sobre el uso de la interseccionalidad en los estudios migratorios en Chile', *Revista Punto Género,* (14): 49–70. Available at: https://doi.org/10.5354/2735-7473.2020.60866 (accessed 4 December 2023).

Rebolledo, L. (2001), 'Mujeres exiliadas: con Chile en la memoria', *Cyber Humanitatis*, 19. Available at: https://cyberhumanitatis.uchile.cl/index.php/RCH/article/view/8876 (accessed 4 December 2023).

Resumen (2021), 'Dirección del INDH dejó fuera de registro a más de 300 víctimas de lesiones oculares por efectivos policiales en el Estallido en Chile', 17 June. Available at: https://resumen.cl/articulos/direccion-del-indh-dejo-fuera-de-registro-a-mas-de-300-victimas-de-lesiones-oculares-por-efectivos-policiales-en-el-estallido-en-chile (accessed 4 December 2023).

Riedemann, A. and Carolina, S. (2015), 'Sobre el racismo, su negación, y las consecuencias para una educación anti-racista en la enseñanza secundaria chilena', *Polis (Santiago)*, 14(42). Available at: http://dx.doi.org/10.4067/S0718-65682015000300010 (accessed 4 December 2023).

Rivas, C. (2021), 'President Piñera signs decree for the armed forces to collaborate in migration control', *Diario Financiero*, 12 January. Available at: https://www.df.cl/noticias/economia-y-politica/pais/presidente-pinera-firma-decreto-para-que-las-ffaa-colaboren-en-el/2021-01-12/115557.html (accessed 4 December 2023).

Salinas, S. and Liberona, N. (2021), 'Violencia de género en el tráfico de migrantes. Efectos psicosociales y agencia de las mujeres migrantes clandestinas', *RIEM*, 10(2): 51–77. Available at: https://doi.org/10.25115/riem.v10i2.4885 (accessed 4 December 2023).

SJM (2020a), 'Migration in Chile, Bill on Migration and Foreigners: 5 Fundamental Proposals'. Available at: https://www.migracionenchile.cl/wp-content/uploads/2020/06/5_propuestas_fundamentales_PL_de_Migraci%C3%83%C2%B3n.pdf (accessed 12 January 2024).

SJM (2020b), 'Migración en Chile. Anuario 2019, un análisis multisectorial', Santiago, Chile. Available at: https://www.migracionenchile.cl/wp-content/uploads/2020/09/MIGRACION-EN-CHILE-V6.pdf (accessed 4 December 2023).

SJM (2021), 'Casen y Migración: Una caracterización de la pobreza, el trabajo y la seguridad social en la población migrante (Informe N°1)', Santiago, Chile. Available at: https://www.migracionenchile.cl/wp-content/uploads/2021/10/Informe-CASEN_compressed-2.pdf (accessed 4 December 2023).

Sørensen, N. and Gammeltoft-Hansen, T., (2013), 'Introduction', in (eds) Nina Sørensen and T. Gammeltoft-Hansen, *The Migration Industry and the Commercialization of International Migration (Global Institutions)*, 1–23. New York: Routledge.

Stang, F. (2020), 'Legislating Blindly, with Urgency, and in a Situation of Exception: The Processing of the Migration Bill', *El Mostrador*, 20 July. Available at: https://www.

elmostrador.cl/noticias/opinion/columnas/2020/07/20/legislar-a-ciegas-con-urgencia-y-en-situacion-de-excepcion-la-tramitacion-del-proyecto-de-ley-de-migraciones/ (accessed 4 December 2023).

Stefoni, C., Báltica, C. and Blukacz, A. (2021), 'Migraciones y COVID-19: Cuando el discurso securitista amenaza el derecho a la salud', *Simbiótica*, 8(2): 38–66. Available at: https://doi.org/10.47456/simbitica.v8i2.36378 (accessed 4 December 2023).

Stefoni, C., and Brito, S. (2019), 'Migraciones y migrantes en los medios de prensa en Chile: La delicada relación entre las políticas de control y los procesos de racialización', *Revista de Historia Social y de las Mentalidades*, 23(2): 1–28. Available at: https://doi.org/10.35588/rhsm.v23i2.4099 (accessed 4 December 2023).

UNHCR (n.d.). 'Ayuda Chile: Ingreso a Chile'. Available at: https://help.unhcr.org/chile/ingreso/ (accessed 4 December 2023).

UNHCR (2020), 'Tendencias globales. Desplazamiento Forzado en 2020'. Available at: https://www.acnur.org/60cbddfd4 (accessed 21 October 2021).

UN Women (2020), 'Cash Transfers and Gender Equality: Improving its Effectiveness in Response to the COVID-19'. Available at: https://lac.unwomen.org/en/digiteca/publicaciones/2020/05/respuesta-covid-19-transferencias-monetarias (accessed 4 December 2023).

12

Organizing from the Heart: Migrant Domestic Workers' Resistance in Malaysia during the Covid-19 Pandemic

Liva Sreedharan and Yen Ne Foo

1. Introduction

Domestic work is a significant source of employment for women migrant workers in Malaysia. The sector is characterized by high levels of informality, the private nature of workplaces, low wages, and exclusion from the labour rights and social protections afforded to workers in other sectors. Migrant domestic workers (MDWs) in particular face a shortage of decent work, have limited ability to organize effectively and bargain collectively, and are exposed to the risk of violence and harassment. These inequalities, which MDWs routinely experience, were further exacerbated during the Covid-19 pandemic.

The public health crisis negatively impacted MDWs' working and living conditions and their ability to remit money to families (Lim 2020). It also brought to the fore anti-migrant sentiments as MDWs reported being discriminated against and stigmatized as virus spreaders (Hector and Pereira 2020, Fishbein 2020). Anti-migrant attitudes manifested in the government's pandemic response policies,[1] including large-scale arrests and deportations of undocumented migrants (Human Rights Watch 2021, The Straits Times 2021), stricter enforcement of immigration laws, exclusion of migrant workers from pandemic assistance plans and prohibition on renting low-cost housing to migrant workers (Hisamudin 2020).

Although these measures reflected increased biopolitical control by the state and the expansion of an ongoing authoritarian trend, the pandemic was also a period in which transformative policies for MDWs emerged in Malaysia. The crisis acted as a portal into labour policies that expanded social justice for

MDWs. Amid an authoritarian landscape, MDWs displayed tremendous resilience and increased their capacity to organize and mobilize against heightened inequalities. Organizing led to the strengthening of existing MDW associations and the formation of a new one.[2] This created a support network for workers to navigate everyday rights violations and vulnerabilities, spread awareness about MDWs' rights and expand the spaces where they could claim rights through policy advocacy. Organizing also led to substantive policy changes, specifically an expansion of the coverage of national social protection schemes to include MDWs.

This chapter examines how MDWs in Malaysia experienced the Covid-19 pandemic, taking into consideration multiple oppressions embedded in class, gender, migrant status and racial hierarchies. It looks at how Malaysia's sociopolitical context, characterized by anti-migrant regimes, and the country's pandemic response policies contributed to (re)producing and exacerbating MDWs' precarity during the public health crisis. As a second line of inquiry, we examine how MDWs resisted the rising inequalities they experienced during the Covid-19 crisis by organizing and advocating for progressive policy transformations.

Data for this case study was collected using a mixed methods approach. It included a review of existing literature on domestic workers as well as semi-structured interviews with the leaders of two domestic worker organizations, namely the Association of Nationalist Overseas Filipino Workers in Malaysia (AMMPO) and Persatuan Pekerja Rumah Tangga Indonesia Migran (PERTIMIG), which translates to the Indonesian Migrant Domestic Workers Association. Both are affiliates of the International Domestic Workers Federation (IDWF) and organized MDWs prior to Covid-19. A representative from the IDWF was also interviewed for this study.

2. MDWs in Malaysia: A precarious life

As of May 2020, there were 129,980 documented MDWs in Malaysia while an estimated 200,000 were believed to be undocumented (Ke-Arah 189, 2021). As in many parts of the world, MDWs in Malaysia live in the shadows of the country's restrictive immigration and labour governance regimes. Each of these regimes differentially includes MDWs in their spheres of control and reproduces socially constructed roles and relationships between women and men, nationals and migrants, and the rich and the poor.

Immigration regulations dictate which migrants can access Malaysia's domestic work market. The gendered and racialized nature of the sector is an outcome of Malaysia's labour migration regulations, whose provisions only allow women between the ages of twenty-one and forty-five from an approved list of countries who have been certified as physically fit and who have passed security clearance to be employed as MDWs, also referred to as foreign domestic helpers (Immigration Department of Malaysia 2021). The requirement that only women of reproductive age be employed as MDWs is a reflection of a labour market that sees care and domestic work as extensions of a woman's duty as a citizen (Hierofani 2021, Anderson 2000).

Based on the nationalities of the MDWs they are hiring, prospective employers have to meet certain income thresholds and make personal bond payments[3] to Malaysia's Department of Immigration. This places MDWs in a hierarchy of desirability while giving employers with greater financial resources more hiring choices. For example, to hire a MDW from Indonesia, a prospective employer must have a monthly net income of 7,000 Malaysian Ringgit (MYR) (US\$1,570.33) and make a personal bond payment of MYR250 (US\$59.72). Hiring a MDW from the Philippines would require a monthly net income of MYR5,000 (US\$1,194.32) and a personal bond payment of MYR750 (US\$179.15) (Immigration Department of Malaysia 2021). These criteria not only determine which racialized subjects are suitable for hire but also reproduce inequities and power imbalances between MDWs and their employers as well as between MDWs from different countries.

What's more, the immigration regime's control over MDWs' mobility extends beyond their entry into the labour market to how they move within it. Once employed, MDWs in Malaysia have limited labour market mobility and agency. The Visitor's Pass (or Temporary Employment Pass) is a work permit that ties a MDW to a specific employer; no change of employer and/or employment is allowed except with the permission of the immigration department. This limits the ability of MDWs to leave exploitative working conditions or negotiate the terms of employment. In the event of violence and exploitation, only the immigration department has the power to transfer the MDW to a new employer on humanitarian grounds. The work permit is valid for twelve months and may be renewed annually for a period of up to ten years.[4] However, renewal is at the employer's discretion and subject to the worker's fitness for work, which must be proved by passing a medical examination and a mandatory pregnancy test. If the MDW is pregnant, the employment contract is terminated and the worker is repatriated.

Malaysia's labour laws leave the domestic work sector largely unregulated. The Employment Act 1955, which is the foundational legislation that governs employer-employee relations in the country, relegates domestic workers to a subclass without many of the standard labour rights and protections afforded to other workers. Provisions of the Act that regulate the number of working hours, paid days off, holidays and leave days; the payment of overtime wages; and maternity benefits do not apply to domestic workers. They are also excluded from other laws that protect workers from exploitation, including those that govern the payment of the minimum wage and establish national standards for employer-provided accommodation. Such exclusions affirm a broader appraisal of domestic work: it is seen not as 'real' work but as a form of 'service' and is, therefore, not subject to rational economic calculations of exchange and use values (Chin 2003).

The absence of regulations for the domestic work sector engenders power imbalances between the employer and the MDW in that the employer alone determines the wages, the quality of work and the living conditions of the MDW. This exposes MDWs to substandard working conditions and labour rights violations, which are compounded if they are undocumented or working informally without government-approved permits (Human Rights Watch 2004). In severe cases, MDWs in Malaysia have been exposed to conditions that amount to forced labour and other forms of violence and harassment (Napier-Moore 2017). Given the power imbalances within employment relationships, MDWs who attempt to negotiate better working conditions or report errant employers risk losing employment and a place to live and may be handed over to the immigration authorities.

Traditionally, organizing and collective bargaining have allowed workers to manage unequal power dynamics with employers. However, Malaysia does not have any registered trade unions for domestic workers, and previous attempts to establish one were unsuccessful.[5] Migrant worker associations in the country are also not formally registered. Further, the characteristics of domestic work are such that it does not conform easily to the standard industrial relations model. There is little recognition of the fact that domestic workers are labour rights holders and employers' homes are sites where labour relations play out. On the one hand, the maternalist dynamic of domestic work means that MDWs are often seen as 'part of the family', undermining latent work relations (Anderson 2000). On the other hand, the positioning of domestic workers as a subclass in the Employment Act 1955 implies that they need to show loyalty or deference. In both contexts, organizing by MDWs could be seen as a personal affront to employers (Hobden 2015). Domestic work is also highly decentralized, meaning that MDWs are spatially isolated from each other and dispersed in multiple households with individualized contracts with their respective employers. To organize collectively, they have to come together in a shared public space, which is logistically challenging because of the high degree of control employers are able to exercise over MDWs' working hours and freedom of movement. Among MDWs who are undocumented or working informally, organizing and moving in public spaces come with the added risks of arrest, detention and deportation.

To work around some of these issues, MDW associations in Malaysia, such as AMMPO and PERTIMIG, have adopted a mode of organizing that focuses on micro-level mobilization of MDWs. This typically begins with building safe spaces for workers to convene and share experiences with each other. Although there is a designated organizer, the structure of the MDW associations is not hierarchical. These women-only environments allow MDWs to compare notes on employers and working conditions and share their day-to-day lived experiences of being a woman, a migrant and a domestic worker in Malaysia. Meetings are usually conducted on Sundays in informal settings such as restaurants, public parks, churches and homes of MDWs.

3. Covid-19 as 'security threat' and Malaysia's 'securitized' pandemic response

Malaysia detected its first Covid-19 case on 25 January 2020 and, thereafter, experienced recurring waves of infection. From the beginning, the government of Malaysia described Covid-19 as a national security threat (National Security Council Malaysia 2020)[6] and an 'unprecedented crisis' (Prime Minister's Office of Malaysia 2020a) that poses a 'serious' and 'major threat to the economic life of the people' (Prime Minister's Office of Malaysia 2020b, Malaysia Central 2021). The government's pandemic response was presented as a 'fight' that must be won (Prime Minister's Office of Malaysia 2021) and a collective responsibility. In line with the framing of Covid-19 as a security threat, all pandemic-related policy making was led by the National Security Council chaired by the prime minister. A Compliance Operations Task Force, which included the police, the army and other enforcement agencies, was established to monitor compliance with Covid-19 prevention measures (Ministry of Health Malaysia 2020).

On 18 March 2020, the government introduced an expansive regime of mobility control known as the Movement Control Order (MCO), which outlined three key measures. The first was the implementation of border controls, characterized by the closure of all entry points and international borders save for approved reasons for travel.[7] The second was the implementation of controls on the freedom of movement within the country, marked by the closure of non-essential workplaces, public and private business establishments, and schools; a broad stay-at-home order; and restrictions on inter-district and inter-state travel. This precipitated a significant loss of income and jobs, especially among daily wage earners and informal sector workers. The third was the prohibition of public gatherings and the promotion of physical distancing.

In high-risk locations with Covid-19 infection clusters, an Enhanced Movement Control Order (EMCO) was put in place. Movement in and out of EMCO locations was prohibited, except for emergencies, and residents were subject to mandatory Covid-19 tests. Depending on the number of Covid-19 cases at any point, the government tightened or relaxed the restrictions using different iterations of the MCO and EMCO (Hashim et al. 2021).[8]

Enforcement of these restrictions relied on increased police presence in civilian spaces. In the early phases of implementation of the MCO, the Royal Malaysia Police (RMP), with the support of the Malaysia Armed Forces (MAF), conducted roadblocks, stationed personnel at inter-state checkpoints and patrolled certain areas to control day-to-day mobility. Inter-district and inter-state travel had to be authorized by the police and other law enforcement officials, who could issue fines for non-compliance with MCO regulations.

On 12 January 2021, the government declared a state of emergency on the pretext that it needed 'certain powers' to curb the pandemic effectively (Prime Minister's Office of Malaysia 2021). The Emergency (Essential Powers) Ordinance 2021 (EO), which was in place until 21 July 2021, further increased the powers of security personnel while suspending accountability mechanisms. The EO gave the MAF policing powers, allowing its personnel to arbitrarily impose fines and detain those in violation of MCO restrictions. It also empowered law enforcement and border control officials to 'arrest illegal immigrants and anyone who encroaches on our national borders' (Malaysia Central 2021). Concurrently, it provided officials immunity against prosecution and allowed the prime minister and chief ministers to unilaterally pass supplementary budgets, including for the enhancement of security measures, without the legislature's approval. Parliament and state legislative assembly sessions were suspended, as were elections for one state assembly and several vacated parliamentary constituencies, removing not only a check-and-balance tool but also any potential challenge to the government's hold on power.

Part of the state's pandemic response was to position migrants as sources of the Covid-19 virus and, consequently, as security threats. The working and living conditions of migrant workers made it challenging for them to practise contagion prevention measures and access health services. The first set of EMCO restrictions was implemented in buildings with large numbers of migrants.[9] Under its cover, the state conducted immigration raids to arrest undocumented migrants (Kanyakumari 2020, CodeBlue 2020). Images of barbed wires and security personnel guarding entrances implied that the contagion threat in the form of migrant bodies had to be isolated and then removed from public spaces. Similarly, inspections for compliance with the national standards for employer-provided housing and amenities often involved raids on migrant workers' accommodations (The Straits Times 2020). Targeted at migrant workers in general, children and the elderly, if found, were also arrested.

Enforcement activities and media images of arrests optically linked migrants with Covid-19 risks and contributed to anti-migrant discontent (Latiff and Ananthalakshmi 2020). The rhetoric of migrants as threats was reinforced when the immigration detention centres, where migrants are held pending deportation, became hotspots for Covid-19 outbreaks (Wahab 2020b). Over the course of the pandemic, the state tapped into anti-migrant sentiments and tightened its immigration control regime. In March 2020, despite the guarantee of non-retaliation towards migrant workers who sought Covid-19 testing or treatment based on their immigration status, the authorities conducted crackdowns in which 2,000 people were arrested (Al Jazeera 2021). As the number of large-scale raids rose, the state increased the capacity of prisons and detention centres (Chung 2021) and suppressed dissent towards this policy through media censorship and criminalization of journalists on the basis of Malaysia's Communications and Multimedia Act 1998 (Al Jazeera 2020, Lakhdhir 2020). The immigration department asked the public to identify and report undocumented migrants via hotline numbers and its official Facebook page. Netizens were commended for efforts to report 'illegal immigrants'.[10]

Immigration raids were conducted alongside the implementation of the Labour Recalibration Programme and the Return Recalibration Programme to regularize or repatriate undocumented migrants.[11] The Labour Recalibration Programme, in part, sought to use migrant workers to fill labour market gaps in key economic sectors such as construction, manufacturing and plantations; domestic work was excluded. While there was no reason provided, this exclusion was consistent with the treatment of domestic work and domestic workers within existing labour and migration policy frameworks. This situation exposed the duality in Malaysia's labour migration approach, which perceives migrant workers simultaneously as security threats and as embodied labour necessary to secure the economic well being of the state (Harun 2021). Other discriminatory policies included reminding property owners to not rent their premises to migrants, and prohibiting migrants from engaging in certain types of businesses and securing employment outside their approved permits (Bavani 2020). Migrant workers in essential services and domestic work were expected to work longer hours without adequate physical and social protections. With the exception of MDWs, they also had to undergo mandatory Covid-19 screening to return to work, though the same was not required of Malaysian nationals (Lee 2020).

4. MDWs during the pandemic: Pushed to the brink

Successive stay-at-home orders and the closure of educational institutions during the pandemic forced many MDW employers and their children to remain at home. This not only intensified MDWs' workloads but also substantially increased the hours they spent in the confined spaces of their employers' homes. This had two implications. Firstly, live-in MDWs in particular were subjected to greater surveillance and control over their time and freedoms by employers. Secondly, MDWs in general faced increasingly precarious working conditions, which further devalued domestic work.

Employers' standards of hygiene in their homes changed due to infection risks. MDWs were not only expected to shoulder the additional burden of meeting those standards but were also prevented from leaving their workplaces and fraternizing with others for fear that they would bring the virus into employers' homes. School closures meant that MDWs had to provide additional care for employers' children. MDWs interviewed for this study spoke about being tasked with caring for the sick and elderly without the provision of adequate personal protective equipment (PPE) such as masks and gloves.[12] Needless to say, they had to purchase their own PPEs for work.[13] With the domestic work sector not being subject to the legal limits of regular and overtime work hours[14] and the requirements of minimum wage[15] and overtime pay, MDWs were rarely compensated for the additional hours of work or the risks they took on.

Additionally, MDWs and their employers were specifically excluded from the pandemic-related economic assistance provided by the state. Employers who lost jobs or experienced salary deductions transferred this financial burden onto domestic workers through deductions in or non-payment of wages. Live-out MDWs suffered a loss of income because they were unable to travel to their workplaces due to movement restrictions or lost jobs due to the fear of contagion. At times, the loss of income among live-out MDWs led to food deprivation, the inability to pay rent and eviction from their homes (Wahab 2020a).

MDWs who obtained full wages on time were unable to remit money to their families as these services remained closed during partial and full lockdowns. Many did not know how to remit money online. This had a knock-on effect on the ability of families of MDWs to meet their basic needs in their countries of origin (ILO 2020).

Outside the world of work, MDWs were grappling with challenges in accessing support services. MDW organizations, such as PERTIMIG, the IDWF and AMMPO, saw a sharp rise in complaints from MDWs over termination of employment, food deprivation, long working hours, abuse and violence, and eviction and deportation during the pandemic. The increase in violence and harassment came at a time when social, health care and access to justice services were reprioritized to respond to the pandemic. Non-governmental organizations (NGOs) that provide services to migrant workers were deemed non-essential and not allowed to operate during the MCO periods.

Barriers to accessing services were likely intensified due to increased police presence and other markers of law enforcement in public spaces. Police roadblocks, patrols and random stops to check for compliance with Covid-19 measures made day-to-day movements perilous for MDWs. As mentioned earlier, the securitized nature of Malaysia's pandemic response positioned migrant workers, especially those who were undocumented, as security and public health threats. Not only were migrant workers at risk of being arrested during immigration raids, but there was a tacit awareness on the part of law enforcement that such workers were obvious (and easy) targets for random stop-and-checks. Given the sweeping discretionary powers granted to security personnel, most migrant workers were powerless to object to police stops and document checks. Research participants reported that MDWs were deterred from and deliberately avoided leaving their homes for these reasons. Workers who experienced violence or other kinds of crises were hesitant to seek support services. The result was that MDWs, already isolated from most social connections because of the nature of their workplaces, were locked in by the pandemic.

Central to the precarity of MDWs was their reliance on migration status to validate their standing and worth in Malaysian society. Consular services and immigration offices were closed through most of the lockdown periods. Whenever reopened, they experienced a surge in applications related to permits and passport renewals. MDWs often depended on their employers to prepare the paperwork and go through the necessary administrative processes to enable them to legally work and stay in Malaysia. During the pandemic, MDWs and their employers were unable to renew their documents on time, putting them at risk of arrest, detention and deportation for not complying with immigration requirements. Many MDWs whose work contracts had expired were unable to return home due to the closure of international borders. This group of workers often continued to work for their employers without pay. Others saw their permits expire as they waited for flights to their countries of origin. State policies to regularize undocumented migrant workers excluded MDWs, underscoring the continued gender-based discrimination and inequalities experienced by them.

5. MDWs' resistance to an authoritarian landscape

Malaysia's highly discriminatory and oppressive labour and immigration regimes limited the autonomous space for MDWs to connect with others, form social networks and collectively organize. Yet, even amidst this authoritarian landscape, MDW organizations adopted multiple strategies to resist the barriers to organizing and leverage the impact of their resistance.

5.1 Redefined safe spaces for collective communities

Prior to the pandemic, MDW organizations hosted weekly or fortnightly meetings to provide a safe space for workers to meet, connect and develop a sense of community with others outside of their employers' homes. Attendance at these meetings varied based on the distance and cost of travel and the ability of MDWs to get days off. Because the domestic work sector is not regulated, many MDWs do not have fixed and paid days off. As such, their ability to leave the workplace is subject to employers' discretion. Attendance among undocumented MDWs was inconsistent because many feared being stopped by law enforcement officials while travelling to and from meetings.

During the pandemic, when restrictions on daily movements and full or partial lockdowns were in place, MDWs began conducting these meetings virtually. This not only altered the medium through which they connected amongst themselves but also redefined (and widened) the shared public sphere for collective organizing. Virtual meetings offered more than just a safe space for sharing and connecting. By removing the need to travel, they allowed MDWs to gather without the risk of arrest and detention. Thus, the decision to participate in meetings became a matter of choice as MDWs were less limited by the fear of losing their jobs or encountering law enforcement officials.

To be sure, mobilizing and organizing online came with its own challenges, as the cost of internet data, poor internet connectivity and long working hours posed questions of accessibility. But these hurdles were not insurmountable. With the support of the IDWF, a MDW coordinator was recruited and stationed in Malaysia to spearhead organizing efforts. Frequent consultations between the coordinator and the IDWF led to strategic and locally relevant decision making on community mobilization. A few months into the nationwide lockdown, some MDWs formed a committee to empower other members of MDW organizations to convene online. Committee members taught others how to download and use virtual meeting platforms like Zoom on mobile phones. Because meetings were just a click away, MDWs could participate while they were at work and did not have a day off. Besides, virtual meetings could be arranged with fewer resources, allowing MDW organizations to convene more regularly and target workers from more distant geographies.

The virtual format also acted as an equalizer between MDW organizations and other labour migration stakeholders. During the pandemic, MDW organizations regularly coordinated with CSOs and strategically joined meetings with civil society coalitions working on advancing the rights of domestic workers in Malaysia. The coalition meetings exposed MDWs to the politicized language of workers' rights, collective organizing and labour solidarity and provided them with a useful frame of reference for self-representation.

Of the CSO coalitions the MDW organizations participated in, two are notable: the first is the Labour Law Reform Coalition (LLRC), which, as the name suggests, focuses on labour law reforms, including the amendment of legislation such as the Employment Act, while the second, Ke-Arah 189, is a coalition of CSOs advocating for domestic workers' rights in line with the ILO Domestic Workers Convention, 2011 (No. 189). MDWs interviewed for this study said that being part of a coalition offered psychological empowerment, especially when they had to make their case to power holders such as government agencies. When participation was mediated through a virtual platform and included other CSOs, MDWs were able to better represent themselves through verbal interventions as well as virtual functions such as polls, chat boxes and comment boxes.

Over time, MDWs evolved from participants to conveners and leaders of these settings. On their own or in collaboration with other CSOs, they carved out new spaces to speak about their experiences and demand regulations for the domestic work sector and inclusion in social protection schemes. It became apparent to state and non-state stakeholders that the participation of MDWs was critical in shaping policies for the domestic work sector. As the PERTIMIG representative interviewed for this study put it,

> Now that the government understands how connected we are with MDWs on the ground, they specifically invite us to meetings and consultations. Our input helps them make relevant policy decisions for MDWs because it is informed by MDWs themselves. One of our successes was the inclusion of MDWs in social security (August 2021).

Because they represent the unmediated voices of MDWs, these organizations were invited to contribute to policy dialogues on labour laws and domestic workers' rights with countries of origin embassies or high commissions and the Malaysian government. In some of these meetings, the Ministry of Human Resources (MOHR) committed verbally to providing domestic workers with paid days off, enacting legislation for their protection and including them under the Social Security Protection Scheme of Malaysia's Social Security Organization (SOCSO).[16]

5.2 Strengthened community consciousness in a time of crisis

The virtual safe spaces nurtured the individual and community consciousness needed for sustained MDW organizing and mobilizing. The weekly gatherings offered a sense of community and solidarity amid the isolation of the pandemic. As MDWs spoke of their own pandemic experiences, it became clear that especially those who were undocumented and excluded from state-sponsored aid were struggling with food and income insecurities. Community organizers learnt that the food aid given by embassies to their nationals did not reach many workers. This provided the impetus for MDW organizations to mobilize members and allies.

With the support of the IDWF, PERTIMIG established a hotline and used social media platforms, such as WhatsApp and Facebook, to gather requests for and coordinate the distribution of food aid. A database catalogued the requests, separating those made by MDWs from other migrant workers, and food aid deliveries were coordinated accordingly. To mitigate the risk of arrests associated with travelling during the pandemic, PERTIMIG sought a letter of authorization from the Embassy of Indonesia. Food was distributed door-to-door by MDW leaders within the same locality. When it was not possible to distribute food personally, MDWs used private sector food delivery services. Along with customized food aid packages, an information pack containing leaflets about

MDWs' rights and PERTIMIG's activities and gatherings was included in the deliveries for MDWs. Recipients were then invited into a WhatsApp group, offering them inclusion in a mutual aid community of MDWs and reminding them of the value of organizing. Those who were not MDWs received food packages with general information about PERTIMIG and were asked to share its hotline with the MDWs they knew.

This process led to the development of a collective leadership as individuals who were part of MDW organizations worked together towards a shared goal of reaching and empowering more MDWs. For example, AMMPO expanded its organizing to the state of Penang. PERTIMIG, established in December 2019 with thirty members, grew to have over 130 active members over the course of the pandemic. In June 2021, PERTIMIG hosted its first founding congress online to establish a leadership structure and constitution. Through participatory democracy, members nominated, campaigned, delivered speeches and voted virtually for their elected leaders. PERTIMIG also received requests from MDWs in other regions of Malaysia for weekly organizing programmes.[17] The organization's sustainability was driven by the fact that its leaders were domestic workers themselves and its advocacy was informed by the experiences of MDWs.

Illustration 12.1 PERTIMIG members practicing outreach during training for organizer. *Photo by PERTIMIG.*

Illustration 12.2 AMMPO leaders completed public speaking training. *Photo by AMMPO.*

5.3 Sustained resistance and policy change

The work of MDW organizations precipitated the emergence of domestic worker activists among MDWs who could articulate their interests and contribute to the advocacy agenda. MDW organizations used the coalition meetings they participated in to advocate for policy change based on their lived experience. They also strategically used the media as an ally, offering a much-needed grassroots perspective on the situation of MDWs during Covid-19. Issues such as the deprioritization of domestic workers' welfare and the heightened risks experienced by them during the pandemic were featured in alternative media channels, which helped shift the negative perception of and public attitude towards domestic work and domestic workers.

The IDWF, AMMPO and PERTIMIG, along with other CSOs, jointly advocated for the inclusion of domestic workers in Malaysia's social security schemes. This was both strategic and opportunistic because the indiscriminate nature of Covid-19 infections made it clear that domestic workers, like other workers, faced risks of employment-related injuries during the pandemic. In this environment, domestic workers urgently needed some social security, even if they were deemed undeserving of full labour rights.

These advocacy efforts resulted in the extension of social security coverage to domestic workers, including MDWs, starting 1 June 2021 (PERKESO 2021). With this, MDWs became entitled to coverage under the Employment Injury Scheme, which provides compensation against any accident and/or occupational disease arising out of and in the course of employment.[18] Employers shoulder the responsibility of registering MDWs and contributing 1.25 per cent of the wages due to them towards the scheme. Although this is an important step forward in securing decent work for MDWs, there are notable exclusions. MDWs, who hold temporary employment permits, are excluded from the Invalidity Scheme, which provides benefits for invalidity or death unrelated to employment, and the Employment Insurance System, which offers unemployment benefits.[19]

Recognizing that policy change alone has a limited impact on the ground, MDW organizations mobilized to translate this reform into action. They continued dialogue with the SOCSO to push for expanding the number of MDWs registered under the above-mentioned schemes and removing barriers to social security access for MDWs. Through these dialogues, AMMPO and PERTIMIG lobbied the SOCSO to proactively reach out to employers to encourage registrations. They also advocated for establishing a complaints mechanism to hold errant employers accountable, making registration a prerequisite for obtaining and renewing a MDW's work permit and including MDWs in the Invalidity and Employment Insurance Schemes. The SOCSO has said that it will consider the proposals and bring them up for internal discussion.

6. Conclusion

The pandemic response policies of the Malaysian government and the expansion of its authoritarianism exacerbated the precarity experienced by women migrant workers in the domestic work sector. The pandemic, however, was also fertile ground for ushering in transformative and progressive policies for MDWs. The organizing by MDWs in Malaysia shows that the Covid-19 crisis presented opportunities for resisting gender-based inequalities, intersectional discriminations and a migration policy that reinforced the exclusion and criminalization of migrants. Workers tackled exploitative and precarious situations and successfully advocated for tangible political and policy outcomes. The move from physical to virtual meetings expanded and created safe spaces for MDWs to come together and develop collective leadership, and work closely with other allies to represent themselves at various policy platforms and push for their rights as workers. The increasing relevance of digital access and justice in exercising workers' rights was also highlighted by domestic workers in Jamaica (Constable, this volume) and migrant and feminist grassroots organizations in Chile (Stefoni, Liberona and Salinas, this volume).

One clear result of this persistent organizing was the expansion of the Employment Injury Scheme under the national social security scheme to cover MDWs. Another was commitments from the MOHR to regulate the domestic work sector through legislation and from the SOCSO to further lower barriers to social security access for MDWs. Although this was yet to materialize at the time of writing (January 2023), government buy-in is apparent and opens up the space for continuous policy exchanges informed by MDWs themselves. This is not to say that organizing during the pandemic was without its challenges or that the everyday risks that MDWs face have been eliminated. Rather, this chapter revealed that when innovative strategies are adopted, collective organizing is possible, even among small and marginalized communities that face significant structural obstacles and even in the context of rising authoritarianism.

Notes

1 Anti-migrant policies such as arrests and deportations of migrants, especially undocumented migrants, existed before the pandemic. However, their enforcement intensified during the Covid-19 crisis, with the first large-scale raid and arrest of migrants taking place in May 2020. These policies are not specifically targeted at MDWs or migrants of specific nationalities.

2 The *Persatuan Pekerja Rumah Tangga Indonesia Migran* (PERTIMIG) was formed in December 2019. However, it held its first founding congress on 13 June 2021 for members to elect its leadership.

3 Employers of MDWs are required to pay a personal bond as a form of guarantee in the event that the worker absconds. The bond ranges from MYR250 to MYR1,500 based on the nationality of the worker employed.

4 Malaysian immigration requirements mandate that every migrant worker undergo a medical examination annually for the first three years of their employment in the country. After the first three compulsory medical examinations, each migrant worker is required to undergo a medical examination once every two years of their stay in Malaysia, that is, the fourth, sixth, eighth and tenth year. Every test has to be

completed three months before the expiry of the work permit. Migrant workers who are 'skilled workers' and have been in Malaysia for ten years may extend their work permits for a period of three years. This does not apply to domestic workers.

5	In 2007, the Malaysian Trades Union Congress attempted to register a national domestic workers' association, but the application was rejected without clear reasons. In 2014, a second attempt to register the association at the Registry of Societies of Malaysia was similarly rejected.

6	Malaysia perceives national security as 'being free from any threat, whether internally or externally, to its core values'. The National Security Policy identifies 'illegal immigrants and refugees' as a factor that can 'threaten the peace and security of the nation'.

7	In March 2019, the government announced that it would close its borders for international travellers. However, exceptions were made for Malaysian citizens returning from abroad, permanent residents, holders of diplomatic and official passports and long-term pass holders working in the country's essential services sector. These restrictions were subsequently relaxed as the pandemic progressed.

8	The government implemented the MCO in various phases since the start of the pandemic.

9	The first EMCO were implemented in Selangor Mansion and Malayan Mansion where many residents were non-nationals.

10	For example, see this post on the Malaysian immigration department's Facebook page: https://www.facebook.com/imigresen/photos/a.540547279345065/ 3680683188664776/?type=3&source=57&locale=ms_MY&paipv=0&eav=AfaRpVDi hfilq4nYQ8YB3DJagC7w3Q1dSoy1oE_tKl2Uhyh5hfsOMg1B_-CL4PT-gy4&_rdr.

11	The Recalibration Programme comprises two main programmes: the Labour Recalibration Programme and the Return Recalibration Programme. The former is a process to regularize undocumented migrants for employment while the latter is aimed at facilitating the voluntary repatriation of undocumented migrants to their countries of origin.

12	Interviews with PERTIMIG and AMMPO.

13	Interviews with PERTIMIG and AMMPO.

14	Malaysia's Employment Act 1955 caps normal work hours at eight hours a day and six days a week.

15	See the National Wages Consultative Council Act 2011, which establishes the mechanism for setting the minimum wage. The latest minimum wage rate was set by the Minimum Wages Order 2022 (P.U. (A) 140). Like all its predecessors, it explicitly excludes the category of 'domestic servant'.

16	Interviews with MDW organizations, August 2021.

17	Interview with the IDWF, December 2022.

18 Benefits under the Employment Injury Scheme include cost of medical treatment for employment-related injuries and diseases, temporary and permanent disablement benefits and allowances, access to physical or vocational rehabilitation centres, and funeral and education benefits.

19 Domestic workers who are Malaysian nationals, permanent residents and temporary residents are not excluded from the Invalidity Scheme and the Employment Insurance Scheme. These schemes require contributions from both the employer and the employee.

References

Al Jazeera (2020), 'Al Jazeera Journalists Questioned over Malaysia Documentary', 10 July. Available at: https://www.aljazeera.com/news/2020/7/10/al-jazeera-journalists-questioned-over-malaysia-documentary (accessed 10 October 2021).

Al Jazeera (2021), 'Fear of Arrest Among Undocumented Risks Malaysia Vaccine Push', 6 August. Available at: https://www.aljazeera.com/news/2021/8/6/mixed-messaging-in-malaysia-leaves-migrants (accessed 30 July 2021).

Anderson, B. (2000), *Doing the Dirty Work? The Global Politics of Domestic Labour*, London: Zed.

Bavani, M. (2020), 'Do Not Hire Illegal Foreign Workers', *The Star*, 1 May. Available at: https://www.thestar.com.my/metro/metro-news/2020/05/01/do-not-hire-illegal-foreign-workers (accessed 30 July 2021).

Chin, C. B. N. (2003), 'Visible Bodies, Invisible Work: State Practices toward Migrant Women Domestic Workers in Malaysia', *Asian and Pacific Migration Journal*, 12(1–2). Available at: https://doi.org/10.1177/011719680301200103 (accessed 30 July 2021).

Chung, N. (2021), 'Immigration to go after Undocumented Migrants during Lockdown', *Free Malaysia Today*, 29 May. Available at: https://www.freemalaysiatoday.com/category/nation/%202021/05/29/immigration-to-go-after-undocumented-migrants-during-lockdown/ (accessed 10 October 2021).

CodeBlue (2020), 'Ismail Sabri Doubles Down on Nabbing Undocumented Immigrants', 26 May. Available at: https://codeblue.galencentre.org/2020/05/26/ismail-sabri-doubles-down-on-nabbing-undocumented-immigrants/ (accessed 30 July 2021).

Fishbein, E. (2020), 'Fear and Uncertainty for Refugees in Malaysia as Xenophobia Escalates', *The New Humanitarian*, 25 May. Available at: https://www.thenewhumanitarian.org/news/2020/05/25/Malaysia-coronavirus-refugees-asylum-seekers-xenophobia (accessed 10 October 2021).

Harun, H.N. (2021), 'Government Expanding Labour Recalibration Programme to Include Foreigners', *New Straits Times*, 22 April. Available at: https://www.nst.com.my/news/nation/2021/04/684474/govt-expanding-labour-recalibration-programme-include-foreigners (accessed date 10 October 2021).

Hashim, J. H., Adman, M.A., Hashim, Z., Radi, M.F.M. and Kwan, S.C. (2021), 'Covid-19 Epidemic in Malaysia: Epidemic Progression, Challenges, and Response', *Frontiers*, 7 May. doi: 10.3389/fpubh.2021.560592 (accessed 30 July 2021).

Hector, C. and Pereira, A. (2020), 'End Discrimination against Foreigners and Migrants in COVID-19 Responses', *Malaysiakini*, 30 June. Available at: https://www.malaysiakini.com/%20announcement/532379 (accessed 10 October 2021).

Hierofani, P.Y. (2021), 'Productive and Deferential Bodies: The Experiences of Indonesian Domestic Workers in Malaysia', *Gender, Place & Culture*, 28(12): 1738–1754. doi: 10.1080/0966369X.2020.1855121 (accessed 10 October 2021).

Hisamudin, H.A. (2020), 'Don't Rent Your Property to Illegal Migrants, DBKL Tells Homeowners', *Free Malaysia Today*, 27 May. Available at: https://www.freemalaysiatoday.com/category/nation/2020/05/27/dont-rent-your-property-to-illegal-migrants-dbkl-tells-homeowners/ (accessed 10 October 2021).

Hobden, C. (2015), 'Domestic Workers Organise – but Can They Bargain?', ILO. Available at: https://www.ilo.org/wcmsp5/groups/public/@ed_protect/@protrav/@travail/documents/publication/wcms_345704.pdf (accessed 12 January 2024).

Human Rights Watch (2004), 'Help Wanted: Abuses against Female Migrant Domestic Workers in Indonesia and Malaysia', 16(9). Available at: https://www.hrw.org/reports/2004/indonesia0704/indonesia0704simple.pdf (accessed 30 July 2021).

Human Rights Watch (2021), 'Malaysia: Raids on Migrants Hinder Vaccine Access', 30 June. Available at: https://www.hrw.org/news/2021/06/30/malaysia-raids-migrants-hinder-vaccine-access#:~:text=(Bangkok)%20%E2%80%93%20The%20Malaysian%20government's,for%20vaccine%20equity%20among%20nations (accessed 10 October 2021).

ILO (2020), 'Protecting the Rights of Domestic Workers in Malaysia During the Covid-19 Pandemic and Beyond', Working Paper. Available at: https://www.ilo.org/asia/publications/WCMS_748051/lang--en/index.htm#:~:text=This%20note%20explores%20the%20impact,of%20domestic%20workers%20in%20Malaysia. (accessed 30 July 2021).

Immigration Department of Malaysia (2021), Foreign Domestic Helper. Available at: https://www.imi.gov.my/index.php/en/main-services/foreign-domestic-helper-fdh/ (accessed 29 July 2021).

Kanyakumari, D. (2020), 'Putrajaya Defends Detention of Illegal Immigrants During COVID-19 Pandemic', *Channel News Asia*, 27 May. Available at: https://www.channelnewsasia.com/asia/malaysia-covid-19-defend-detention-illegal-immigrants-930676 (accessed 30 July 2021).

Ke-Arah 189 (2021), 'Case Calls for Domestic Workers' Act', *The Star*, 20 May. Available at: https://www.thestar.com.my/opinion/letters/2020/05/20/case-calls-for-domestic-workers-act (accessed 30 July 2021).

Lakhdhir, L. (2020), 'Troubling Cases of the Malaysian Government Criminalizing Speech', *Malaysiakini*, 13 July. Available at: https://www.hrw.org/news/2021/04/29/

troubling-cases-malaysian-government-criminalizing-speech (accessed 10 October 2021).

Latiff, R. and Ananthalakshmi, A. (2020), 'Anti-Migrant Sentiment Fanned on Facebook in Malaysia', *Reuters*, 14 October. Available at: https://www.reuters.com/article/ uk-facebook-%20malaysia-rohingya-idUKKBN26Z0BP/ (accessed 30 July 2021).

Lee, C. (2020), 'All Foreign Workers in Malaysia Must Be Screened for COVID-19 starting Jan 1', *HRM Asia*, 31 December. Available at: https://hrmasia.com/all-foreign-workers-in-malaysia-must-be-screened-for-covid-19-starting-jan-1/ (accessed 30 July 2021).

Lim, L.L. (2020), 'The Socioeconomic Impacts of COVID-19 in Malaysia: Policy Review and Guidance for Protecting the Most Vulnerable and Supporting Enterprises', ILO. Available at: https://www.ilo.org/asia/publications/WCMS_751600/lang--en/index. htm (accessed 30 July 2021).

Malaysia Central (2021), 'Speech Text of The Special Announcement of Emergency MALAYSIA 12 January 2021'. Available at: http://www.malaysiacentral.com/ information-directory/speech-text-of-the-special-announcement-of-emergency-malaysia-12-january-2021/ (accessed 30 July 2021).

Ministry of Health Malaysia (2020), Updates on the Coronavirus Disease 2019 (COVID-19) Situation in Malaysia, Press Statement, 25 June. Available at: https:// covid-19.moh.gov.my/terkini/062020/situasi-terkini-25-jun-2020/Kenyataan%2520 Akhbar%2520KPK%2520COVID-19%2520(25%2520Jun%25202020)%2520-%2520EN.pdf (accessed 30 July 2021).

Ministry of Human Resources (2019), 'Proposed Employment (Domestic Employee) Regulations 2019', 3 April. Available at: https://www.mohr.gov.my/index.php/ en/97-public-online-engagement/1023-proposed-employment-domestic-employee-regulations-2019 (accessed 30 July 2021).

Napier-Moore, R. (2017), 'Protected or Put in Harm's Way? Bans and Restrictions on Women's Labour Migration in ASEAN Countries', ILO. Available at: https://www. ilo.org/asia/publications/WCMS_555974/lang--en/index.htm (accessed 30 July 2021).

National Security Council Malaysia (2020), The National Security Policy. Available at: https://www.mkn.gov.my/web/wp-content/uploads/sites/3/2019/08/English-National_Security_Policy.pdf (accessed 10 October 2021).

Prime Minister's Office of Malaysia (2020a), 'Teks Ucapan YAB PM di Konvensyen Setengah.Tahun Pentadbiran Perikatan Nasional', 1 September, Available at: https:// www.pmo.gov.my/ucapan/?m=p&p=muhyiddin&id=4600 (accessed 24 January 2024).

Prime Minister's Office of Malaysia (2020b), 'PM's Speech at the 36th ASEAN Summit', 26 June. Available at: https://www.pmo.gov.my/2020/06/speech-at-the-36th-asean-summit/ (accessed 30 July 2021).

PERKESO (2021), 'Employer Circular No.5 Year 2021: Extension of Social Security Coverage to Domestic Workers'. Available at: https://www.perkeso.gov.my/images/

pekerja_domestik/Employer%20Circular%20and%20Appendix.pdf (accessed 30 September 2021).

The Straits Times (2020), 'Malaysia Detains Hundreds of Foreign Workers in Major Raid on KL Wholesale Market', 11 May. Available at: https://www.straitstimes.com/asia/se-asia/malaysia-detains-hundreds-of-foreign-workers-in-major-raid-on-kl-wholesale-market (accessed 19 December 2023).

The Straits Times (2021), 'Malaysia to Deport Thousands of Undocumented Indonesian Migrants amid Pandemic', 11 June. Available at: https://www.straitstimes.com/asia/se-asia/malaysia-to-deport-thousands-of-undocumented-indonesian-migrants (accessed 19 December 2023).

Wahab, A. (2020a), 'Migrant Workers and Covid-19 Outbreak in Malaysia', IkmasWorkingPaper 3/2020, University Kebangsaan Malaysia. Available at: https://www.ukm.my/ikmas/wp-content/uploads/2020/12/IKMAS-WP-3_2020-Andika-Migrant-Workers.pdf (accessed 30 July 2021).

Wahab, A. (2020b), 'The Outbreak of Covid-19 in Malaysia: Pushing Migrant Workers at the Margin', *Social Sciences & Humanities Open*, 2(1). Available at: https://www.sciencedirect.com/science/article/pii/S2590291120300620?via%3Dihub (accessed 19 December 2023).

Are we still in this together? From a period of Shared Global Precarity to a New Era of Structural Violence and Localised Crises

Masaya Llavaneras Blanco and Damien P. Gock

This book is going to press in October 2024, over a year after the World Health Organization declared the end of the COVID19 pandemic in May 2023. When we started the collective process that led to the production of this volume back in 2020, we understood it as a way of bearing witness to the responses to the system shock that the pandemic brought to the structural aspects that sustain our lives collectively. In that way, this book is an exercise in documenting and making sense of what was happening in the governance mechanisms at play, centering Southern responses to a global emergency experienced by all, albeit in different ways.

But why does it matter to write about this now that the pandemic is mostly framed as a rare period followed by a generalised pretence of being *back to normal*? First, while we acknowledge that the pandemic was experienced differently depending on location, class, gender, ability, citizenship status, etc., we believe that it was a rare period of shared precarity in which most of the world experienced a significant halt in normalcy. We are moving back into a context of multiple localised (yet interlinked) crises, in which relatively spared centres of global power adopt an *out of sight out of mind* approach. In this context of normalised structural violence, the pandemic represents an important point of reference to understanding how life and death, access to health and everyday livelihoods are interdependent transnational processes. Second, contrary to the aspiration of some of having returned to the previous status quo, we find ourselves in a new one characterised by the normalisation of emboldened authoritarian practices and biopolitical control, increasing nationalist rhetoric and disregard for multilateral governance spaces, all of which was further enabled and exacerbated by the pandemic period. Third, despite the serious implications of the latter (or, even more so, because of them), we see special value in examining the practices of radical care and collective organising across differences among migrants, non-migrants, workers, and others that emerged in the context of the pandemic. Among them we find a wide diversity of forms of organising vis-à-vis the state locally, nationally and transnationally; as well as different ways of engaging institutions and also mobilising beyond them. All of these remain urgent points of reference to reflect on coalition-building and transnational solidarity in the current context.

Our multi-pronged analysis was built on the long-time mobilisations and past analyses that DAWN has undertaken about 'development siloes' at multilateral spaces and Southern Feminist organising. In the last two decades, DAWN has advanced complex and interlinked South-based Feminist approaches to global development. The urgency of an interlinkage approach became ever more salient in the context of the pandemic in which a global health crisis led to a financial crisis, a crisis of livelihoods and of the multilateral system, in which global mobilities and entitlement to rights were weakened in significant ways.

In the wake of the pandemic, the war in Ukraine and the genocide in Gaza, in the context of the ever-present climate crisis highlight the relevance of these conversations about the interdependent and interlinked nature of crises, and political and policy responses. Now the shared concern about interdependence is increasingly widespread and reaching a wide diversity of political spaces from DAWN to the World Economic Forum (2023). For example, the WEF of 2023 rehashed discussions about the notion of a polycrisis referring to a state in which several crises interact, their causes and processes intertwined and resulting in amplified and compounded effects (World Economic Forum 2023; Allouche et al. 2023).

In conversation with the interlinkages approach, the lens of a polycrisis is useful in looking at the knock-on impacts of the pandemic not only because of the distinct ways in which it interacts with other crises, but also because of the ways these crises reinforce each other (Helleiner 2024). As such, the cases we have put together do this work by looking at the interconnectedness between long-standing macroeconomic, labour, mobility and care crises exacerbated by the pandemic, instead of considering the health crisis as the sole cause for the outcomes we have witnessed. This is consistent with DAWN's past contributions. During the era of the Millenium Development Goals, DAWN noticed that state programmes targeted at the sexual and reproductive health of women, for example, created *silos of intervention*, where the focus was on indicators and targets, rather than on implementation of intersectoral and interlinkages approaches in policy directions (Reddy and Sen 2013; DAWN 2010). The silos of intervention did not improve the sexual and reproductive health (SRH) of women; conversely, the approach exacerbated the SRH issues and resulted in a proliferation of population control initiatives and damaging population control discourse aimed at the poor. By approaching the pandemic crises in an interlinked and intersectional way, we provide alternatives to linear analyses and 'single crisis interventions' that are harmful or, at the very least, continue the status quo where the poor, women, girls, undocumented migrants, LGBTQI+ and other marginalised folk are impacted the most.

As a Southern Feminist effort, the writing of this book was also concerned with the political directions available to us in this conjuncture. Building on Roy's (2020) now famous text, we approached the pandemic moment as a potential portal into a period of transformation. Without false illusions, we contemplated different scenarios in which the state and the private sector responded to the moment, open to the possibility of witnessing feminist transformations in global power structures. After all, the pandemic caught us at a time of global governance fragmentation and severe inequality (Llavaneras Blanco and Rosales 2020). This urgent sense of opportunity was shared across movements globally, when calls to action and system change emerged across movements and institutions (see for example the Feminists for a People's Vaccine Campaign, and Oxfam's Inequality Kills Report). It was in this period that the need to revitalise multilateralism emerged as a priority in the UN General Secretariat, assuming that the pandemic crisis would serve as an opportunity to rethink and restructure the global governance mechanisms as we know them through the recent Summit of the Future.

Nevertheless, more than a year after the official end of the pandemic, and despite the potential, hopes and actions for system change, we face a further weakened multilateral system. We are approaching three years since the Russian invasion of Ukraine, with 29,731 casualties in Ukraine, almost 11,000 dead and 19,000 injured in the last year alone. Figures are thought to be much higher (UNODA 2024). In tandem, we recently passed one year of the Israeli attack in Gaza, which has destroyed 68 per cent of cropland and road networks, and more than half of Gaza's homes, all universities, and 87 per cent of school buildings. In one year the war has killed at least 42,227 people including nearly 16,765 children, while injuring close to 100,000 people with access to only 17 of 36 partially functioning hospitals (Al Jazeera 2024). We bear witness to these wars in which the sustainability of life is ever more perilous, especially in the context of longstanding occupation and a severely weakened multilateral system.

In the midst of these perils, we are reminded of Roy's portal. Have we moved on from the cusp of possibilities for a truly transformative world? The answer remains elusive. We hope that these twelve case studies by Southern feminists nurture reflections about the role of the state and social mobilisation; austerity and the need to shift macroeconomic logics towards prioritising the sustainability of life; about feminist digital justice and the political potential of care.

References

Allouche, J., Metcalfe, S., Schmidt-Sane, M., Srivastava, S. (2023) Are we in the age of the polycrisis. Institute of Development Studies. Available at: https://www.ids.ac.uk/opinions/are-we-in-the-age-of-the-polycrisis/[Accessed 15 October 2024]

Al Jazeera (2024) *Israel-Gaza war in maps and charts: Live Tracker, AJLabs.* Available at: https://www.aljazeera.com/news/longform/2023/10/9/israel-hamas-war-in-maps-and-charts-live-tracker [Accessed 15 October 2024].

DAWN. (2010). MDG 5 Maternal Mortality: In need of rescuing from the depths of a silo. Statement by Development Alternatives with Women for a New Era. 22 September 2010. Available at: https://www.dawnfeminist.org/library/in-need-of-rescuing-from-the-depths-of-a-silo [accessed 15 October 2024]

Feminist People's Vaccine. (2024). https://feminists4peoplesvaccine.org/ [accessed 16 October 2024]

Helleiner, E. (2024) Economic Globalization's Polycrisis, *International Studies Quarterly*, Volume 68, Issue 2, June 2024, sqae024, https://doi.org/10.1093/isq/sqae024 [accessed 15 October 2024]

Llavaneras Blanco, M., and Rosales, A. (2020). Global Governance and COVID-19: The Implications of Fragmentation and Inequality, E-International Relations. Available at: https://www.e-ir.info/pdf/83300 [accessed 17 October 2024]

OXFAM. (2022). *Inequality Kills: The unparalleled action needed to combat unprecedented inequality in the wake of COVID-19.* Oxfam. https://doi.org/10.21201/2022.8465

Reddy, B., and Sen, G. (2013). Breaking through the development silos: sexual and reproductive health and rights, Millennium Development Goals and gender equity - experiences from Mexico, India and Nigeria. *Reproductive Health Matters*, 21(42), 18–31. https://doi.org/10.1016/S0968-8080(13)42743-X [accessed 15 October 2024]

Roy, A. (2020, April 3). The pandemic is a portal. *Financial Times.* [accessed 7 December 2022]

United Nations Office for Disarmament Affairs (UNODA) (2024) Briefing to the United Nations Security Council threats to international peace and security. Statement by

Mr. Adedeji Ebo, Director and Deputy to the High Representative for Disarmament Affairs. Available at: https://front.un-arm.org/wp-content/uploads/2024/01/Statement-to-the-Security-Council-Threats-to-International-Peace-and-Security-Mr-Ade-Ebo-22-January-2024-.pdf [accessed 16 October 2024]

World Economic Forum (2023). This is why 'polycrisis' is a useful way of looking at the world right now. Available at: https://www.weforum.org/agenda/2023/03/polycrisis-adam-tooze-historian-explains/ [accessed 15 October 2024]

Index

Please note that the following abbreviations have been used – *f* = figures/diagrams; n = end of chapter notes; *t* = tables; page references in *italic* refer to photographs.